# Effective Learning
## for
# Effective Management

### Glenna E. Sutcliffe

*Structured Learning Courses*

**Prentice Hall**

New York   London   Toronto   Sydney   Tokyo

First published 1988 by
Prentice Hall International (UK) Ltd,
66 Wood Lane End, Hemel Hempstead,
Hertfordshire, HP2 4RG
A division of
Simon & Schuster International Group

**1988 Prentice Hall International (UK) Ltd**

Printed and bound in Great Britain by
A. Wheaton & Co. Ltd, Exeter

---

*British Library Cataloguing in Publication Data*

Sutcliffe, Glenna E.
    Effective Learning for Effective Management
    1. Management — Study and teaching
    I. Title
    658.4′007        HD30.4

    ISBN 0-13-244229-9
    ISBN 0-13-244237-X pb

---

1 2 3 4 5    92 91 90 89 88

# Effective Learning
# for
# Effective Management

For Derek, who noted, amongst other things, Alberti's comment in the 15th Century: *Very often, ignorance of the way to learn, more than the effort of learning itself, breaks the spirit of men who are both studious and anxious to do so*

*Alberti, Florentine Architect, 1430*

# Contents

# Preface

It would be impossible to acknowledge all the influences that made me want to write this book. My initial introduction to the subject of 'study skills' in Poynton High School, Cheshire led on to a further investigation of how they are relevant in many areas of life apart from the academic. Material written by Alan Mumford, Peter Honey and Peter Russell was invaluable as was the help and encouragement given by many training officers and managers that I have met in my work as an independent trainer. A rather stunned family gave me moral support as did Clare Butcher (Clare Sproston Associates) who also gave constructive help. And of course without Derek's skills of disk formatting, tea making, spelling, fish and chip collecting, information retrieval, tolerance and patience the final printout would never even have reached the ever-cheerful Maggie McDougall at Prentice Hall.

G.E.S.
*1987*

# ONE

# Introduction

This book is designed for those who want to acquire the skills and techniques of learning and who also want to be effective practical managers. Study skills are not used only when studying but are fundamental to everyday life. Using the memory, reading text books, planning and writing essays and researching projects are the same skills that are needed for remembering facts about clients, reading technical journals and finding and extracting information on which to base company decisions.

Most people enjoy the challenge of study and find it a stimulating activity. I hope that you will find this book enables you to acquire (or brush up) those learning methods needed for study and effective management.

Professional qualifications, management diplomas and degrees, and other forms of higher and further education are all ingredients in the upward movement of those who are aiming high. The successful manager never stops learning and the skills and techniques described in this book should be of value when used for formal study or in everyday managerial situations.

## Using this book

Use this book as a management tool. Make your own notes and comments in the margins, underline passages that are relevant and photocopy exercises that you want to use. Try to overcome any reluctance to write in the book — you should be able to use it in the same way you would use a notebook, a set of instructions or a calculator. There is no 'correct' way to read it, although Chapter Two does give an overview of the strategies for learning outlined in the book. Look through the table of contents or the index and pick out topics which you think would be useful to you. You will find that some of the chapters go together: the two chapters on memory and those on reading strategies are probably best looked at together.

There are exercises at the end of each chapter. The first section contains individual exercises although many of the group exercises could be of use to the individual reader. Personnel and training managers will find that the material can be adapted easily for use in training sessions. The basic information can be used for tutor input, and both the group and individual exercises may be used and adapted freely.

## Management skills and study skills

The classic definition of a manager is someone who:

    plans,
    motivates,
    controls, and
    directs human and physical resources

to achieve a particular end.

It is possible to break down the four basic managerial functions into specific skills. Some of these will include:

    communication;
    decision making;
    organisation;
    staff development;
    forward planning;
    directing and supervising.

The study skills discussed in this book complement managerial skills — many are already possessed by effective managers. There is a two-way traffic whereby learning strategies can enhance managerial practice and management skills can be of direct use in study.

Communicating and listening, making informed decisions, planning and goal setting are skills basic to good management. We all have to write clearly, to listen and concentrate. The ability to transfer a skill learned for one purpose to another shows

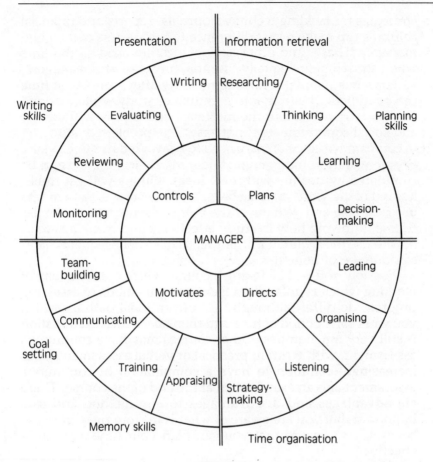

*Figure 1.1*

flexibility and adaptability, both core ingredients in a successful manager.

Many of the skills of successful study are those of good organisation and efficient goal setting. Essay and report writing demand similar skills of research, planning and writing. A well-trained memory is as useful when meeting new clients as it is in the examination room, and effective note-making methods are as important to study and revision notes as they are in the board room or in forward planning. Listen to a senior executive wishing she could read and absorb the amount of background material that has to be dealt with and it will be obvious that knowing how to read at speed and being able to select effective strategies for tackling technical journals, reports and financial columns can make a vast difference to the success of the good manager. These, and other skills which are used all the time when studying, are equally essential for successful managers.

For some people, returning to study after a period of time can be difficult. Getting into a routine of study while working all day, worrying about the mortgage and coping with family and social commitments is not easy. The problem of studying in comparative isolation may need to be worked through. Many people will thoroughly enjoy widening their horizons and be stimulated by dealing with new ideas. Others will get rather less out of the actual material being studied, but see it as a means to a desirable end. Whatever the motive for taking a particular course, knowing how to study effectively and being aware of how to use the acquired learning skills in any subsequent career can only be of benefit.

Possibly you will be taking a course which entails a way of working which is unfamiliar. Examiners' methods of assessing progress do differ, although the conventional path by which you work for a period of time and then take a final examination is still very much in use. Other courses may have continuous assessment, with written, practical or verbal assessments. It is increasingly common to have a combination of continuous assessment and an examination at the end of the course. There are advantages and disadvantages to any method and it is important that you are aware of what is in store right from the beginning to ensure that you can plan your time and study effectively.

## Different ways of study

*Open learning* is a method of learning whereby the student works at his or her own pace. This has obvious advantages but still needs a good deal of personal organisation. Open learning courses range from the fairly elementary instruction manuals for young, unqualified trainees to highly sophisticated degree courses.

*Action learning* is usually a combination of practical and written work based on real-life managerial situations which have to be resolved. An ability to record information quickly and to collect relevant information for use is often an element in this type of learning.

*Distance learning* (what used to be called correspondence courses) is still very popular and in it all the skills of study are important, especially that of organising time effectively. Some external university degrees rely on this approach with occasional meetings with a tutor as well as summer schools and occasional lectures. This method is used by the Open University which not only awards degrees but also has a wide range of diploma and non-examination courses. Much of the material is provided on television and radio.

An *in-company course* can be as short as an afternoon discussion on introducing new company regulations, or it may be a custom-made internal course run over several months. Many courses which are run internally are on-going, and workshops and discussion groups will reflect the group's understanding and experience.

An honest assessment of your own strengths and weaknesses is a good start to any course of study. If you know yourself well, you will be able to plan the most effective way of exploiting your strong points and bolstering up the weak ones. Most new ventures are fairly daunting at first and this is especially so when the end result is a pass or fail based on an examination. It is important to have confidence in your own ability from the very beginning.

Do not be deluded into thinking that if you have passed the first flush of youth you will find studying very much more difficult. On the contrary, you may well find that your experience of life and your own particular interests and job give you a definite edge over a younger and less experienced person. Age is a state of mind, not a series of cut-off points decided by fate. If you are interested and motivated, your chronological age will not be a major factor. This is not to say that it will not be hard work — it will be, but not an insuperable task.

Maybe you have a specific problem; the partially-sighted or hearing-impaired person may have to discover ways of overcoming these particular disabilities. Handicapped people may need to make special provision for wheelchair entry into lecture rooms or find equipment which will enable them to fulfil the course requirements properly. Tell your tutor of any particular needs you may have.

Successful learning depends on motivation and good study skills as well as ability and hard work. You may have bought this book to help you obtain a professional qualification or to become a more effective manager. Whatever your reasons, use the text and exercises to help you realise your full potential.

Personnel or training managers, who might be using the book as part of a company training course, are free to use any of the exercises as they stand or to adapt them for individual or group training sessions.

# TWO

# Strategies for learning

To be successful, a student requires a combination of ability, hard work and effective study methods. The psychologist, C.A. Mace says that intelligence plus some special ability contributes 50 per cent to success, hard work and effective study 40 per cent, and chance the remaining 10 per cent.

We can take the 50 per cent of general intelligence and any special ability for granted. If you have been accepted as a student on your chosen course, it is unlikely that your mental ability will let you down. The 10 per cent of success that depends on luck is out of your control ... this leaves the 40 per cent of successful achievement that is due to hard work and effective learning methods.

Determination and hard work can be easier if you have organised your study time well and have thought about your short-term and long-term goals. Many of the strategies and techniques of learning are skills which you may already have and, by analysing how you learn and how you carry out various tasks at work, you will be able to use these skills more efficiently.

## Motivation and attitude

Your attitude and approach, whether for work or study, can make a great deal of difference between successful conclusions and those which are unsatisfactory. There will, inevitably, be times when you will feel thoroughly disenchanted at the prospect of getting down to work, especially when you are studying by yourself. Recognise that this can happen and aim to get *something* done, even if it is not as much as you had hoped. In other words, you are readjusting your goals from

ELEM—B

7

short-term to even shorter-term, but this is preferable to doing very poor work or abandoning your course altogether.

Many factors affect achievement, and motivation is an important element. Some of the reasons for poor motivation may be that:

> you would really prefer not to be taking the course;
> you do not find it particularly interesting;
> you have personal problems;
> you are in poor health;
> you are an active person and find it difficult to sit and work;
> you are basically lazy.

Many different pressures are put on people to improve their qualifications and status. Some of the pressures come from within ourselves and some from others. There may be financial or career pressure, pride, family or peer pressure, even insistence from your manager or supervisor at work. It is more sensible to decide *before* you commit yourself whether what you have set yourself to do is really essential to your life and happiness. If you are having doubts but intend to stay with it, it will be even more important to manage the workload efficiently, as enthusiasm for the course may not be strong. If you have a negative attitude towards study, you will have constant problems and will get little out of the course. Luckily, most people are able to find interest and enthusiasm for their studies and gain a great deal out of completing them satisfactorily.

Keep the things which motivate you most to the forefront of your mind. They will perhaps include:

> better chances of promotion and pay;
> the recognition of your achievement by family, boss and friends;
> the desire to complete the course;
> more interesting and challenging career prospects;
> the need to be more independent.

There are many other things which motivate people besides these — think about what really motivates *you*.

If you do find that motivation is at a low ebb, there are steps that can be taken. Do not let yourself drift into neglecting your work — it is very hard to reclaim any time that you lose.

Here are some positive steps that can be taken when

motivation is poor:

(a) make a sensible timetable and stick to it;
(b) set short-term goals and stick to them;
(c) check your physical health;
(d) check that your study environment is suitable;
(e) 'lose' yourself in your work if you have personal/emotional problems;
(f) work for a set time, and then *stop*;
(g) assess your progress to date, looking for positive points;
(h) if concentration is low, work in short, rapid bursts;
(i) make a real commitment to work hard; tell a relative or friend who will help you keep your resolution;
(j) ask your tutor for help and advice.

Most people begin a course with a positive attitude towards the work involved and find that they are reasonably well motivated. Do not despair if you occasionally lose motivation. Unless you have real problems, this will only be temporary and you will continue to enjoy the stimulus of widening your horizons. Keep an open mind and try to explore all the different facets of the subjects you are approaching.

An enthusiastic mind, an inquisitive nature and an ability to solve problems are signs of an alert student as well as a successful manager. If you can learn to use your mind so that you can take new ideas on board and assess the potential in any learning situation, your future studies and career prospects will seem bright.

## Learning styles

No two managers have the same managerial style and no two students have the same learning style. Because of this, some methods of learning will appear easier than others. For example, many people prefer talking through a problem with colleagues or fellow students, trying out different ways of working and learning from experiments. Other people will find that listening to a lecture on theory and then researching the information alone will be more effective.

Sometimes it is assumed that learning is irrelevant to our daily life and work, but the good manager goes on learning all the time, keeping up with new ideas, technology and circumstances. An understanding, however superficial, of the way in which you learn can be profitable.

Most of us are biased towards one particular style of learning but can use other ways occasionally. If you can exploit your own particular learning style and also become competent in other styles, you will be able to learn more effectively.

If students develop a certain style of *learning*, it follows that lecturers, compilers of open-learning manuals or writers will have certain *teaching* styles. This is something to take into account when studying because it may be easier to learn from someone who has a complementary style. Be aware that you may have to make more effort with some materials than with others. For example, this book is written, for the most part, in a way that an analytical learner may find familiar. However, most of us are capable of learning (and communicating) in more than one way and, even if you are not basically an analytical learner, the style of this book should not present you with any problems.

Look at the four groups below and ask yourself which group (or groups) you seem to fit into.

## Practical learners

These people use known facts to solve problems. They like to test theories by putting them to practical use and by relating theory to practice. They enjoy 'hands on' experiences. They are not happy with 'fuzzy' ideas. They like quality allied to utility.

*Strengths*   practical application of ideas

A favourite question of theirs would be, *How does this work?*

## Analytical learners

These learners are more interested in ideas than in people. They like to think problems through, step by step. They are good at research, planning and assembling information and value sequential thinking. They like to fit details into an overall concept. They probably enjoyed the traditional school or college atmosphere.

*Strengths* creating intellectual concepts

A favourite question would begin with *What . . . ?*

## Action learners

These people often learn by trial and error. They look for hidden possibilities in things. They like variety and change and are adaptable and flexible. Sometimes they are intuitive rather than logical in the way in which they solve problems and come to conclusions.

*Strengths* taking action, carrying out plans

A favourite question is, *If . . . ?*

## Concept learners

These learners are interested in people. They are imaginative and innovative. Good at listening and sharing ideas, they want to be involved in their work and study. They are always looking for the meaning behind action and thought. They like to work in a co-operative way.

*Strengths* innovation and imagination; working with others

A favourite question is, *Why does this happen?*

> Do you recognise yourself in any of these learning styles?
> What are your greatest strengths?
> What kind of situation helps you to learn best? Is it people? Practical experience? Books?
> What makes it more difficult for you to learn?
> What are your personal learning goals?
> What sort of questions do you ask?

To find out more about learning styles get a copy of *The Manual of Learning Styles* by Honey and Mumford (see bibliography).

By thinking about the way you learn and asking questions about yourself, your motives and attitudes, you build up an understanding of your own strengths and weaknesses in a learning situation. Knowing how you learn is useful, not only for study but also in your role as a manager.

It has been suggested that successful managers and senior executives have strong experimental skills and are always interested and flexible in their approach to life. They constantly seem to be asking the question, What has been learned from this?

An inquiring mind and a positive attitude towards work will enable you to complete your course with confidence and apply your knowledge and understanding to your future career.

## An overall strategy for study

### The syllabus

The key word here is *overall*. Before you read the first book or write the first assignment, it is important that you have a clear idea of the content of the entire course. Read through the syllabus and note all the main topics. It can be useful to jot down a rough list of things you feel you already know something about, and another of the topics which appear to be completely new.

You may find that the syllabus and the course content do not always match up. When a flexible research course or a self-managed learning project is under way, the course can be constructed as the studies proceed. The tutor and the student may decide together the way they think the work should be undertaken.

As you read through the course, unfamiliar material will begin to integrate with the known. If you have noted titles, headings, and key words that refer to new material, you will soon find that your mind starts assembling the jigsaw of knowledge and you will note the relevant topics subconsciously even before you begin working on them. This receptive awareness means that your brain is picking up these words and ideas wherever they occur, for instance in a newspaper article, a television programme or a colleague's conversation. When you begin detailed study of these items, you will find that you have already gained a good deal of information about the subject.

As you read through the syllabus, getting an overview of the entire course, ask yourself the following questions: What do I already know about the subject? What other subjects I am interested in are relevant to the course? Where does my everyday experience fit into what I am about to learn in detail? Question all the time: the more questions you ask the more you will open your mind to new ideas and see new horizons.

If you know which topics are coming up in the course, you will become aware of information relating to them. This is very useful, as you can begin to collect references, articles, statistics and so on, which can be filed away until you need them. An informal file of references and notes about information you have come across is invaluable. Another useful exercise is to compare different syllabuses from other similar courses to identify the most important themes running through your course.

When you have read through the syllabus for your course, assess the skills you will need in order to learn effectively. There may be skills which are not covered in this book. For example, can you read and interpret statistics? Can you use a computer program? Can you make, use and evaluate a sophisticated questionnaire? The basic learning methods often need other skills as well and it is sensible to try and identify which skills you may need for any specific course.

**Your tutor**

Whatever type of course you are taking, whether in a college, or with open or distance learning, your tutor will be a vital part of your learning experience. You will need to know what she or he expects of you and your work. A good relationship between tutor and student can be a great help. With distance learning, it is obviously more difficult to communicate easily but, even so, your tutor will welcome requests for help and advice. This is, after all what their job is all about. Never leave it too late to ask for help in any area in which you are experiencing difficulty.

**People who can help**

Your family and friends can give you immense support when you are studying. Take all the assistance you can get. A husband or flatmate who takes over the shopping, or a friend who lets you talk through a project, are invaluable 'aids to study'.

However independent you are as a person, do not despise help from others.

Take every opportunity to meet other students taking the same course. Try to arrange regular meetings for discussion and self-help sessions. People learn from each other, and having others to bounce ideas off is mutually beneficial. Talking through an idea or a project is often more useful than all the other study skills and techniques that you have acquired. You learn by thinking and doing, and it is important to be able to express your thoughts in words. By verbalising your ideas, you can usually see the flaws in an argument (or someone else will) and can rethink or reword your ideas. In discussion groups you usually have to lay your ideas and theories on the line. For some people this is difficult, but overcoming any initial diffidence is worthwhile because of the very real benefits to learning.

In a self-help group each student should be willing to:

(a) attend as regularly as possible;
(b) join in the discussion as often as possible;
(c) take responsibility for arranging the details of the meetings in turn.

The preparation for a group meeting is in itself a form of learning. How you operate each session will depend on the needs of the group but could include: an exchange of views about a passage in the course modules, a discussion arising from a lecture, sharing the results and comments on a set assignment, talking through a practical project, helping to devise a question-naire and so on. Another session could be in the form of a seminar where the group will come prepared to discuss a specific topic. In this case they will probably have:

(a) reread and brought their own notes;
(b) read and thought about the relevant course material;
(c) noted down problem areas;
(d) noted down questions to bring up in discussion;
(e) written brief notes on their own understanding of the subject.

This preparation will have involved reading and writing. The third stage, speaking, is very important for learning. When you can put your ideas, arguments and conclusions into words it is more than likely that you have learned and understood the concepts involved. Even admitting that you are unsure of a point is valuable — others may have the same difficulty and sharing and hammering out the problem will lead to a much better understanding. Even for those with no problems or doubts, getting a fresh viewpoint on the subject and widening perspectives is a valuable exercise.

## Practical working strategies

### General organisation

If you are taking several different subjects or topics in one overall course you will need to organise your equipment as well as your time and mind.

*Planning ahead* Books or articles that are needed for reference, as opposed to the set books you will already have, may have to be borrowed from a library. Give yourself plenty of time to get this background material. If other people have the books out, you could miss information which would make the difference between an indifferent assignment and a first class one. You will find it useful to photocopy short articles, graphs, statistics and so on well in advance.

*Background material* Keep a box file for reference material which might be useful. For example, press cuttings, colour supplement articles, advertisements, radio/TV comments, photocopies of reports, handouts from other parallel courses that you acquire, computer printouts, etc.

*Files* Your study files record your progress throughout the course. They are likely to contain at least some of the following:

    notes taking during lectures or broadcasts;
    notes made from books;
    photocopied passages and articles;
    handouts from lectures;
    notes given for radio or television broadcasts;
    completed essays and assignments;
    essay plans;
    completed exercises or tests;
    diagrams, graphs, maps, tables, etc.

If you neglect to organise this material, life can get very complicated. The organisation involved in fitting in newly-made notes, removing irrelevant material and retrieving information to use for a particular purpose will help you learn and memorise the material.

How you organise the 'software' is up to you — there are advantages and disadvantages in most methods. Below are a few ideas which you could adapt or adopt.

*A working file*  It may not be convenient to carry around a bulky file and many people prefer to have something in which they can keep the material in current use. If you only study at home, this will be irrelevant as all your notes should be to hand, but, if you do work in the office or go to occasional seminars, a working file could be useful.

*Subject files*  Few courses have only one narrow topic. It is far more likely that you will need a file for every subject. If you try to keep all the material together it can easily get mislaid and misplaced.

Within each subject file the material can be organised in one of three ways:

*Topics*  Using file dividers, arrange the notes in sections each one dealing with a topic or specific area of the main subject.

*Chronological order*  As you study a particular topic your notes and any handouts etc. are filed in that order.

*Material*  Notes, essays, handouts, printed notes, worked problems, for each subject are in different sections of a file (or could have a file each). The material could be arranged in either chronological or topic order.

How you decide to file your notes will depend on the way your mind works and the way in which the course is structured. Take into consideration that you may need to retrieve material quickly for an assignment or revision.

It may seem excessive to have an index or a table of contents in a file but it can cut down time taken in searching through your notes for a particular reference that you need. If you decide to do this, get into the habit of entering new items each time you put them into the file. File dividers can also be used to note down what each section contains. Listing references is important and you might find that having a section for them in each file you use is convenient. A simple reference system is to use a 'highlighter' pen and colour code the top of each page. Writing the page topic in colour is useful when you want to look a particular point up quickly or need to revise for an unexpected test or group session.

Some people prefer to use a small notebook for this. Without some form of recording device, useful references can be completely lost or you can spend an inordinate amount of time in searching for just the right quote or vital statistic that is not exactly where you thought it would be.

*Cross referencing*  Where material is common to more than one area it may be useful to have a simple system for cross referencing. It you are using a reference notebook this could also contain information about where different aspects of the same subject are to be found. Notes on a file divider or index sheet will tell you where other items are stored. For a very long thesis or course it may be more convenient to use a card index system.

*Computer filing*  If you have access to a personal computer with word processing facilities you may decide to store your basic information on disk. You will not need to be told that it is essential to have back-up disks in case of power cuts or accidentally hitting the wrong key. You may only use the WP for writing the assignment or report but you will still need a back-up disk unless you make sure that you have a print out for quick reference. A computer facility for noting down ideas, storing information and filing material is only as good as the operator. Some people use a computer in the same way that others use a pen and paper. For essays and reports, a WP is probably the best thing since sliced bread. You are unlikely to come across problems with your tutor but make sure that any material to be submitted to an examining board is in a format that is acceptable to them.

## Case study

Asante Adofo has recently taken over as the head of a small department in a graphic design company. He enjoys solving problems at work and his bias is towards action learning. His open learning course is in business studies but he finds it hard to cope with research and listening to lectures. However, as a new head of department, he realises that he needs to be able to collect data and explore new subjects if he is to be on top of his job and get further promotion. He has taken time to organise a good filing system and has initiated a fact-finding project which will help his staff by making important information instantly available.

While studying, he joined a self-help group and found it

extremely valuable for learning material he found difficult to absorb. Because of his experience of working and learning with a small group, and through the theoretical study of team building, he is trying to develop a working team within his department. He has the problem of having to manage both people and resources while not wanting to lose touch with his own talents as a designer. Asante is learning to work in co-operation with his staff and recognises that they also have different styles of learning and working. This understanding means he can often assess what sort of material or instructions will be most helpful to them when they need to absorb new information about specific jobs.

## Individual exercises

1 Check the list of skills that you need for your course. Make an action plan to ensure that you know where to get help in acquiring any new skills and where you can learn about them.

2 Establish a notebook in which you can jot down information, conjectures, references, ideas, etc. about the subject you are studying. Impress your tutor by adding extra material that is not to be found in the set books. (Always state the source of such references.)

3 Try setting up a self-help group at the start of your course. If you are on a distance learning course ask your tutor for details of people living near to you. If there are others in your company who are studying, see if you can arrange a meeting place at work on a regular basis. If you cannot arrange group meetings, try contacting other people by phone for an exchange of views and ideas.

4 Think about the way in which you learn. Make a list of how you feel you learn material most successfully. For example:

*Memory* How do you memorise particular material? Do you use: Repetition? Write it out? Association of words and concepts? Any other methods?

*Reading* How do you tackle a new text? Do you read slowly or quickly? Do you sample and skim? Do you make notes from the beginning?

*Note making*   Do you make copious notes? Do you jot down key points only? Do you copy out important passages? How do you arrange the notes on the page?

*Information processing*   Do you think in a logical, step-by-step manner? Do you collect all the information you can find first and then go through it? Do you try to see all the angles and possibly some that are not there in the first place?

In other words, you are thinking about how you think and learning about how you learn. To know more about learning to learn, look at the bibliography for books that expand on the theory of learning.

## Group exercises

This chapter briefly and rather superficially discusses different ways of learning. A lighthearted set of problem solving exercises can often be useful to point out the way in which individual group members approach and solve problems. If you want to extend these exercises, Edward de Bono's *Five Day Course in Thinking* (Pelican) can supply further ideas.

Try some of the problems and exercises below with a group, which can be of any convenient size. Use your sense of drama to tell the stories in the first three exercises. The group leader can answer questions, but must not volunteer any information. The exercises are not new by any means and some of the group may know them already. These people should keep quiet and try to analyse how the group arrives at the answer. Answers are on page 22.

1   *The sad case of the hanging man*

When his friends realised that Tom was missing they set off to look for him. Leaving the little Moroccan town where they were staying, they followed the tracks of his open truck through the desert until they found it outside a wartime pillbox far into the desert. The truck had an almost full tank of petrol and the keys were in the ignition.

The concrete pillbox was 20 feet in diameter, and a thick concrete floor and ceiling made it impregnable. The friends, fearing for Tom's safety, broke down the locked door and discovered Tom slowing swinging from a hook embedded in the centre of the ceiling. He was quite dead! The ceiling was 12 foot high. There was nothing else in the pillbox at all except for a few grains of sand that had blown through the small gap under the door. Hastily, they cut him down and discovered the key to the locked door in his pocket. With no windows and a locked door, how did Tom die?

2  *The fire on the cliff*

Mary left her car in the lane and walked to the edge of the cliff where a plateau of grass made a fine sunbathing area. In front of her was a steep drop over sheer cliffs to a rough sea. Behind her, apart from the narrow lane down which she had wandered were high cliffs, quite unclimbable. The many gorse bushes were an added hazard, especially as she had left her clothes in the car and was only dressed in a bikini.

Waking from a sundrenched sleep, Mary smelled smoke and was horrified to realise that her way back to the car was cut off by raging flames. In front of her was the sheer drop into the sea (she could not swim!) and behind her the fire and unscaleable cliffs. Will she survive? How?

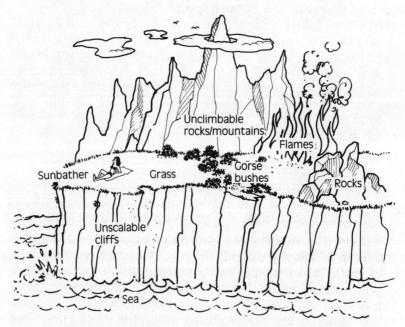

**Figure 2.1  Illustration of the fire on the cliff**

3 *Nine dots*

Figure 2.2 shows nine dots. Ask the group to draw four continuous lines, which must connect up all the dots. The lines must be straight.

This exercise shows the mind's tendency to impose order and organisation on information. It also shows that we can become very rigid in our thinking, unable to see beyond the obvious and the stereotype.

**Figure 2.2**

4 *The bottle game*

This exercise is designed to test the creative and lateral thinking abilities of a group. There may be some surprising leaps of imagination. This exercise is best done when the group is relaxed and uninhibited. Points to make are:

(a) Problem solving usually requires creativity and imagination combined with logic.

(b) By stretching the imagination and looking beyond the confines of the obvious it is easier to grasp an unfamiliar point of view and of prejudging a situation.

Ask each member of the group to make a list showing the uses to which you can put a bottle. Do *not* specify what type of bottle. Most people will assume that you mean a glass, wine or milk bottle. It could, of course, be plastic, stone or metal; as large as a house or small as an ant.

If someone has made a list consisting only of things that could be put *into* the bottle (e.g. wine, milk, sand, marbles, oil, leaves, old socks, beer, feathers, etc.) this is as correct as anything else. You did not specify particular uses.

Group discussion can bring some bizarre results. Try asking the group to think about what you could *not* use a bottle for.

The object does not have to be a bottle. Try a brick, paper clip, daffodil, ping-pong ball . . . .

5 *The liferaft game*

Opportunities for testing group logic, problem-solving strategies and even compassion are provided by the Liferaft Game.

The scenario is this: the liferaft is far out to sea and there is only enough food and water for three people. Who do you throw into the shark-infested sea? The managing director? The head of finance? The office boy? The MD's personal assistant? Who would be of most value? A variation is, who should be made redundant first, but this can cause problems!

6 *The survival course*

A similar exercise is the Survival Course.

Four people are in the Scottish mountains on a survival course. The group must first decide what each person's rucksack should hold, and on the age and occupation of each person.

One person (decided by the group leader) gets hypothermia because of the terrible conditions.

The following decisions have to be made:

(a) Will they abandon the victim and head for home?
(b) Will some one/two stay with the victim?
(c) Who will go for help? Why them?
(d) What will be taken/left from the contents of the four rucksacks?

This exercise can be made as elaborate as you want by using more people and introducing various hazards.

**Answers**

1 He had taken a block of ice with him in the back of the

truck, stood on it and jumped off, having placed a rope around the hook. The ice had melted in the hot desert air and any water had trickled out under the door.

2 Mary pulls up a gorse bush, lights it from the fire and burns the grass around her. With another bush she beats out the flames to make a fire break. Here she waits until the fire has died down when she can make her way back to her car.

3

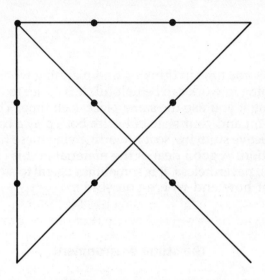

*Figure 2.3   Solution to Exercise 3*

# THREE

# The physical factors

Spending some time in thinking and planning where and how you are going to work can be helpful. It is easier to concentrate on studying if you use the same place each time. The physical environment and your state of health both play a considerable part in effective studying so it is worth giving these factors some consideration. A good deal of the material in this chapter will be obvious; nevertheless, it is sometimes useful to stop and look critically at how and where you study.

## The study environment

A room that can be used as a permanent base is an advantage. The fewer the distractions, the easier it is to work. It is best to have an area where books and other study materials can be left. If you have young children it may not always be possible to leave things around, but using the same place for your work helps you to get into the right frame of mind for productive study.

Whether the room you choose is a bedroom, dining room or study, the main essential is that you can remain undisturbed. For many people it is important for the place to be relatively quiet. You may have to point out to your family or flatmates that when you are working, only an earthquake is sufficient excuse for a visit. There are people who can work effectively in the midst of distractions, but most of us need to be able to settle down in a certain amount of guaranteed peace and quiet.

With some planning, your study area will be a place in which you can find stimulation and enjoyment in what you learn. However, co-operation from those you live with is an important ingredient in helping you to work well.

When deciding where to work you should take into account the sort of person you are. If the idea of working in complete solitude appals you then being close to other people will not be a problem. However, there are some people who find the everyday background noise in any family irritating. In this case it would be better to work in a bedroom. Having decided on where to work, look at some of the physical factors which could affect the way in which you work.

## Temperature

It is as difficult to work in a room that is too hot as in one that is too cold. The suggested temperature for those doing mental work is between 60 and 70°F. The all-round warmth of central heating is easiest to work in. Electric and gas fires are less easily regulated for overall warmth and tend to be turned up rather too high; thus they can have a soporific effect. Paraffin heaters are cheap to run, but many people find that the smell is unpleasant to be with for any length of time. Whichever form of heating you use, perhaps the most important item to check is the dryness of the atmosphere. The head can feel stuffy and the skin can get very dry if some moisture is not introduced. This can be done with a humidifier, or even a small bowl of water near the source of heat.

## Ventilation

Having clean air with a little movement in it is more important than the actual temperature of the room in which you work. It is important to make sure that you have a good supply of oxygen. If you try to study in a stuffy atmosphere you will probably find it difficult to concentrate and to produce high-quality work. Lack of concentration, sleepiness and a strong inclination to give it all up can often be traced to inadequate ventilation.

Oxygen is essential to brain function. The brain uses 25 per cent of the average person's oxygen intake even though it is only a fraction of the body's weight. When we breathe, oxygen is taken into the system and carbon dioxide is expelled. In a room with insufficient ventilation the air is breathed over and over again, and each time the oxygen content is reduced considerably. As more carbon dioxide accumulates the student will begin to feel headachy and slightly sick. It is obvious that under these circumstances the brain will not be working very efficiently.

Make sure that there is a good supply of air. Open the windows occasionally even in winter so that the air circulates. The trick is to arrange matters so that you have fresh air without having to sit in a howling draught. Good ventilation and a reasonable working temperature are both important for working well, so it is worth spending some time and thought on getting them right.

## Furniture

The importance of a good oxygen supply has been mentioned. For your body to benefit from all the pure air now available, think about how it actually enters the lungs. If you are not sitting in a reasonably upright position the lungs will not be able to take in sufficient oxygen to enable the brain to function well. A desk or work surface that is not comfortable to write or read at will hinder (and lengthen) study. Your work will be more productive when you sit so that there is no undue strain on the back, and your lungs are able to take in a good supply of air. You will also find that you do not get so tired either mentally or physically.

Check that when you are sitting at your desk your knees are right under the work surface, and your feet flat on the floor. When your arms are placed on the desk top they should be parallel to your thighs and the floor, and your shoulders should not be raised. Raised shoulders cause muscular tension and discomfort. Experiment until you feel you have got the right combination of chair and desk. If you are sitting properly there will be no undue strain on your body, and your lungs will be drawing sufficient oxygen into the bloodstream to make your brain function effectively.

It is useful to have a well-designed adjustable office chair. Some of the more modern chairs are designed so that the seat is tilted forward. This has the effect of making the back very upright, and cuts out much backstrain. Notice also the seat length. If the seat is too short the thighs will not have sufficient support. If it is too long you will not be able to use the backrest properly, and the feet may not be placed on the floor so that they balance the body. This relationship between the seat and the work surface is crucial for comfort and to efficient, less tiring study. It is important that you spend some time on getting it right.

The work surface should be large enough for books and other equipment to be spread easily. Reference books, subject files, spare paper, pens and so on should be within easy reach when needed. A shelf above the desk or a bookcase to the side is useful. It means that you can reach out for what you want instead of having to search around for books and equipment.

In addition to course materials, the shelf could also contain a small alarm clock. This is a useful piece of equipment, as we shall see in a later chapter. The elements of time and memory in study planning are important.

## Lighting

Good lighting is extremely important. The strain of working under inadequate or wrongly-placed lighting will lead to inaccurate and inefficient results.

There are three main sources of light: *daylight, incandescent* lighting and *fluorescent* lighting. Good daylight is the most satisfactory light, provided there is no glare from bright sunshine.

*Incandescent lighting* is the most common type of lighting to be found in the home. The worst type to work under is the ceiling light with a small bulb. A desk lamp is much easier to work with, and an adjustable anglepoise lamp is far better than a fixed table lamp. Remember that for small or detailed print, or for formulae, you will need more light than for larger print. A 60 watt bulb should be about right. Experiment to make sure that there is no glare. An opaque shade is best so that the light is directed onto the work and not into your eyes. Note also that many books have shiny paper which can give off a strong glare. If you have a shelf over the working surface, a small strip light (usually fluorescent), suitably shaded, can be most effective. The pool of light over the student's desk, with the rest of the room plunged into darkness, may look dramatic but a more sensible approach is to try to achieve an even distribution of light. One solution is to have the light turned towards the wall onto a white sheet of card. The reflected light gives a diffused but even spread of light. As with seating, you may need to experiment with lighting until you get the most comfortable lighting conditions for your purpose.

*Fluorescent lighting* is used in many places, as it gives a strong illumination for less cost than other forms. This type of lighting can be very fatiguing to work under, and you may find that if you use it you cannot work for quite so long. The almost undetectable flicker affects some people quite considerably. The glare factor is also greater with this form of lighting. However, there are some people who find that this is a good light to work under, with the overall lack of shadow an advantage. The best thing to do is to experiment, and to note your comfort, or lack of it, when working in different conditions. The aim should be to have lighting that gives a general distribution of even background light, with a more directed source of light for closer work.

When placing desktop lighting, you should be looking for a position which will not cast any shadows on whatever you are studying. Thus, if you have an anglepoise lamp on the desk, make sure that it is placed on your left if you are right-handed, or on your right if you are left-handed. Good, well-placed lighting will be of little use if you are having difficulty with seeing. At the start of your course it may be a good move to go to your registered ophthalmic optician for a checkup. Even small visual defects that under normal circumstances cause no trouble can become significant when reading habits change. Eyestrain will make it difficult to study comfortably and efficiently.

## Reference books

Collect a set of reference books. These do need to be easily available and up to date. For example, a 1923 dictionary will be less than helpful. Words change their meaning over the years and new words are constantly being added to the language. A thesaurus is a subject-based, extended vocabulary list which can be immensely helpful when searching for just the right word when you are writing an essay. A dictionary and a thesaurus could form the basis of your reference shelf. In addition, you will need to add the set books for your course, and possibly specialised subject dictionaries for your particular area of study. Do not let these books stray — buy the rest of the family their own dictionary if necessary. Your books are your tools; they need to be on hand so that time and effort are not wasted searching for them.

Basic reference books could start with:

Shorter Oxford Dictionary, or
Collins English Dictionary (use as a mini encyclopedia);
Roget's Thesaurus;
a dictionary of abbreviations;
Oxford Dictionary of Quotations;
Keesing's Contemporary Archives (details of political, economic and social events);
British Standards Yearbook (information about British standards);
Whitaker's Almanac (current events in government).

## Noise and study

The noise level can affect work quite considerably. Noise is very tiring and, especially if you are studying after a day's work, a high level of sound can lead to indifferent work and loss of concentration. As with lighting, it is important to find the right level for you. Some people find that complete quiet is essential for studying, while others need a little background sound to aid their concentration. The purist will say that all sound should be eliminated, but from a practical point of view this is very difficult. Regular background noise, such as the hum of traffic or the sounds in a factory, can easily be ignored after a while. It is the sudden, unexpected noise or conversation that is the most distracting. If you have to work at home, where children may be playing, dogs barking and the telephone ringing, you may want to mask these sounds with others of your own choice.

Again, experiment to find the best way for you. Background music can mask the outside world somewhat, but you will need to find music which you find pleasant, at a level which does not stop you thinking about your work. The radio is not always suitable, since music may be interrupted by a disc jockey or announcer; your attention will be attracted instantly to the sound of a voice even though you may have little interest in what is being said. Music with a very heavy beat is also distracting, although you may not be aware of it at the time.

If noise is a problem ask yourself:

(a) can you eliminate the noise?
(b) can you remove yourself from the noise?
(c) can you mask the noise?
(d) can you change the time of your study to avoid noise?

If all else fails, ask you local chemist for some ear plugs! This is a serious suggestion — plastic earplugs are often used by night workers trying to sleep during the daytime.

## Working outside your home

With many open-learning programmes it may be necessary, or even desirable, to do a certain amount of studying at work. The same conditions of study still apply; again, it is important to try to use the same place each time so that your mind quickly accepts that you are in a working environment. If the study area is your own office desk, the familiarity could help you to settle down, since you are used to the noise and movement of your workplace. The snag is that unless you have told everyone that you must not be disturbed, you may find that interruptions are frequent. Privacy is essential, and you may have to help your colleagues to understand that there are times when you must not be disturbed. Have your calls redirected, and have a 'do not disturb' sign on the door if you are lucky enough to have an office of your own. Sometimes it may be convenient to use a colleague's office. The advantage of this is that you may be able to get away from people who need to talk to you. Co-operation and a little secrecy from your colleague could pay off. If the office is in a different department so much the better.

Look around the building in which you work for quiet rooms that are only used occasionally. The board room is often used only spasmodically: get permission to use this when it is not timetabled for important meetings. Not only do you get privacy, but also a chance to try out the managing director's chair for size! In larger companies the training manager or the personnel officer may have rooms that are allocated for private study sessions.

If you are working regularly in a room that is not your own, make a checklist of the items you need, ensuring that your briefcase includes all the material you require for a study session. You will be wasting your time and effort if you have to spend time going up and down corridors in search of vital books or new file paper.

Another place which has distinct possibilities is the public library. Of course, you will need to work according to opening times, but most libraries have a reference room which is quiet and has the advantage of having suitable reference books easily available. If you do use your local library, try to sit in the same place each time. As mentioned before, this familiarity is a signal to the brain that it is time to study. There will always be some movement within the library but you will soon get used to this. One point to think about is the ventilation; in many places intended for public use the rooms can get too warm. Make friends with the librarians and they may even keep your favourite seat. Certainly, a co-operative librarian who knows just where to get information quickly is worth his or her weight in gold.

Wherever you decide to work — and it may be a combination of several places — think carefully about the physical environment in which you intend to work. Although most of the things we have considered may seem rather unimportant, it is certainly easier to get down to productive work in a suitable study area than one in which you are constantly irritated by minor problems.

## Personal health

The physical conditions in which study takes place will have a direct effect upon concentration and work effectiveness. Moreover, a definite relationship has been found between physical fitness and a high performance level. People in poor health usually have such a low energy level that it is difficult for them to achieve the results that they want. Physiological factors affect concentration, and therefore study. As an example of this, the body will make certain adjustments which result in relaxation and possibly sleep, immediately after a heavy meal, or on entering a warm room after exercise in the cold, fresh air.

Body and mind are closely interrelated, and the effect of bodily conditions on the mind has been very well documented. On the principle that prevention is better than cure, and without turning into a hypochondriac, it is wise to think a little about your own health. Use common sense, lead a reasonably regulated life, and all will be well — literally.

An understanding of one's own physical make-up is useful. Some people function better in the morning while others enjoy working at night. Capitalise on this when working out study timetables and a working routine. After all, there is no real reason why you should not study quite happily at three in the morning if this works for you. Good study habits are mainly a matter of common sense and organisation. When planning out your workload, make sure that you do not neglect your health, and that you have built in time for exercise.

A very high proportion of conventional students at our universities appear not to take sufficient exercise. This proportion may be even higher for those who are both holding down a job and studying. Without going to ridiculous extremes, you can ensure that you do get some exercise each day. Try leaving your car a fair distance from work and walking the rest of the way. Use a bicycle instead of a car. Spend several hours each weekend in the garden if you have one, or in a place where you can get some fresh air and recreation. Exercise does not have to be strenuous to be effective, but if you are keen on sport anyway, do not abandon all sporting activities because of your commitment to your course.

Some people are very affected by the weather and this may have to be taken into consideration. If your mind seems to seize up in some weather conditions and you are prone to headaches, it might be worth looking at the various ionisers that are on the market. For some people, charging the air with negative ions can make a good deal of difference to their comfort and alertness of mind.

This is not the place to go into the sense or non-sense of smoking, but note that you can acquire serious respiratory diseases through smoking, and the constant pollution of your working environment will cut down your ability to think clearly.

If common sense says don't drink and drive, it will also tell you not to sup and study. Even a small amount of alcohol will impair your judgement and reduce your concentration.

The use of effective time planning will be covered in the chapter on time organisation. However, do remember to make time for friends, hobbies, sporting and leisure pursuits, and any other activities important to human happiness. You may have to curtail some of these activities in the short-term, but do not lose sight of what you eventually want out of life.

## Case study

Christine Allenby is the managing director of a small but well-established firm of builders' merchants. Christine took over the business on her father's retirement. The business, though fairly busy, had been run on very traditional lines. She is determined to make it more efficient and successful.

While on a business studies degree course, Christine took a student counsellor's advice and thought through her needs for an organised and efficient study environment. One look at her father's office convinced her that she needed to rethink the whole office area. She took the principles of efficient study organisation into her office, and with the willing help of her secretary resited desks so that light and access became easier. She also arranged for a better ventilation system, and got a lighting engineer in to give advice on general office illumination. A commercial-weight carpet helped with the noise problem. Her secretary's comments on the filing system (paid invoices on the shelves, unpaid on the desk, orders on the floor) were noted and a new filing system has been installed. Christine is convinced that paying attention to the working environment makes for higher productivity, more efficient customer service and better staff relations. Next she tackles the yard!

## Individual exercises

For effective and productive work it is important to pay attention to the physical conditions under which you study.

Use the two checklists below to see how you rate. Are you studying in conditions which will enable you to achieve good results?

### Study area checklist

1 *Physical conditions*
   (a) Can you be sure of a reasonably undisturbed place in which to work?
   (b) Is the room well ventilated, neither too hot nor too cold?
   (c) Is your clothing loose and comfortable?

2 *Desk or work surface*
   (a) Is your desk large enough to spread out all your books,

papers and equipment?

(b) If the books, etc. have to be cleared away, have you a permanent shelf, cupboard or box in which to keep everything?

3   *Chair*
Can you sit comfortably at the work surface, ensuring that you are at the correct height and that your lungs can take in sufficient oxygen?

4   *Lighting*
Do you cast a shadow on your work? Is there too much glare from your table light? If you are right-handed, is the light coming from the left, or vice-versa?

5   *Equipment*
Have you sufficient paper, rough notebooks, pens, calculators, etc. to ensure that your work is not hindered?

6   *Reference books*
Have you a set of basic reference books which are relevant to your course?

**Checklist of good study habits**

*How do you rate?*

Answer true or false to the following statements.

1   I try to choose a time to study when I have no other work, or other domestic or leisure pursuits.
2   If I choose to have background music, it is suitable and not too loud.
3   I sit in an upright position so that I am comfortable and get enough oxygen.
4   I study at a time when my mind and body are as fresh as possible.
5   Before I begin, I make sure that I have collected all the things I will need.
6   I do not use planned study time to ring friends, watch television, do crosswords, etc.
7   The room where I work is well ventilated and has a reasonable temperature.
8   I try to plan study times on a regular basis.
9   I make sure that all my notes and assignments are well organised, meaningful and legible.

10 I check the meanings and implications of all new words, and consciously extend my vocabulary.
11 I am alert to the varying places from which I can get information (magazines, television, specialists, museums, etc. as well as libraries).
12 If I do not fully understand a topic I obtain immediate help from my tutor.
13 I consciously apply study techniques and learning strategies to my work.
14 I try to relate what I have learned about any subject to things learned elsewhere, and to everyday life.
15 I structure my study sessions sensibly.
16 I make a positive effort to read any graphs, diagrams, illustrations, etc. which are part of my course material.
17 My notes from written sources are always in my own words except where I need to quote material.
18 I enjoy my studies.

## Group exercises

1 The study area checklist can be used as a basis for discussion. People will often arrange home study areas in a sensible fashion but will put up with inadequate seating and lighting in a noisy, ill-ventilated office.

Good working conditions are similar to good study conditions. Being aware of the importance of the physical factors involved in thinking, planning and studying can be a fruitful exercise.

2 The good study habits checklist can also be used for discussion. Below are a few further points raised by students, which could also be used for discussion.

(a) I find it really hard to concentrate.
(b) I'm way behind schedule.
(c) My problem is working in fits and starts, it's difficult to work regularly.
(d) Compared with the others I seem to do far less (or more).
(e) Priorities are the difficulty: whether to do the report for the MD or the essay for my tutor.
(f) I'll never get through it all.
(g) It's impossible to get going after a day's work.

(h) I never know how long to take over my assignment.
(i) The relevant background material never seems available.
(j) I tend to fall asleep as soon as I pick up a book.

When students realise that other people have similar problems they become more confident in looking for solutions. A group discussion will often help the individual to think through a particular study problem and hopefully come up with an answer.

3 The following exercise will help individuals in the group to assess their own reaction to working under noisy conditions.

*Materials:* sheets of paper printed with random numbers from 1 to 9
a loud rock cassette with a heavy beat
*Group size:* any size

(a) Supply each person with a printed sheet of random numbers.
(b) Instruct the group to print the word *phenomena* in the margin and write under each letter the numbers 1—9, as follows:

P H E N O M E N A
1 2 3 4 5 6 7 8 9

(c) Tell the group that when you give the signal they are to look at the random numbers and, working along each row, write down the appropriate letter under each number as in the sample in figure 3.1.

**Figure 3.1**

Give them a three minute session while playing the cassette at full volume. (Not popular with colleagues in adjoining rooms!)

(d) Leave this exercise for at least 15—20 minutes.
(e) Repeat the exercise but this time using the word *principle*, as follows:

    P R I N C I P L E
    1 2 3 4 5 6 7 8 9

This time the group must try to complete the exercise for the same amount of time in silence. (The same sheet of A4 paper can be used for each session.)

This exercise is useful, in that it shows how distracting very loud sounds, especially those with a heavy beat, can be when they are trying to concentrate.

Discussion within the group will often lead students to rethink their method of study, although it must be said that, as individuals vary so much, the exercise has little scientific value. Used as a talking point it can be helpful.

# FOUR

# Listening

The ability to communicate and learn is essential for all human beings, and one of the most neglected skills of communication and learning is listening. We spend a high proportion of our time in listening to others, face to face, on the telephone, or when listening to the radio, tape recordings, etc. It has been estimated that in managerial communication, writing takes up 9 per cent of time, reading 16 per cent and talking 30 per cent, but at least 45 per cent of time is used in listening. It has also been estimated that over 70 per cent of oral communication is misunderstood or forgotten. Certainly between one third and one half of what we hear is lost within approximately eight hours unless we take steps to retard this forgetting process. In this chapter we will be concerned with listening effectively, so that we can reduce the likelihood of mishearing information and the difficulties this can entail.

## Listening is more than hearing

*Collins English Dictionary* says that *hearing* is 'the faculty or sense by which sound is perceived' but that to *listen* is to 'concentrate on hearing something, to take heed, to pay attention'. Listening is a positive skill although too many people think of it as a passive and rather negative activity. It is, however, a complex psychological process which involves interpretation of material and understanding its significance. Merely allowing words to enter the ear is not listening; however, 'in one ear and out the other' is often the norm. In our childhood we receive a good deal of help with reading, writing and talking, but very little is done about teaching us how to listen.

Our early childhood experiences often lead to bad listening habits. Teachers are sometimes bad listeners; they tend to talk at great length, not always realising that the child has switched off because of unanswered questions, a short concentration span or poorly-structured lessons. Parents are also sometimes guilty of talking *at* rather than *to* their children. This is important to remember when thinking about study listening in later life. Think about your own attitude towards listening — to material which has association with study, for example.

Within any organisation, poor listening can lead to inefficient daily work, and ultimately to staff dissatisfaction, customer loss, bad labour relations and major policy mistakes. Acting without adequate information and understanding is a recipe for disaster. If an organisation is to be successful, feedback from staff, customers and clients is essential. Good listening is a crucial managerial skill. To make any decision, however trivial, the manager has to have alternatives to act upon. Listening to others and assessing the opinions and information acquired is vital for the health of the organisation. Good relationships are built on day-to-day communication, and this is a two-way process, where listening is equally as important as talking.

It is asking for poor results to go through any course of study without the ability to assess, structure and make decisions about what to do with the material available. Much of the information dispensed in a course is in the form of lectures, radio or taped information; it may also come from group discussion and conversations with knowledgeable colleagues. If you have not learned how to listen properly, much of the spoken information will either pass you by or be misunderstood.

Perhaps the key to good listening is to have an open mind. We hear what we want to hear in many cases. Our prejudices, beliefs and expectations often determine what is heard. We tend to block out the ideas and words that we do not want to hear. Openness of mind is an essential part of learning and thinking. The person who has enough self-confidence in his or her own ability to learn will accept new ideas and concepts, selecting those which are of value to him or her. Thus, a basic respect for others is necessary; and it is as important when listening to a lecture or a taped piece of information as it is when having a conversation while at work or at home.

Because they sometimes feel guilty at 'wasting time' just sitting listening, students often skimp the time needed for listening to tapes and broadcasts, believing that they should be able

ELEM—D

to pick up the information very quickly. This is even more evident when the student is listening to another student, tutor or colleague. The supposition is that if you do not grasp the message in a very short time, you are intellectually inadequate. Acquiring good listening habits will help you take in material far more quickly and with more accuracy. Listening is like any skill: it takes practice to reach a competent level. The student and the manager who take time to listen to other people's opinions, ideas, prejudices and worries will learn a great deal about the subject or person they are investigating.

Critical faculties are sharpened when you listen carefully to other people's ideas, and your own opinions and ideas can only benefit from listening to others. But listen with intelligence, and in a positive manner. Listening is a skill and a discipline. It requires control, both intellectual and emotional. Hearing only becomes listening when you are totally involved with the auditory experience and interpret it correctly.

Messages are not conveyed by speech alone. We need an awareness of how people use their bodies to give information as well. When listening to others or using our own signals to show interest (or boredom), we communicate, using body language to express these feelings. This is an important part of listening. The alert student will be able to pick up clues from the way other people use their bodies to convey messages.

When a speaker wants to emphasise a point that she feels is particularly important, she will probably show this by leaning forward slightly, raising the shoulders and looking around the room quickly. She may make emphatic movements with the hands, tap on the table and alter the tone of her voice. We recognise these non-verbal clues instinctively, but it is helpful to try to analyse them and to be aware of how movements back up spoken language. Even in a lecture, the listeners contribute a good deal to the communication process by looking alert, nodding at appropriate moments, leaning slightly forward and smiling occasionally. There are few things more unnerving than to be speaking to someone who does not respond in any way.

In small groups or on a one-to-one basis, try talking to one another with little or no eye contact. Even when this is pre-arranged it can be very frustrating. Speakers who feel that their audience is not attending to them find it difficult to speak well, and may even dry up altogether. Active listening is an essential to good learning. If you are uneasy about looking people in the eye, try looking them in the bridge of the nose — if you are a reasonable distance away this works very effectively without making you feel embarrassed!

Try to become aware of non-verbal clues. You will find that both the verbal and physical signals given out by a speaker will help you to make more effective notes, to pick up the main thread of an argument and to have a shrewd idea of when the speaker is not too sure of his or her own stand. Identifying these clues will be of value outside the area of study. Non-verbal behaviour that accompanies speech gives you information about the subject, and your own body language will encourage a speaker to be more interesting and forthcoming.

The three main areas where the student has to listen carefully are when:

(a) listening to taped instructions/lectures and radio broadcasts;
(b) listening to lectures;
(c) listening in seminars and group discussion.

With a little imagination it will be obvious that these three areas are similar in form to many daily listening situations at work: listening to a telephone conversation or taped message from a colleague in the field; listening to the chairperson's speech; taking part in a meeting where you will be expected to participate, and so on.

We will now look at these three main situations and consider how best to listen carefully in the different circumstances.

### Listening to radio and tape

Once the tape recording or radio is turned on, most students feel at a disadvantage because the speaker is not visible. We rely on the non-verbal clues given out to us by a speaker much more than we realise. These clues of expression and gesture are now unavailable. For those who listen regularly to the radio life is somewhat easier, but a very high proportion of people nowadays get most of their information from television, or in written form. The concentration required for listening without visual clues is more intense and consequently more tiring. You may find that you have to work in rather shorter time spans. It is always worth taping a radio programme and this will be assumed in the paragraphs below.

Listen to the tape once (twice if you can spare the time) without taking notes or worrying about learning or memorising the content. In this way you will get an overall picture of the subject and know what aspects of the topic to expect when you listen in more detail. At this time, you should be mentally reviewing what you already know about the subject, and how the tape will fit into the general pattern of information that you are building up over the course.

Read through any notes that have already been given with the tape, or from any broadcast before listening as a preview of content. As you listen the second (or third) time, try to pick out the key phrases and themes. How you actually take notes will depend on the method which seems most appropriate for the material, and your own choice. The chapter on note making will introduce you to various different methods of notation.

If you find that the information is difficult to grasp, stop the recording so that you can go back over your notes and consolidate and explore what you have heard.

If you are unable to tape a broadcast and so have only one bite of the cherry, take very brief notes, possibly just jotting down key words. Time spent in writing means less efficient listening. You can write notes after the programme has ended.

When listening to the radio or to a tape, sit in a comfortable chair — but watch your reactions. If you settle down to listen in the chair in which you usually relax or watch your favourite 'soap', you may find that your mind wanders. This is because both your mind and your body are in a place which is not associated with study. If you do not want to sit at your desk, sit in a comfortable chair in a room that you do not associate with relaxation.

Television programmes and videos present their own problems. A visual presentation, especially where the pictures are vivid and the graphics are exciting, can become more important than the intended message. Often this does not matter, since with the extra dimension of visual stimulus you will possibly get a more rounded view of the subject. There are, however, times when detail, which is important for real understanding of the topic, is lost because you are concentrating on the pictures and not on the speech. This is where a VCR is useful, as it lets you go over the programme several times, looking for different points at each viewing.

## Listening to lectures and meetings

Even during a distance-learning course there is often an opportunity to attend a lecture given by an expert in your field. This lecture may last anything up to an hour and a half, and this time span is hard to cope with. You are not going to be able to concentrate at the same level throughout the talk and you will have to take steps to counter this loss of concentration. There are several practical things which you can do to help you to get the most out of the talk.

*Movement* When you find that your attention seems to be wandering, shift your position very slightly. Even a small movement of the body will help. Total physical inactivity can make positive listening very difficult. Shrugging the shoulders, moving the facial muscles and flexing the muscles of the body will all help. Do take care that the speaker is not aware of any facial movement, however. It is rather offputting to have a member of your audience grimacing as if in pain as you launch into your most dynamic delivery. Dropping a pencil is also a good ploy, but again you owe the speaker the courtesy of being as unobtrusive as possible. You can also relax by rolling your eyes and blinking, preferably while your eyes are looking downwards!

*Mental preparation* Before you go into the lecture, go over in your own mind what you already know about the subject. Find out about the speaker and his angle on his topic. Discuss with other students what you expect to get out of the lecture. In other words, go into the talk with some background understanding. You may find it useful to think of a few questions that you would like to be answered. Most lectures are one-way affairs, but there may be time for questions at the end. Be prepared for this and use the opportunity whenever it arises.

*Note taking* A knowledge of the room that the lecture will take place in is a great help. You may find that you are able to write notes quite easily because the room has desks or chairs with writing boards attached. But this is not always the case, and balancing a few sheets of A4 on your lap while trying to write down important points is not easy. A clipboard or a small notebook may be more appropriate than a ring file or loose sheets of paper. Seating has already been mentioned, but it is worth thinking about it again, especially if you know that the room will get hot or is dimly lit. Make sure that you are in the best possible position both physically and mentally to profit from the speaker's words.

## Active listening

You will get very little out of the lecture if you are not thoroughly and actively involved in listening to it. Once you sit back and think your own thoughts you have lost the opportunity to learn from the experience. Very often a subject which you may assume to be complex and difficult will become clear when you force yourself to follow the argument, and make a real effort to understand. Listen with empathy so that you listen to what is being said and not what you want or expect to hear. Never prejudge speakers because of their appearance, manner or importance.

A very real danger is to switch off early on because you have decided the subject or the speaker is of no interest. It is easy to jump to the conclusion that the speaker will add nothing to your knowledge and therefore that there is no reason to listen properly. This, of course, may not be true, and in any case the discipline of listening, arguing (mentally) and reviewing the speaker's message is in itself part of the learning process.

In lectures, as in textbooks, the core ideas are the important ones. Look out for the main themes and try to identify them early on. If you have been able to do some background work on the talk before you arrive, this will be of help. A lecturer will often give a topic or theme sentence at the start of each section of the talk and this sentence will sum up the ideas which follow. Sentences like these are worth listening for as they provide a heading for notes. If you are lucky, the lecturer will also make a brief summary at the end of each section or at least at the end of the lecture. Do not expect dozens of major themes. It is far more likely that the speaker will only attempt to introduce one or two main themes and a few subsidiary topics. Most of the time will be spent in giving supporting details or explanations of the thesis. Learn to spot the major points by looking for verbal and non-verbal clues that the speaker will give.

In the case of verbal clues, certain 'signal' words and phrases will help you to keep track of the way the speaker's mind is working, and to take notes. For example, the speaker will possibly use some of these phrases when introducing new ideas:

*A major development . . .*
*There are two reasons why . . .*
*And most important . . .*
*First . . . Second . . . Third . . .*
*I feel strongly that . . .*

When introducing supporting material these phrases may be used:

*On the other hand . . .*
*In contrast . . .*
*As an example . . .*
*Similarly . . .*
*Furthermore . . .*
*Also . . .*
*For instance . . .*

A summary or conclusion could be signalled by:

*Therefore . . .*
*In conclusion . . .*
*From this we can deduce . . .*
*Finally . . .*
*To sum up . . .*

Some lecturers will give very clear signals about the things they consider extremely important. They may say:

*The important thing here is . . .*
*Remember that . . .*
*The basic argument states . . .*

The majority of speakers will write lecture notes out and deliver them in a fairly logical way. However, they do not necessarily follow them slavishly. They may add personal comments and extra examples that occur to them as they talk, and they may even tell the occasional joke. The student's task is to disentangle the main themes from the subsidiary ideas, and to leave out the supporting material (and irrelevancies) unless they seem valuable.

Listening is an active and positive skill, not just a matter of filling the ears with sound. The good listener has a quick heart action and a faster circulation of blood, and shows a small rise in body temperature. These are signs of a person using a good deal of energy. It is impossible to be passive and a good listener. Concentration is essential if you are to understand the message fully. You can help yourself to concentrate by preparing beforehand, making sure that you are not too physically tense, and taking the lecture environment into consideration.

There are also things that you can do to keep yourself alert during the talk. You should be looking for the main themes, and for any subsidiary topics. The speaker's ideas should be making you think around the subject. Try to anticipate what is coming next. React to the statements in a critical way, and try to link what is being said with your own knowledge of the subject. If you use your imagination to empathise with the speaker you will find that it is easier to concentrate on his or her ideas. Develop your critical faculties, and, as you think about the subject, agree or disagree with the concepts being presented. Alert listening will improve your ability to absorb, remember and learn, especially if you are thoroughly involved with the speaker and the subject.

A real danger may be that you find some of the ideas given out stimulating and thought-provoking. This is, of course, a good thing; the danger lies in going off at a tangent and missing the next thing that is said. You can overcome this to some extent by the way you make your notes. If you are making linear notes, have a different colour of pen to jot down your own reactions. If you do this you will be able to read them afterwards and think about them seriously, but will not lose the thread of the lecture. Some people prefer to have a margin down the right-hand side of the page on which to record their own thoughts. When making pattern notes (see the chapter on note making) a separate colour, a different type of printing or even a separate heading will record your personal reactions.

Although it is important to keep pace with the speaker, you can capitalise on your speed of thought, which is on average four times that of the rate of speech (about 125 words per minute). Because you think so quickly, you can mentally question, summarise what has been said and anticipate what is to come. Some speakers have long pauses in their delivery. Try not to let your mind drift away during these pauses. This is the time for anticipating coming ideas or summarising the significant material that has already been given.

The experienced note maker will never take notes as if taking dictation. Writing down everything that is said is not just a waste of time: it usually means that you have little chance to absorb the full meaning of the talk. You will end up with a mass of notes, but very little idea of their significance. It is better to take no notes and really listen to the speaker than to write down every word but leave the lecture with no real understanding of the subject.

As you listen to the speaker you can involve yourself even more if you think of examples that will illustrate the points the lecturer is making. If you note them down as well they may be useful for written assignments that come up in the future.

Question the speaker in your mind. The more you feel personally involved in the talk, the more you will learn. By forming a question in your mind you are helping your mind to organise the material that you hear. You could also jot down the questions in order to use them in any question-and-answer session at the end of the lecture. It is virtually impossible to keep a well-formulated question in the mind as you listen intently to an interesting lecture. If you really want to know the speaker's thoughts on the subject, note the question down, and then quickly focus your mind on the next thing that is being said.

All speakers, unless they are very insensitive, are aware of audience reaction and respond to an interested and alert audience. If you want to get the best out of a speaker it is necessary to show him or her that you are interested in what is being said. The speaker will use the voice and body to gain attention and you should respond in a positive way by facing the speaker squarely; look directly at the speaker and use facial gestures to convey non-verbal messages. Watch a lecturer carefully and see how gestures and tone of voice are used to emphasise particular points. You will find that you can pick up clues about the significance of what is being said more effectively than if you just hear the words and ignore the attitudes and enthusiasms of the speaker, as expressed by non-verbal messages. If you yourself are interested in a particular point, you will unconsciously tend to lean towards the speaker. A smile of appreciation or a nod of understanding will indicate that you have not in fact died, but are interested in what is being said. This will encourage any lecturer to give of her or his best, and everyone will benefit. It cannot be stressed too often that communication is a two-way process, and that listening is an active and positive part of it.

When you are taking notes in a lecture, do not be put off by what a fellow student is noting down. People are different in their approach, background knowledge and understanding, and they organise their thoughts differently. A key word which will be meaningful to you may not suggest the same train of thought to your neighbour. Stick to your own ideas, even though comparing notes later and discussing the lecture after it has finished is an extremely useful learning technique.

Try not to be distracted by whispering in the audience, the person with the bad cough, the latecomer going to his seat. These things are only likely to distract you if you let them. Train yourself to come back to the speaker even when you have momentarily let your attention slip. More difficult to cope with are the mannerisms, appearance or voice of the lecturer. Concentrate on the content of the talk and not on any irritating or disturbing things about the speaker.

In a long talk you will find that there are times when your attention wanders, unless the speaker is exceptionally interesting and dynamic. If you have been listening well and really thinking about what you hear, it will not be a complete disaster if you switch off for a few seconds. The trick is to switch off at a moment when you can afford to, rather than miss a vital point of the talk. If you listen for the signals from the speaker that were referred to earlier in this chapter you will be able to select a time when it is reasonably safe to let your mind relax for a moment. With practice, you will be able to take a short break and still not lose the thread of the lecture. Fortunately, most lecturers will repeat the points they want to make more than once.

A head full of ideas, conversations, letters and gossip will prevent clarity of thought. Try to clear your mind of outside thoughts before you go into the lecture or talk. You will get more from the lecture if you prepare thoroughly and review what you already know. Your mind is not a blank page, so go to the talk with a framework of ideas on which to build. Good listening will create the conditions necessary for the mind to sort out, restructure and digest what you hear.

### Tutorial and small-group listening

The opportunity to meet in small groups and to exchange ideas with other students and colleagues should never be missed.

This is a vital part of the learning process, and the art of listening is never more important than in this situation. Many people can carry on a one-to-one conversation with ease and are happy to sit through a talk and benefit from it, but find it difficult to meet in a smaller discussion group. Some people, especially if they have a prepared paper to submit, find it difficult to listen to others as they are completely preoccupied with what they themselves are going to say. Prepare such material really well, and then forget about it while you listen to the other members of the group.

In group listening you have to be very alert to the styles of speech, thought patterns and experiences of other people. Sometimes it is difficult to follow and take part in the discussion fully because you hear words and arguments with which you disagree strongly. If you respond to a word or concept in a negative manner, this will be a real block to effective listening. You may lose the thread of the discussion and fail to develop a fuller understanding.

There may be people in the group who are difficult to handle because they argue in an emotional way, interrupt the speaker, and are suspicious about other students 'stealing' their ideas; or they may have so little self-regard that they say little or nothing. All these people can make group discussion very difficult. In a tutorial this is not your problem but that of your tutor. Within a self-help study group you may have to do some negotiating if you are all to benefit from listening to each other. To make sure that you have grasped an important point within a group discussion or tutorial, try to paraphrase the content. This helps others to clarify their own thoughts as they listen to their ideas being summarised, and it will also help you to think through the material and classify it in your own mind. In addition, it will serve as a springboard for further exploration of the theme.

## Questioning

Sometimes you will want the speaker to give you more information, or to clarify a point. It can be very frustrating if you do not get a full response. Part of the reason may be that you are not phrasing the questions in the right way. Asking questions is part of the manager's function. Use the following questioning methods for asking questions in lecture situations or in group sessions. The suggestions below are, of course, only a simplified approach to questioning techniques.

*Statement (or summary) questions* rely mainly on your tone of voice for a response. They are useful in small groups, or on a one-to-one basis. Statement questions ensure that you have summarised the information properly and check that the speaker has not been misunderstood. For example:

> 'So, there are five basic needs in Maslow's hierarchy of needs?'
> 'What we seem to have decided so far is . . .?'

*Open questions* encourage the speaker to 'open up'. Sometimes follow-on questions can then be asked to get more information. Open questions are useful when you want the speaker to expand on a point or explain it more completely. For example:

> 'Can you tell us more about your attitude to delegation . . .?'
> 'What happened next . . .?'

*Closed questions* usually get a one-word answer. They are helpful in establishing specific facts, but little use for getting the speaker to expand on a subject. For example:

> 'How old were you then?'
> 'Did you tell Mary about the management development meeting?'

## Good and bad listening

Below are some of the key points about negative and positive listening. Use them as a guide to assessing your own listening skills.

*Negative listening* means:

> (a) making up your mind that the subject will be boring before you have really tried to master it;
> (b) being too critical of the speaker (strange accent, unusual appearance, irritating mannerisms, etc.);
> (c) listening only to the parts of the talk which you find of interest;

(d) deliberately interrupting the speaker;
(e) daydreaming;
(f) letting things distract you (noise, movement, heat, light, etc.);
(g) switching off when you come to anything unfamiliar (new words or concepts);
(h) sleepiness or poor physical condition.

*Positive listening* means:

(a) deliberately looking for interesting points in the lecture;
(b) trying to ignore a bad speaker in order to get through to the message;
(c) not getting side-tracked into thinking of other things that the speaker's words remind you of;
(d) trying to establish the key points of the lecture;
(e) looking interested (the speaker will react to an interested audience);
(f) making a determined effort not to be distracted by outside noise or movement;
(g) becoming involved in the meaning of what is being said;
(h) keeping pace with the speaker and not lingering over points that were made a few minutes before;
(i) moving slightly if your attention seems to be wavering (total physical inactivity makes listening more difficult);
(j) writing down the key words of the talk where appropriate;
(k) being receptive, not being afraid of new ideas;
(l) thinking of questions you could ask if you disagree with the lecturer;
(m) trying to anticipate what is coming next (even if it is wrong, your mind will be actively involved and alert);
(n) in a long talk, not worrying if your mind appears to slow down (move, blink, switch off for 20—30 seconds and then go back to active listening);
(o) preparing yourself before the talk, by reviewing what you already know of the subject;
(p) putting yourself in the speaker's place, making sure that you hear what is being said rather than what

you want to hear (the practised listener will question, summarise and read between the lines);

(q) capitalising on your speed of thought. Most people talk at about 125 wpm. You can think at at least four times this rate. Use this to your advantage for questioning, summarising and so on. You can:
   — anticipate what is coming,
   — summarise what has been said,
   — question the speaker and listen between the lines (use clues given by body language, tone of voice, and so on).

## Case study

David Masters is head of a newly formed research and development department. He is now responsible for a staff of ten people as opposed to his previous position at a university, working with just one other colleague, and engaged in pure research. As a rather retiring person David found talking to his staff quite difficult. He realised that it was not enough just to ask them to take on particular tasks, and in any case he found that some people were obviously unhappy about their work. Inexperienced in handling staff, he applied the principles of research to his own situation and looked at all aspects of the daily routine. He came to the conclusion that lack of real communication was the major problem and concluded that, as communication is a two-way process, it was necessary for him to listen as well as request. Dredging up from his mind the advice he had been given about positive listening as a student, David started to listen with empathy, taking time to analyse not only the words he heard but also tone of voice, body language and even brief silences. After a while his staff responded to his increasing listening ability and he found that the people he thought were obstructive were often full of stress. He was able to respond with sympathy, and in one case with practical help. By listening creatively he was able to see that some staff did not understand how he envisaged the development of their department. He found out that they were uneasy about their own positions in the future. Listening effectively did not solve all his difficulties, but made it possible for the department to operate much more happily and efficiently.

## Individual exercises

1 Practice listening to an audio tape on an unfamiliar subject. Listen to it carefully and afterwards make brief notes on what you heard. Play the tape back with your notes in front of you. Check that:

(a) you have grasped the main outline of the subject;
(b) you have noted accurately at least some of the detail;
(c) you can tell someone else what the tape was about.

2 Choose another tape, also on an unfamiliar subject. This time take notes as you listen. Check afterwards that your notes reflect the overall meaning of the subject and that a high proportion of the detail is correct.

These two exercises aid listening, concentration and comprehension. It is advisable to choose unfamiliar topics as it is easier to assess your progress when you do not have a lot of background knowledge. Tapes on allied subjects can also be used; for example if your field is in accountancy and finance, choose material from personnel or industrial relations.

The next two exercises require the co-operation of others. The first exercise is to demonstrate how impossible it is to listen to more than one speaker at a time if you are to absorb what is being said.

3 *Stereo headphones*

Three people are needed. Two people get as near to the third as possible, and talk into his or her ear at close range. A non-stop flow of speech is needed, on any subject under the sun. The speakers should talk for about sixty seconds.

The person in the centre will probably have found that their attention switches from one voice to the other. Sometimes this is because a key word will trigger off a series of thoughts, sometimes because one voice is louder, more persuasive or more insistent than the other. Analyse why you listened more to one voice than the other. What linked you with one more than another? Was it volume? Friendship? Interest? The importance of the speaker to you?

The conclusion may be drawn that a head full of conversation, ideas, letters, agendas and stray thoughts will hamper clarity of thought. This obviously has implications for the working situation as well as for study.

4 *Summarising*

Three or four people are needed for this exercise.

The first speaker begins to talk on any topic and carries on for three or four minutes while the others listen. (Use an egg timer so that the speakers do not get too carried away.) The second person must summarise accurately what has been said. Then they themselves go on to speak on a new subject. This is in turn summarised by the next person. Those people listening but not summarising should check the accuracy of the summary and challenge any detail they feel is incorrect.

5 Listen to a serial on the radio and try to predict the outcome. Write down your ideas and listen to the next episode to check whether your prediction was credible.

6 Recall from memory the last conversation that you had with your wife, optometrist, boss, secretary.

7 The next time that you have to listen to a lecture or speech, or when in a general meeting, use the following method to help you listen and concentrate. Divide your notepaper into four columns. Use column 1 to note the speaker(s), column 2 for any questions the talk raises in your mind or that you want to raise with the speaker, column 3 for any general points that you think of, and column 4 for any specific points that you want to remember.

## Group exercises

1 *Materials:*  copies of the 'listening checklist', below
  *Group size:*  any number

Use the checklist below, which has been adapted from the points for negative and positive listening given earlier. The checklist may be used as a basis for discussion and to reinforce the material in the chapter. Point out to the group that it is easy, but pointless, to 'cheat'. If they are honest with themselves they will have a good chance of estimating their listening ability fairly accurately. Group members answer the questions *yes* or *no*. Count each *yes* as one point.

After the checklist has been answered, the following points can be made:

(a) If all the questions were answered with *yes*, then it is unlikely that the person was being absolutely honest. Listening is hard work and no one listens well all the time.

(b) A score of 5 is fairly realistic. It is useful to identify which questions had a *no* answer. This often says something about the person. Perhaps concentration is a problem. Is personal prejudice hampering effective listening? A general discussion can often lead to a reappraisal of listening abilities, and a desire to improve the skill.

(c) If any scores were well under 5 then the group member was either being very modest or is too concerned with his or her own prejudices to be able to listen effectively to others.

The discussion needs to be led carefully and sensitively, but increasing the awareness of the group to some of the elements of good listening can only be useful.

A summary of good listening attributes could include:

being prepared to listen;
being interested;
keeping an open mind;
listening for key points;
listening critically and examining each point;
concentration;
effective note taking.

*Listening checklist*

(a) Do you always take the speaker seriously, even when the talk is boring and repetitive?

(b) Do you sit where you can both see and hear the speaker?

(c) Do you consciously try to work out the key points and logic of what is being said?

(d) Do you pay due attention to the speaker, and make an effort to look interested?

(e) Do you always ignore irritating mannerisms, accent or appearance in the speaker?

(f) Do you always allow for your own prejudices and emotions when evaluating what you hear?

(g) Do you 'listen between the lines' and observe the body language underlying the feelings of the speaker?
(h) Do you really think about what is being said?
(i) Do you always refrain from interrupting whenever you hear something that you know to be wrong?
(j) Do you never let tiredness, heat, noise, movement etc. distract you when you are listening?

2 *Materials:*    two video recordings of opposing viewpoints (e.g. party political broadcasts or a recorded discussion programme)
  *Group size:*    6—10

Run through the video recordings, inviting the group to take notes and then to recount in as much detail as possible what they heard.

Prejudices and allegiances can be very strong — you will need to handle this exercise with care! Political emotions can take over from the main discussion about listening skills, but with a tolerant group this can be a valuable exercise.

Replay the videos after the group have recounted what they thought they heard. How accurate were the accounts?

*Points to look out for* the use of emotive language and its effect upon what we hear; the use of body language to emphasise particular ideas; the use of visual images to distract the listener from or towards what is being said; verbal clues given to signal a key point

3 *Materials:*    shapes on thin card from template based on A4 (see figure 4.1)
  *Group size:*    5—7 in each sub-group

This exercise illustrates aspects of non-verbal communication. Listening with the eyes is an essential counterpart to listening with the ears.

(a) Supply each group with a set of cut shapes. Each person should have two or three pieces.
(b) Ask the groups to assemble the pieces into an oblong. They must not speak to each other at any time, and must therefore try to communicate in other ways.
(c) Set a time limit of five minutes.
(d) After the set time the groups can come together and discuss the way in which they were able to communicate.

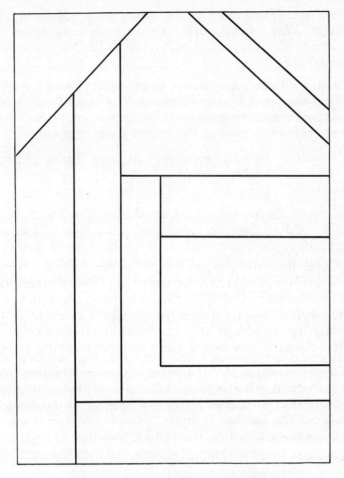

*Figure 4.1   Template for Exercise 3*

Discussion will probably follow several paths:
   How do we communicate non-verbally?
   Do relationships within the group matter?
   What other methods of non-verbal communication are
      there?
   What thinking/learning styles and skills appear to be
      important for:
      — completing the exercise?
      — spatial skills?
      — observation?
      — memory?

Were some members of the group more dominant than others? Was this because they were more aggressive? Or better at communication? Or more skilled in memory and spatial skills?

Gestures, facial movements, grunts and groans are all part of the way people communicate. The aim of this exercise is to make students aware of how important it is to consider these things as well as the actual words spoken.

4 *Materials:*   two identical sets of lego bricks or similar building blocks
  *Group size:*   pairs sitting back to back

Taking it in turns, each person makes an object with the lego bricks. When they have finished, they take it in turns to describe to their partner how it has been put together. As they speak, the partner attempts to make a matching object. This is easier said than done. Clarity of instruction and good listening skills are essential.

5 *Materials:*   prepared newspaper articles
  *Group size:*   any size

Select a newspaper or magazine article that will take about 4–5 minutes to read. Go through it and underline the following words: *the, to* and *when.* Ask the group to listen carefully as you read it, and to count the number of times each of these words occurs.

Read the article out, then check answers. Do not let the group use paper and pencil. Check that they have not added *too* to their score.

Using a passage of similar length, read it through, but leave out several words that you have selected beforehand. (Choose some key words and some less important words.) The group must work out and record the missing words, or words that make sense in the context.

# FIVE

# Memory (1)

The next two chapters will be concerned with memory. Most management education is to do with researching information and with decision-making exercises. Nevertheless, the ability to recall information when required is a useful managerial quality. This chapter is an attempt to describe a little of how the memory appears to work. The following chapter includes many well-known memory techniques and mnemonics. These should help you to retain and recall the material that you need to remember, for whatever purpose.

Many different processes are involved in human memory, and memory has various functions. It provides us with an identity, a name, a family. Daily recognition of people and places is due to stored memories, and without a memory for past experiences it would be impossible to know whether our favourite food was chicken vindaloo or beans on toast. We would have to try them out each time to see whether or not they were appetizing. But most of all, our memory enables us to learn, not only in the formal sense, but for personal growth and a wider understanding of the world in which we live. Memory by itself is not, of course, enough. We need to be able to use stored memories for assessing and understanding other people's ideas, for original thought, and for selection and arrangement of information in order to reach an intelligent conclusion.

## Memory function

Memory function can be divided into different areas:

  (a) *survival memory* (breathing, sleeping, heartbeats, etc.);

(b) *sensory memory* (taste, touch, smell, sight, sound);

(c) *skills memory* (walking, speaking, driving, typing, etc.);

(d) *factual memory* (Who wrote Hamlet? What was the date of the Battle of Hastings? etc.);

(e) *episodic memory* (from trivial to important, from remembering one's wedding day to burning the toast this morning);

(f) *semantic memory* (understanding the meaning of words and therefore the meaning of concepts).

For the student, the most important of these (apart from the obvious advantages of heartbeat and breathing memory skills!) is the semantic memory. If you have a limited vocabulary it is impossible to think an idea through or to understand meaning and function. For example, a child of three may know that if you turn the ignition key the engine of a car will start and a journey can begin. But the child has not got a wide enough vocabulary or understanding of the meaning of words to describe the workings of an internal combustion engine. As her experience widens with her comprehension of engineering words, she may become able to understand the practical application of the principles of engine design. The same thing happens to adults who are confronted for the first time with a computer. Unless they have acquired a working vocabulary and an understanding of the meaning of specialist jargon, they may still expect a 'menu' to include starters, main course and dessert, and think that 'modes' and 'zones' are something to do with fashion or geography.

Good memory and concentration go together. A well-trained memory, which any motivated person can acquire, is an asset in all aspects of life. The trained mind will remain alert and be aware of everything going on around it, and thus will be able to think and plan in a creative way. Contrary to popular myth, memory need not decline after the age of twenty. An alert mind which is used constantly and which is skilled in the arts of memory retention and recall will have little difficulty in remembering whatever is required. Research done at Newcastle University by the North East Age Research Team suggests that alert people who suffer temporary lapses of memory are not cracking up, but are probably experiencing one of the side effects of leading a full and interesting life.

The brain has more than enough capacity to store all the

information that we need, and the skill of retrieving this information on demand is certainly not beyond the average intelligent person. Provided that an organised attempt has been made to store and classify the material, a well-organised and well-used memory need not deteriorate with age.

However, we do need to take positive steps to retain those things which are important for us to remember. It is essential to transfer this material from short-term to long-term memory; otherwise what we have learned will soon disappear.

When we learn, we build on past experiences. Some facts are learned and then stored for future use. Some facts are computable; we work them out indirectly by using already-stored information. To gain maximum retention and recall, it is important to see any subject as a whole. A bird's eye view which shows the entire landscape will highlight the relationships between various elements and make it easier to apply known facts to new concepts. It is much easier to do a jigsaw if you have seen the picture.

## Concentration and memory

Most students are concerned about concentration when learning. As with all aspects of study, involvement and motivation are key elements in successful learning. When you have got into the right mental set and have confidence in your brain's ability to think, learn and remember then you stand a good chance of concentrating on what you are learning and being able to retain it for recall on demand. There are, of course, some things which will work against good concentration and good remembering. Although these will be mentioned in other parts of this book it is worth stating them again, as they are so important.

*Mental set* This is concerned with getting yourself into the right frame of mind, with organising yourself so that you are able to spend the appropriate amount of time on what you have to do; it involves making certain that before you start to study material, especially material which you eventually want to recall, you have marshalled all the ideas you can about the subject.

*Goals* You know what you need to learn and are clear in your mind about the steps you need to take. Examples include short-term goals such as completing an essay, and long-term goals such as obtaining a professional qualification. Set yourself realistic short-term goals for each study session, as advised elsewhere in the book. A twenty minute period of productive and concentrated work is better than two hours of uninvolved study.

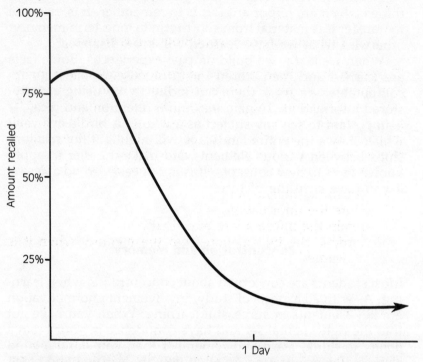

*Figure 5.1 Curve of learning and forgetting: human recall rises for a short while after learning and then falls steeply. 80% of all detail is forgotten within 24 hours*

*Attitudes* A positive approach to your work is essential for success. Confidence in your own ability combined with awareness of the benefits of what you have embarked on will help overall memory skills. It is noticeable that people who are interested in a topic have little difficulty in remembering quite complicated material. Are there some subjects that you find difficult to recall? Perhaps you need to awaken an interest in that area. Ask yourself if you sometimes dismiss an idea because you are not in sympathy with its basic principles.

*Stress* If you are full of stress, your chances of retaining and recalling what you are learning are very much reduced. Try to deal with anything which is causing you a problem before you begin to work. It may be that you have a general feeling of anxiety; you will then need to sit down to isolate the difficulties and try to solve them. Acceptance of a problem is better than worrying away at it while you are trying to concentrate.

## Learning, storing, retaining and retrieving

The graph shows how learned material soon leaves the memory. You must arrest this process if you want to retain the information. By classifying and organising the material well, and by using various memorising techniques, it is possible to halt memory decay. The relationship between time and the memory process is discussed elsewhere in the book.

When learning anything it is necessary to be able to:

learn the information,
store the information,
retain the information, and finally to
retrieve the information from the memory when it is wanted.

## Learning

It is difficult to remember material that has not been thoroughly learned and understood. Make certain that you do not pass on to a new topic until you are confident that you have really learned what has gone before. This is where a good overview of a subject is essential. The pieces of information should slot into the overall pattern. Test yourself informally as you go along so that you are sure that you have understood the work really well.

## Storing

Learn to make good notes. You will find that the process of organisation and selection, and the need to make them clear and interesting will help you to memorise them. Remember that when you put things into your own words you are helping the learning and the memory process.

## Retaining

You will be able to retain more of what you are learning if you organise and classify the material, and review your work frequently. Regular review helps to transfer the information from the short-term to the long-term memory.

## Retrieving

However much is stored in your memory, it is of little use if you cannot get it out when you need it for a seminar, examination or assignment. Mnemonics and memory systems can help with retrieval, and they will be discussed in the next chapter. Retrieval will be much easier if you select key words, classify the material, and use your study time effectively.

We all know that constant repetition aids memory. The nursery rhymes and tables that we learned as children are still part of our mental equipment. In order to put information into the long-term memory, this technique of repetition (known as 'overlearning') can be used. If you know the material 'inside out' because of constant repetition, you will find that retention and subsequent recall are much easier.

### Classifying and organising material in the mind

We organise what we must learn by relating new information to our existing knowledge. Unrelated material tends to be difficult to recall, as there seems to be no trigger or point of contact to start the memory functioning. When consciously trying to remember something, it is essential to have an overview of the whole subject, course or syllabus. This will allow new knowledge and thoughts to fall into place more successfully.

Make a definite effort to group new facts and concepts together; arrange them (on paper perhaps) in sequence whenever possible. Of course, it is important to be able to summarise this information in a succinct way. The use of key words and phrases is essential for efficient memorisation.

To summarise:

(a) The memory is more efficient, and concentration is better, when the items we want to recall have a relationship, pattern or structure.

(b) New information is more easily learned when it relates to existing knowledge.

(c) When disorganised material is received in the mind, the positive act of classifying it enhances the memory and learning process.

(d) Organisation of material can only be carried out if the main (key) points and priorities are recognised.

Psychologists tell us that it is unlikely that the brain holds everything that it has ever perceived and understood. We probably have a filter system by which we retain only the information which is of use or interest to us. Sometimes we retain this material for a brief moment, in the short-term memory. After this transient selection process, information may go into permanent storage, where retrieval is theoretically possible at any time.

As we know, the amount of information stored is so large that retrieval is a major problem. The reason why young people are assumed to have better memories than adults is because they have less to sort through when attempting to retrieve a fact, name or idea. As with all information systems (libraries, computer data bases, etc.), getting information out is often a matter of analysis and questioning. The key to retrieval is often a question. For example:

'What were you doing on Tuesday afternoon at three o'clock in the first week of October, two years ago?'

Before you read any further, try to remember just what *you* were doing then. Initially this seems an impossible retrieval problem, but when you start asking yourself questions, the script could go like this:

'Let's see, that was the year we had the late holiday in Scotland! We motored up on the last Saturday in September. Mary got married on the Friday.

It rained all over the weekend. The weather changed on the Monday. Surely we spent the first few days on the beach because it was so hot?

On the Wednesday we went to Fort William, so on the Tuesday we were on the beach all day.

I forgot to pack my costume — so I didn't swim on

Monday. On Tuesday morning we went into Oban. In the afternoon we swam.

I remember how cold it was in the sea, but the sand was very hot. We fell asleep after lunch. In the middle of the afternoon we decided to take the ferry over to the island. It goes at four o'clock — so at three o'clock we must have been packing up the picnic things and taking them to the car before leaving.'

By taking an overview of the year in question and then using a process of question and answer, it becomes possible to establish what happened on a certain day. This example only gives a rough idea of how the recall process works but it is obvious that the association of words, experiences and emotions all play an important part in the retrieval process. When attempting to retrieve information for learning purposes, the same basic process is gone through. But leaving the associative words to chance leads to poor and inadequate remembering. The choice and use of key words is a vital element in study techniques. The problem with recall is finding a starting point. Key words provide the trigger which will enable you to recall information more easily.

### Key words

Key words, as the name implies, unlock the memory and the imagination, and are the keys to understanding. A strong key word will bring to mind other words and ideas associated with it.

These important trigger words help recall. By looking for them and identifying them in what you are studying or reading you will increase your chance of remembering ideas and information. List key words or note them down and you will then be able to use them in a positive way when revising or memorising. The act of selection is part of the learning process. If you have not completely understood a passage, any key words that you find and eventually use will not have strong enough associations, and will only be of limited use.

In any paragraph of an article or book you will find that there is a key *sentence*. Often it will be the first sentence, but not in every case. Try to identify this key (or thesis) sentence, and select the key words from within it. Both for note making and memory work this identification is crucial. If you are thinking out ideas yourself, the same thing applies. Select the key words and ideas which encapsulate your thoughts.

The selection and interpretation of a key word will depend to a great extent on the individual experience and knowledge of the student. Your choice of key words will not always be the same as a colleague who is studying the same material, although a high proportion of them will, of course, be the same.

Key words come up again in the next chapter on memory techniques, and in the section on note making.

## Case study

Moira Hill is a busy executive who has to go abroad fairly frequently. Parking at an airport so often can cause a problem when she arrives back late at night. Where is her car? Of course, she could note down the parking area in her diary each time she travels. But being human she is often in too much of a hurry to catch the plane to do this.

Her salvation is to take her mind back to the events leading up to her departure, and to bring to mind deliberately her movements before leaving: movements in the office, the drive to the airport, the time of day, the clothes she was wearing, the appearance of the car park and any landmark like a set of stairs or some memorable graffiti on a wall. By imaginatively recreating the scene, Moira finds that as she walks through customs she can usually remember just where she left the car. Because Moira finds this method successful, she subconsciously notes landmarks, unusual views from the parking areas and other details, and builds up in her sensory memory a picture of where her car is parked. In this way she can retrieve the memory, and the car, when she needs to.

## Individual exercises

1  In the house you lived in, two houses ago, was the keyhole on the right-hand side or the left-hand side of the front door?

2  Read through a newspaper article underlining the words you consider to be key words. List the words. Several hours later try to reconstruct the article using these key words. Check the passage to see if you were accurate.

Initially the tendency is to underline far too many words. With practice, you will choose only the essential key words. This exercise may also be used after you have acquired the skill of speed reading, as a check on speed and accuracy.

3  Spend some time thinking about a familiar subject. Classify the information in a way that could be used for recall.

### Group exercises

1  *Kim's game*

This is an old childhood favourite, but still a very effective memory training exercise. Emphasise the need to try to classify or group the objects.

*Materials:*    a tray with a random assortment of about 20 items
*Group size:*    small enough for each member to be able to see the tray easily

The tray is placed in front of the group for one minute and then removed. Each member of the group lists the items on the tray. Replace the tray and check the results.

Points to note: It is easier to remember items when:

(a)  the memoriser mentally 'sees' the position of each item on the tray;
(b)  the items are classified in some way. For example: paper clips, pen, stapler (office equipment);  comb, hair clip, purse, handkerchief (personal property); sugar cube, cup, biscuit, spoon (coffee break items);
(c)  a memory system has been used (see Chapter Six).

Use the tray again but substitute new items for at least six of the original items. Retest.

The way in which the group coped with recall can yield useful discussion material. Sharing individual methods of remembering will usually encourage other group members to try out new methods for themselves.

2 *Poster exercise*

*Materials:*    a large coloured poster with at least 15 different elements (travel posters are useful) a check list of all the elements on the poster

*Group size:*    any size that can see the poster clearly

Display the poster for ten seconds. Ask the group to write down each item they remember seeing. Allow three minutes maximum. Run through the correct list. Group members add items they have forgotten.

Before showing the poster again, ask the group to give each item on the list a number and then to draw an outline of the poster, showing the position of each item in the appropriate place. Show the poster again and allow the group to check on the position of the items.

Discussion will reveal that it is easier to remember the positions of the items rather than to list them. It may also show that some people 'link' items together through their own personal associations.

# SIX

# Memory (2)

This chapter is concerned with practical ways in which the memory can be trained. Some of the systems will appear easy to cope with, while others will appear awkward. Take what is useful, and adapt systems and mnemonics to suit your own learning style and needs. We all remember things that are important to us. This is because we are involved or interested. Using a memory aid to reinforce what we need to recall is an easy process and one which makes daily life considerably simpler.

## Training the memory

As we saw in Chapter Five, it is essential that material we want to remember is classified and organised in our minds. Pattern note making (in Chapter Seven) is helpful for this.

Part of the memory is a data base. This is the part where material is encoded, and where concepts and inter-relationships are stored. The other part of the memory is the interpretive part, which is responsible for retrieving information, evaluating new material, answering questions and solving problems.

Nearly every situation involving memory requires a trigger to start the retrieval process. Sometimes this may be the deliberate use of a mnemonic; at other times an evocative smell or sight will bring the memory back. When you want to recall anything it is important to find the right initial trigger image or key word; this will start the chain of associations which will bring what you need to remember to the forefront of your mind. Many highly successful people have trained their memories. It is a definite advantage to be able to remember, not only facts and figures, but also names and faces, and facts about staff and clients. The good manager will also be able to remember exactly what she or he has to complete during the day. The recall strategies which are used for study purposes may also be used for everyday routine, and for recalling information as it is needed.

Remembering an important fact that you should bring up at a meeting, being able to talk informally without notes, greeting clients by name with comments on their particular interests — these are some of the practical applications of memory-training methods. All these methods can be harnessed for study purposes, but it is essential to realise that recalling isolated facts in an examination will be useless if a true understanding of the subject is lacking.

As with any thinking process, the more your mind is engaged, the more likely you are to learn and to use the information you come across. As you go through this chapter and possibly try out the ways to improve your memory, think about how you could apply the various methods to your own life and work. As with all skills, you will need to practise frequently, and as you practise the techniques, you will begin to find many different ways in which you can use the mnemonics and memory systems in this book. You may well have come across some of the techniques before. People have been using memory-training methods ever since early man wanted to recall just where he stored his favourite spear, or how to remember the number of mammoths needed to satisfy the hunger of the tribe.

Before reading any further, try to remember the following words (do not look back at the page after reading them):

> *blanket; car; tiger; sheet; elephant; bicycle; pillow; ant; truck; roller skates*

How well did you remember them? Perhaps you remembered them quite well, as there are only ten words. But how well would you recall them two hours from now? This would be more difficult. However, if the words were grouped (classified), recall would be far easier. For example:

**items on a bed:** *blanket; sheet; pillow*
**animals:** *tiger; elephant; ant*
**means of transport:** *car; bicycle; truck; roller skates*

By classifying the words under **bed, animals** and **transport** it becomes easier to remember the items in each group. The association of ideas also enables you to make a reasonable guess at missing items. The smaller the category, the more effective recall will be. If you are used to thinking and planning in an organised and structured way, recalling what you need becomes far simpler.

There are three basic ways of remembering facts. The first is repetition of material, either by reading a passage many times or by repeating the material to yourself (preferably aloud). You may have learned your 'tables' this way. If you have put the material into your own words, either in writing or by speaking about the subject aloud, repetition will be even more effective. The information will then become part of your own experience.

Secondly, you can use a simple mnemonic, or a more elaborate memory system. There will be more about this later in the chapter.

Finally, it is crucial that you are aware of the overall structure of the concept. Learning groups of items either by repetition or with mnemonics will be useless if you cannot place them in the correct context. As with the jigsaw, the small pieces fit together and grow into the final picture; and while it is important to keep in mind the colour and shape of individual pieces, it is even more essential to have a clear idea of what the completed picture will look like.

The best way to retain material is to think about it often. It is easier for a manager dealing with problems of company finance to remember the principles of accountancy and economics than it is for a young student, who only knows the theory, and has not as yet had to put the principles into practice.

## Mnemonics

A knot in a handkerchief, a rhyme, an absurd word or picture are all useful in helping us remember things. These short memory joggers are called *mnemonics* and they are part of our everyday life. The word comes from the Greek word 'mnemone', to remember (Mnemosyny was the Greek goddess of memory). A mnemonic is a device that helps us recall items. Mnemonics are short, simple ways of retrieving information.

Examples are plentiful. For example, how do you spell *receive*? The rhyme 'I before E except after C' will spring to mind. The rhyme about the months is part of our childhood: 'Thirty days hath September, April, June and ...'. You will be able to complete it yourself.

This type of memory aid is used for short pieces of information — the sort that often occur in one's studying or in daily life. A number of well known mnemonics will be found in this part of the chapter, but note that any mnemonic you construct for yourself will be far more effective than one you have heard elsewhere, especially for new material.

If you look at the following examples of mnemonics you will see that they tend to fall into various categories:

(a) a visual image (a knot in a handkerchief);
(b) rhymes (Thirty days hath September ...);
(c) initial letters of key words used to form a sentence;
(d) initial letters making up a word.

Below are some ideas for using mnemonics. Do not despise this humble memory aid. Although we are sophisticated people, capable of thinking deep philosophical thoughts and making intricate machinery, the way in which our memory works appears to be extremely simple. A child, who has not lost the ability to 'see in pictures' and to whom all things are exciting and new, can often remember things more clearly than older people. But as any parent can testify, children remember what they want to recall, like the rest of us.

(a) Set the words to music. (Men of Harlech is a good melody, or use a hymn tune with a regular beat.) Tom Lehrer fans will recall his song about the chemical elements; the rhythm and melody help to fix the words firmly in the mind. Hearing the tune brings back the words immediately.

(b) Use symbols as a quick visual mnemonic; for example, an O for 'never ending', a triangle for the Trinity, etc.

(c) Mispronounce the word you want to remember. 'Hear' yourself say the word inside your head. Try mispronouncing *dictionary, policies, decisions*.

As each person's imagination and experience is unique, it is impossible to state that there is only one way to recall material. What is vital is that you look at (and try out) various methods, and use those which work well for you.

Here are some examples of how imagination and word/image association can work together to enable a fact to be remembered. Use the examples to think how to use *your* memory to the full.

*New words*
Take the word *acrimony* which means 'bitterness' or 'sharpness of manner or speech'. Within the word acRIMony is the word RIM. Imagine that you have cut yourself on the sharp RIM of a glass. Use your total imagination. How would it feel? How would you react?

*Foreign words*
*Herren* means 'men' in German. Visualise a group of herrings in neat business suits and bowlers, carrying umbrellas.

*Gato* is 'cat' in Italian. This is easy; it is so like our own word that you could imagine you are saying *cat* with a strong Italian accent. Would it be too confusing to think of the *cat* on a *cake*? (*Gateau* = 'cake' in French.)

*Technical words*
*Umbelliferous* is the word for a family of herbaceous plants with divided leaves and flowers (carrots, parsley, etc.). All these plants, if enlarged could protect you from the sun or rain. Think of an *umbrella* shape. Knowing that the Latin word for 'sunshade' was *umbella* would make the word even easier to remember.

These few examples of isolated facts give an indication of how you can use your imagination, existing knowledge and sense of the absurd to recall words and their meanings.

If you find accurate spelling difficult, use your imagination in the same way. For those of us who are poor at spelling it is important to learn how to spell correctly. Consider *separate* as an example. You will always know how to spell it if you remember that there is 'a rat' in *sep A RAT e*.

There may be occasions when you will need to associate a name with a fact, or a customer with a product, or a writer with a theory. Again a visual image can often be constructed to fill the need. For example, Professor M D Vernon worked in the field of visual perception and reading, giving us the association illustrated in Figure 6.1 and C I Sandström studied facets of childhood. This is quite easy to remember. A mental picture of *children* playing on the *sand* near a *stream* (ström) will be sufficient to link the name with the concept.

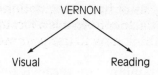

Figure 6.1

Linking names with facts about people is essential for good customer and staff relations, and it becomes simple with practice. For example, *Miss Snow of Turner's Shoeshop* can be remembered if you think of a large pile of snow slowly *turning* on a huge *shoe*. And *Mr Gilbey from the library*, shrunk to midget size, could be sitting on a pile of books inside a gin bottle.

Do you find some of the examples above far-fetched or completely unmemorable? This is quite likely. Your own images would not be so easily dismissed. Other people's imaginations are unique to them. Your own involvement will produce pictures and associations which really stick in your mind.

In all memory training, there must be links, clues or triggers to assist the mind to recall the correct information. The stronger the link the quicker and more effective recall will be. When making mnemonics, or when using any memory systems you will find that if a thing is *funny, ridiculous, exaggerated, absurd* or *sexual*, and particularly if it is *vulgar* or *disgusting*, it will be far easier to remember.

Poetry is easier to remember than prose, so try to rhyme wherever possible. To a small child, the alphabet is at first a long list of arbitrary sounds, but by using a simple tune and subdividing the letters into smaller units it is not too long before the child can recite the entire alphabet with ease. Several different ways of remembering can be deduced, including:

the use of rhyme;
the use of organisation and classification;
the use of mental images — especially ones which are unexpected or absurd.

Mnemonics are of limited use unless the material they relate to is thoroughly understood. When organising and note making for study, use the headings and key words to make mnemonics. Such mnemonics can be used to summarise particular topics or sets of details.

Below you will find a few more examples of well known mnemonics. Using these as reference try to construct some of your own.

The colours of the rainbow are recalled by:

| | |
|---|---|
| **R** ichard | **R** ed |
| **O** f | **O** range |
| **Y** ork | **Y** ellow |
| **G** ave | **G** reen |
| **B** attle | **B** lue |
| **I** n | **I** ndigo |
| **V** ain | **V** iolet |

the hydrocarbon series by:

| | |
|---|---|
| **M** ethane | **M** ost |
| **E** thane | **E** ngineers |
| **P** ropane | **P** refer |
| **B** utane | **B** londes |

arthropods by:

| | |
|---|---|
| **A** rthropods | **A** rthur |
| **S** piders | **S** pits |
| **I** nsects | **I** n |
| **C** rustaceans | **C** arol's |
| **M** yriapods | **M** ilk |

(I told you it was more memorable if it was disgusting!)

The characteristics of all living things may be recalled by using the word GRINMER (to recall the word *Grinmer*, remember all your Grandma taught you):

Growth; Respiration; Irritability; Nutrition; Movement; Excretion; Reproduction

Finally, you will always remember which are *stalactites* and which are *stalagmites* because stalaCtites come down from the Ceiling and stalaGmites come up from the Ground. There are, of course, other mnemonics on the same theme which concern tights coming up and down, but this is a respectable book.

## Memory systems

There are many different memory systems, some of which are fairly elaborate and need considerable practice. The systems included in this chapter can be adapted to different circumstances. Most of them need visual and imaginative skills as well as practice. As we get older, we sometimes lose the immediate visual ability that children have. Nevertheless, it is possible to relearn how to use this side of our brain. Children need little practice as their visual perceptions are strong, but adults have to get out of their mental straightjackets and develop skills of fantasy and perception. As with mnemonics, if a thing is absurd, exaggerated, vulgar or ridiculous it will be much easier to remember.

Our brains are complex, and as adults we are aware of the multitudinous aspects of life. Nevertheless, the basic retrieval and recall techniques are *very simple*. Do not try to make your ideas too complicated and elaborate. Try to be childlike, even childish in your approach. Otherwise you will end up remembering the link, and not the item that you wanted to retain in your memory for eventual retrieval. Simple, uncomplicated ideas are the most effective when using memory systems.

The basis of the first three systems lies in the use of strong visual images. With practice, a good, strong link between the object to be remembered and the 'picture' in your mind will make it possible for you to recall key words every time.

### The number-rhyme memory system

This is one of the 'hook' or 'peg' methods of remembering. In this system the numbers 1—10 are rhymed with words that are easy to visualise and that are not ambiguous, as follows:

| | | | |
|---|---|---|---|
| 1 | *bun* | 6 | *sticks* |
| 2 | *shoe* | 7 | *heaven* |
| 3 | *tree* | 8 | *gate* |
| 4 | *door* | 9 | *vine* |
| 5 | *hive* | 10 | *hen* |

The first step is to make a strong visual image of each of the words that are rhymed with the numbers. 'See' the bun or the shoe or the gate in strong, definite pictures. Each person will, of course, have a different set of pictures in their mind, as each imagination is quite unique. When you have constructed and learned the set of pictures you will find that whenever you say the number, the picture will instantly spring to mind. These pictures will be your constants whenever you use this system. The same images of the bun, the door, or the hive will always be used. If you have real difficulty in making visual images from these words, you may want to use other words that rhyme with the numbers. However, you must make sure that the words can only mean one thing. For example, if your use *sun* as a link with *one*, you may confuse it with a visual image of your *son*.

Other words you could possibly use are: *nun, gun, flea, tor, moor, chive, dive, bricks, Devon, slate, line, pine, pen*.

The main thing to remember is that you must always use the same image. You must always think of the same sort of *bun* and the same colour and shape of *shoe*; the *gate* must always be of the same design, and the *tree* must always be of the same species. Note also that you should make the *gate* as different from the *door* as possible. And if you use *heaven*, do not get carried away with theological ideas of harps and angels; stick to a picture of 'the heavens' — a sky, with perhaps a few clouds floating by.

Once you have got your set of images clearly in your mind it is time for the second stage. You need to use these images as 'hooks' or 'pegs' for the things that you wish to remember. For example, if the first key word that you want to remember is a *fishing rod*, you must visualise the fishing rod and number 1, the *bun*, together. Perhaps the bun will be suspended from the rod as bait, or maybe a huge bun will have a fishing rod stuck into it at an angle.

The second item could perhaps be a *feather*. In this case, number 2 is the *shoe*, so you may 'see' the feather sprouting out of the shoe, or even a feather design in colour on the side of the shoe. Perhaps the feather is floating along, supporting your shoe — use your imagination.

The main thing to remember is that the pictures of the *bun, shoe, hive, hen* and so on remain constant, and the items to be remembered are seen with them.

Of course, you are not likely to want to remember lists of words that start with fishing rods and go on to feathers. Nevertheless, it is quite useful to practise with words which are easy to visualise, and then progress to lists of key words which are important for your studies or your work.

Practise using this system with the list of words below. Once you have gained confidence, make your own list of words: a shopping list, a sequence of key words from your latest unit of study, or a set of words which will remind you of what you must do tomorrow.

| | |
|---|---|
| *table* | *kitten* |
| *feather* | *sauce bottle* |
| *cat* | *wine bottle* |
| *student* | *elephant* |
| *car* | *book* |
| *seagull* | *table lamp* |
| *ruler* | *typewriter* |
| *crown* | *pencil* |
| *cricket bat* | *bucket* |
| *explosion* | *X-ray* |

Test yourself frequently until you are scoring ten out of ten each time.

**The animal alphabet memory system**

This method is also a hook or peg method. With this system you can remember up to twenty-six different items. The procedure is similar to that for the number rhyme system. You get a set of constants and learn these first, then use these constants as hooks for the things you want to file away in your memory. The constants act as the trigger word or image to help you recall items on demand.

Make a list of animals that have initial letters that follow the alphabet, e.g. A = **A**nt, B = **B**ear, C = **C**at, D = **D**eer, and so on. Be careful to choose animals that are quite distinctive. Unless you are very good at wildlife, a deer, a gazelle and an antelope look very alike!

Now suppose the first items on your list were *leaf, petal, stamen* and *stem*:

the *ant* could be carrying a huge *leaf*;
the *bear* could be wearing a skirt of *petals*;
the *cat* could have a crown of *stamens*;
the *deer* could be waving on top of a thin *stem*.

The more ridiculous the image, the more memorable it will be.

A possible list could be as follows, although your own list of favourite animals would be better:

| | | | |
|---|---|---|---|
| A | = Ant | N | = Nightingale |
| B | = Bear | O | = Ostrich |
| C | = Cat | P | = Peacock |
| D | = Deer | Q | = Queen bee |
| E | = Elephant | R | = Rat |
| F | = Fox | S | = Salmon |
| G | = Goose | T | = Toucan |
| H | = Hawk | U | = Unicorn |
| I | = Ibex | V | = Vampire bat |
| J | = Jackal | W | = Walrus |
| K | = Kitten | X | = Xavier (a saint) |
| L | = Lion | Z | = Zebra |

You may know other animals which you can visualise more clearly. Use the list above for suggestions only. Would you find C and K confusing?

There are many peg systems, and all are based on the same visual skills. Practice is the essential ingredient for success. As with all skills, from riding a bicycle to mastering a computer language, familiarity breeds not contempt but confidence.

The next system is as old as the ancient Romans, and has been used for a thousand years or more.

## The locus memory system

(*Locus* means 'place' — from the Latin.)

The first step with this system is to imagine a room that you know very well. Go round it in your imagination, fixing in your mind the location of the furniture, pictures, doors and windows. Using your visual skills, try to superimpose the items to be remembered on top of the things in your room. Go round the room in the same direction each time. Suppose the first things in your room were a television, a bookcase, a fireplace, an armchair and a table, and the items to be remembered were a spreadsheet, a word processor, disk drive, a Qwerty keyboard, and a mouse. You could perhaps 'see' the spreadsheet displayed on the television screen, the word processor surrounded by books on the bookcase, a disk drive burning merrily in the fireplace, a beautifully embroidered Qwerty keyboard taking the place of the cushions on the chair, and a six foot mouse sitting at the table.

Note that this method is quite unsuitable for anyone who has a compulsive furniture shifter in the family!

Try out more than one of these systems, and see which fits into your own way of thinking best. You may find that you use more than one, depending on the things you want to remember. Of course, you do not have to use all ten components of the number rhyme scheme, or the twenty-six animals in the animal alphabet system, or even the full number of items in your room. Nevertheless, the facility is available for you if you want to use it.

## Remembering numbers

Most people find it quite difficult to remember numbers. For some numbers you can use simple mnemonics. Turn the numbers into other things; thus, 17593 could easily become £175.93. Imagine the number to be made of neon tubing which flashes brilliantly against the night sky. Associate the number with a date; thus, 1845 is easier to remember when it is said as eighteen forty-five. If the date is well known, that is better still. Exercise your imagination and you will find that there are many ways of keeping numbers in your mind.

## The number-alphabet memory system

This system is often called the Major System or Grey's System. It has many advantages and can be considerably extended in use. It needs more practice than the methods previously mentioned, but has a much greater capacity.

To use the system for remembering numbers it is necessary to change the numbers into words. This lets you use the visual image of the word as well as the word itself to help you remember. The first stage is to turn numbers into consonants so that words may be made up from them, as follows:

1   *d, t*
2   *n*
3   *m*
4   *r*
5   *l*
6   *j, sh, dg,* soft *g, ch* as in *chair*

7   *k*, hard *c*, hard *g*, *qu*
8   *f*
9   *b*, *p*
0   *s*, *z*, soft *c*

You will notice that there is a link between the numbers and letters:

1   and *t/d* have one downstroke
2   and *n* have two downstrokes
3   and *m* have three downstrokes
4   the word *fouR* ends in *r*
5   *l* is the Roman symbol for 50
6   is a mirror image of *j*
7   capital *K* has two 7's in it
8   the handwritten *f* looks like an 8
9   the reverse of *p* and *b*
0   *z* is in *zero*

Change the numbers into letters and then, by introducing vowels, make them into words that can be visualised. For example, if you want to remember the number 473 the letters could be *r*, then *k/c/g/qu*, then *m*. Now you need a word that includes the three consonants. You can use as many vowels as you need. The word could possibly be *requiem*, and while this is not an easy word to visualise, it is easier to recall than 473. Those people who have trained their memory and are used to memory systems will have no difficulty at all.

To remember longer numbers it may be helpful to split the changed numbers into a series of words. A little ingenuity will produce really memorable chains of key words.

Here are some examples of words from numbers:

3212   M ou N T ai N
7530   K a L a M a Z oo
23940   N u M B e R S

Now try for yourself using 66799, 71342, 450842.

> Could these be:
>
> shish kebab
> catamaran
> royal sovereign?

By using a series of predetermined words it is possible to extend the scheme even further. In this case you need to learn the words, which will take a little time and practice.

| | | | |
|---|---|---|---|
| 1 | *toy* | 6 | *jaw* |
| 2 | *noah* | 7 | *key* |
| 3 | *me* | 8 | *foe* |
| 4 | *ray* | 9 | *pa* |
| 5 | *law* | 10 | *toes* |

Now use these words to remind you of the basic letters and you can begin to build up words to visualise. For example:

| | |
|---|---|
| 11 | **tot** |
| 50 | **lace** |
| 39 | **map** |

Or you can use the system by taking the first letter of each word and making a short sentence or phrase. As an example, consider 1666, which can be transformed into the letters *t, sh, sh, sh*. This was the date of the Great Fire of London, so a suitable phrase could be *To ashes, ashes, ashes*.

Or consider 1917. This was the year of the Russian Revolution. It could be made into *t, p, d, c,* and this could give *The People Demand Communism*. Note that whenever possible, the sentence should reflect the meaning of the numbers.

Remembering telephone numbers can be easy with this method. Suppose you want to remember Mr Butcher's number. If it was 329 8737, it would be quite simple to turn this into a mnemonic by saying to yourself:

Mr nice butcher, very good meat cuts (*m, n, b, v, g, m, c*)

Try turning the following numbers into memorable phrases:

the bank manager   402 5814
the tax office     336 9826

## The chain or link memory system

For remembering daily routine, and for recalling, many people use the chaining or linking method almost unconsciously. Again we will use a list of unrelated items as an example, but this is only for practice. Once you have mastered the skill of this particular method, you will need to organise and classify your words to give you a sensible and meaningful list of things to remember.

Consider the following list:

*book; orange; fork; tree;*
*monkey; stamp; angry; sandwich*

To use the chaining system it is necessary to take the first item and link it to the second, then move on and link the second and third, the third and fourth, and so on.

You could begin by thinking about the book. Perhaps it is an old leather-bound volume with that lovely smell of leather, and faded ink on the pages. You can feel the weight of the volume in your hands. Now think of the orange. Use all your senses of taste and smell and sight to bring the picture to life. In your imagination, put the orange on the pages of the open book and concentrate for a moment on the picture of the two items together.

Leave this image now, forget about the book (it will remain in your short term memory), and link the orange with a fork. This time you must recreate the feel and sight of the shiny table fork; perhaps it could be sticking into the orange and releasing a spray of orange juice. Now leave the orange and, keeping the fork in mind, imagine a large tree blowing in the wind. You are desperately trying to dig it up with your table fork, which is not an easy task. Leave the fork, and concentrate on the tree. From the branches there swings a large colourful monkey. Think of these two items together, and then go on with the monkey, who is trying hard to stick a postage stamp onto an oversized letter. The stamp may well have the familiar face of Queen Elizabeth on it. In the next linking the face on the stamp could be very angry. The Queen could be in three-D, and in the end you may see her angry face biting into a huge sandwich.

Use all the senses you have. Really see the colour of the orange, feel the monkey's fur, smell the breeze that blows the tree about, and feel the smooth metal of the fork.

Now link the following words together and then test yourself:

*pin; crocodile; camera; soup bowl; box;*
*mountain; cloud; anteater; curtain; swamp*

Whichever systems work best for you, always do your best to use your full imagination for all the things you are trying to remember. Colour, sight, sound, feel and taste are all things which will enhance your ability to retain and recall what you need to remember.

### To remember daily routine

List in your mind all the things that you need to do during the day. As you think of them, create the scene in your imagination, with the place, people or things that are involved. Use all your senses to make it feel as though you were really there. Now imagine that each thing you must do is rather exaggerated. For example, you may need to do the following things tomorrow:

take the car into the garage for an MOT;
see the Boss about the holiday rota;
collect your suit from the cleaners;
buy a birthday card for Mary;
see Bill about the bad report that he has submitted.

Using your imagination to the full, think about your journey to work in the car. As you get to the road that the garage is in, imagine a long arm stretching out of the forecourt and grappling with the car. On the hand that grasps the car in its huge grip are the letters MOT, tattooed on the knuckles.

Then see yourself dancing along the corridor, with a wide-brimmed sun hat on your head and a song in your heart. As you go towards the boss's door you flourish the copy of the holiday rota in your hand. Your lunch hour is approaching; imagine walking down the street, window shopping. As you pass the cleaners, a suit with no one in it rushes out and embraces you. It is so pleased to see you that you are forced to enter the cleaners and hand over handfuls of gold coins to have it back.

After you leave the cleaners, you are struck by the immense door of the newsagents across the road. Staggering out of the door are people who are all carrying large envelopes. This will remind you that you have to buy a birthday card for Mary. Go across the road, buy the card, and feel the weight of the card as you too stagger down the road.

Lastly, you have to see Bill about that report. You probably do not relish the idea of telling him how bad it is, and this alone may make you forget to tackle him. Imagine the scene as you go through the office to Bill's desk. Imagine your footsteps thumping on the floor, and Bill cowering, waiting to hear what you thought of his report. In your hand you carry a multi-coloured report, as if it were a great weight. By the time you come to speak to Bill your mind should have adjusted to being rational about the report. You should be able to tell him how he should have structured it, without becoming overheated or ridiculous about the matter.

Create the picture of yourself carrying out the various tasks, within the correct environment, but in an exaggerated manner. You will find that, as the appropriate time or place arrives, your memory will snap into place and you will remember just what you have to do. If there is no definite time or place, the task of remembering is much greater. It is then important to manufacture a specific time and place. If you know that at some time you really must write to Ted, select a place and time, and using all your imaginative powers, see yourself writing the letter. This should be enough to bring guilt feelings when the time and the place coincide, and you will remember that now is the time to get down to the business of writing to Ted.

### The elusive word

How often have you been in the middle of a conversation or sat in the examination room and found that one small fact, phrase or word eludes you? For many this is a familiar occurrence. Most people either give up, or begin to worry excessively about a sudden decline into senility. The problem is not with retention — you know very well that you have the information somewhere; it is with recall. There are various things that can be done, and you will have to think about what works best for your own mind.

The next time this happens to you, try some of the following ideas:

(a) Stop worrying away at the lost word. Think about other words or ideas that are similar and concentrate on them. Often the elusive word comes back when you turn your mind away from it.

(b) If you are a 'word' person, imagine that the sentence is written in front of you as you are speaking. Do not think about what is missing — just try to 'read off' the sentence. This will usually result in *all* the words you need falling into place.

(c)  A similar procedure may work for those who find they are listeners rather than readers. In this case 'hear' the sentence in your mind, and speak the words as you hear them in your head.

(d)  Perhaps the lost words are concerned with past actions, and perhaps you are describing an event. In this case, let your memory flow as you recall other things that happened before and after the event. As you think about these details the information you require will probably spring to your lips.

In other words, you are recreating the event or the words which contain the missing information. By concentrating on the whole, the elusive word will naturally fall into place. By consciously forgetting what is forgotten, your subconscious will deal with it while you think about other things. Unfortunately, there are times when the information seems to come too slowly, for example when you are speaking in a seminar or sitting in the examination hall. Nevertheless, if you do not panic, and are used to using your memory in a positive way, the chances are that the elusive information will surface in time. In an examination, you may well find that as you concentrate on another part of the paper, the missing details come into your mind. Note them down quickly, and use the checking time at the end of the examination to include them in the earlier question.

In Chapters Four and Eight I emphasise the need to listen and read with involvement. If you do this you will be able to store and retain information, and will be able to recall material as you need it.

As with all study and thinking skills, a positive approach and a strong involvement in what you are doing will improve your overall personal effectiveness. This will apply to examinations, career movement and to personal relationships.

## Case study

Bob Wheeldon is a sales representative for a fast-growing computer distributor. Bob has to have at his fingertips information about all the hardware and software that his firm markets. He meets many people in his working week, from important customers to rival distributors and computer manufacturers. He has learned to memorise faces and names, and he uses a

ELEM—G

memory system to help him keep track of the constantly changing items that he has to promote. His ability to plan his time effectively, and to keep efficient and organised notes on his movements and sales, is helping him to get the promotion he deserves.

## Individual exercises

1  Do you recall the meaning of these words:

   acrimony
   Herren
   umbelliferous

   You may have known the words anyway. But do you recall the mnemonic?

   What field did C.I. Sandström work in?
   Who worked on visual perception and reading?

2  Make a list of ten words which are relevant to your studies or life. Put them in rank order, and using the Number Rhyme system, commit them to memory. Test yourself the next day.

3  Using other relevant key words, practise the other methods mentioned in the chapter. Which system do you find simplest to use? You will probably find that one is easier than the others. Stick to that one and practise regularly.

4  The Number Alphabet System needs more practice than the other methods. If it appeals to you, it would be worth looking for a book which contains a more detailed explanation. The bibliography suggests books which are solely concerned with memory.

5  Go through your course syllabus, or a technical dictionary, and select words which you need to be aware of. Learn these words and their meanings early on in the course, even though some of the ideas they represent may not be studied until a later date.

6  Make a mnemonic to remember the six functions of memory.

7   Go through your own notes or textbooks. Use the headings and/or key words in them as a basis for a mnemonic.

8   Note down the type of mnemonic that you find easiest to use. Does it involve rhyme, absurdity, incongruity? What makes one type more memorable than another for you? Try to analyse how your own memory is best helped. Think of an everyday occurrence that you sometimes forget. Make a mnemonic that will stop the forgetting process.

9   Read through a newspaper article, underlining the words you consider to be key words. List these. Several hours later, reconstruct the article using your remembered list of words. Check the passage for accuracy.
    Initially you will want to underline many words. As you gain confidence in your ability to recall from key words, you will not select nearly as many.

10   Spend some time thinking about a familiar subject. Deliberately classify the information in such a way that another person could use for memory practice.

## Group exercises

Many of the individual exercises can be adapted for group work, and there is considerable value in discussions of how people cope with retention and recall.

1   The 'stranger' exercise

*Materials:*     a co-operative 'stranger' to the group
*Group size:*   any size

This exercise needs some co-operation from another member of staff, preferably someone who is unfamiliar to the group. Arrange for the stranger to walk into the training room and to speak to you for a short while. You may perhaps ask them to sit and wait until you have completed what you are doing. The stranger then leaves. About twenty minutes later, ask the group to describe the person who interrupted the session. Ask:
    What did the person look like?
    What was the person wearing?

What was the person's attitude?
What was said?

The exercise is one of observation as well as recall. It can lead to useful discussion about the importance of observation, of having an alert and interested mind, and of having the ability to recall information with accuracy. You can also discuss the fact that recall is often different between men and women, and the reasons for this.

If possible, the stranger should come in during this discussion session so that the group can check their impressions and their efficiency of recall.

2 The 'sequence of events' exercise

*Materials:* two very short stories or descriptive passages
*Group size:* any size

Read through the first passage or story, and ask the group to write down all the events or main points. Most people will do reasonably well, but it is unlikely that all the detail will be recalled. Discuss with the group how imagination can help memory. The group may see how, by imagining oneself involved in the story, or by creating vivid mental images of the events, it becomes far easier to remember all that happens in the story.

Read the second passage or story, and ask the group to use their powers of imagination to the full. They should concentrate on the sights, sounds and also the feelings that come to mind as they listen and create strong images in their memory.

The second passage should be recalled far more easily than the first, and it will remain in the memory longer. It would be useful to ask for an account of both passages in a later session.

# SEVEN

# Note making

We need to take notes for a variety of reasons, including:

storing information;
organising information;
study notes for revision;
notes for seminars and talks;
notes from seminars, lectures and talks;
notes for expansion into written assignments;
notes from written material for reference.

The list could be extended to cover many other areas, from the note saying '3 pints please' to the note saying 'See Jim about pay rise tomorrow'! In this chapter we will be concerned mainly with notes for study purposes. However, most of the different methods of note taking and note making can be used in our work and personal life.

## Notes are not an optional extra

Many students come adrift when they have to write an assignment or begin revising, only to find that the notes they took months before are illegible, disorganised or meaningless. The two main benefits to be gained from efficient note making are:

(a) active involvement which aids learning, retention and recall;
(b) recording information which is necessary for written assignments and revision.

There are several different methods of taking notes. You will have to choose the most appropriate one for your needs. If you are unfamiliar with some of the techniques, try them out anyway. Note making is a skill that needs to be practised. You may find that you eventually use a mixture of methods, depending on the task and your own inclinations. There is no right or wrong way to make notes, only efficient and inefficient ways. How you choose to make the notes will depend a good deal on your personality and the type of learning you are undertaking.

To make effective and intelligible notes, it is helpful to exploit what we know about brain function. The brain tends to work associatively, carrying on many different processes, and integrating and synthesising material as it operates. The left-hand side of the brain, which controls the right side of the body, is concerned with logic, reason, reading, writing, mathematics, analysis, language and sequence. The right-hand side (controlling the left side of the body) is concerned with recognition, pattern, musical appreciation, creativity, rhythm, parallel processing and synthesis.

Because of the emphasis in western education on analysis and logic, many people have not had the opportunity to develop both sides of the brain equally. If we could harness both sides of the brain when we think, note and write, our thinking, speaking and writing would be far more successful. This is not the place to discuss left brain/right brain associations in detail, but it is a fascinating subject and one which opens all sorts of windows in the mind.

The key to effective learning is complete involvement in what you are doing, whether it is note taking, reading or memorising. Even taking the decision to use one note-making method rather than another is part of this involvement.

It is also easier to learn material when you have managed to think it through and put it into your own words. It is therefore essential that you do not 'copy out' notes or passages from books. Of course, there are some quotations and formulae which have to be recorded as they stand. But where concepts or differing views have to be noted, it is important that you 'translate' them into your own personal thought rhythms and vocabulary. Everyone has a different way of expressing things. The same information will be couched in different ways by different people, although the final meaning will be understood by all concerned. Because it is easier to recognise and remember your own patterns of thought, it follows that where you have been personally involved in making the notes, they will be of more use to you than rewriting other people's ideas, or relying on lecture handouts.

There is a school of thought which says that note making in general makes little difference to overall learning performance. From a practical point of view, however, there are few of us who would feel that we could take a course without some notes to back up our memory and thinking processes. The most important thing would seem to be our ability to make meaningful notes, using methods which fit into our own learning styles and which will be useful when we want to revise work done over a long period of time.

There is evidence to show that closely written or dictated notes are of less value than notes which contain key points, clearly selected and structured. Of course, it depends a good deal on the way in which you learn and also the confidence you have in your own ability to take in and process information.

Some lecturers provide handouts for their students. If you are given these before the lecture, read them through quickly to get an idea of the main points. They will then form the basis for your own notes. Do not fall into the trap of thinking that these handouts will be an effective substitute for your own note making. The handout will have been written by someone else, with personal speech rhythms, personal vocabulary and a personal method of organisation. To learn material properly you must make it part of your own thinking, using your own language and thought patterns. Never rely on other people's notes or handouts, except as a source of reference. If the handout is given to you at the end of the talk, the same thing applies. Read it, file it and refer to it. You could use the headings to help you with your own notes. But do not under any circumstances think that they will do instead of your own thinking and noting.

In this chapter we will look at several different ways of note making. Try out those you have come across before, familiarise yourself with differing methods, and you will gradually evolve your own way of working. There is no right or wrong way of taking and making notes. The methods that work for you are the only 'right' ones.

There are five main stages leading to good notes:

1 *Preview* Read all the background material you can find before you attend a lecture or make a note. Organise your listening and note making around what you already know of the subject.

2 *Select*   Note the *key* points in *key* words.
3 *Question*   Use questions as the focal point of the notes.
4 *Organise*   Whichever note-making method you use, ensure that the notes are logical and structured.
5 *Review*   Reread and review your notes frequently.

## Linear notes

Linear notes are the most usual way of producing notes. It is the most obvious method because we read and write in linear form. Notes taken at lectures, from video recordings and possibly from books will probably need to be reworked afterwards if they are to be meaningful. This is not a waste of time, as the process of reworking aids learning and retention. It is important to distinguish between note *taking* and note *making*. Note taking is what you do during lectures, when thinking through a problem or plan, or as you read and write quite informally. Note making on the other hand is the active making of notes, either from a book, or from informal (probably scribbled and unstructured) notes that you have written away from your desk. The notes which you *make* will be the ones which you need for reference or for revision.

The emphasis in the next part of the chapter will be on *making* notes for future use, although note *taking* can, of course, follow similar lines. Linear notes can be in *summary* or *outline* form.

*Summaries*
A summary can consist of a list of key words and concepts, or it may be a closely written précis. Summaries are useful for clarifying thought and for review purposes. They may be difficult to read back at a later date, and it is unwise to rely on them for detailed revision. On the other hand, if you need to commit a sequence of words or thoughts to memory, a keyword summary would be the first stage in assembling material to use with a memory system.

*Outline notes*
There are various approaches to outline notes and most people evolve their own style. One popular approach is to divide the page into two columns, putting the main points on the left-hand

side and supporting details in the right-hand column. An advantage of this method is that you are forced to make a decision as to what the main points really are, and then to make choices about what to add as supporting material. The concentration and thought required helps you to learn the material that you are working on.

Whichever type of note you are making, it is important to select *key words*. Long involved sentences are not memorable, and are of little use in note making. Later in the chapter we will be looking at key words and their selection.

Outline notes are sequential. They are usually divided into headings and subheadings, and the main and subsidiary points are arranged on the page in a straight, linear fashion.

Try to avoid having blocks of closely-written notes which go on from page to page, with no relief from the closely-written text. Considered superficially, a thick file of these notes may tend to give the student a certain confidence. Quantity and weight seem to mean that much work has been accomplished. But this is an illusion as such notes are hard to revise from and difficult to read. They also show that the student has found it difficult to extract the relevant and essential points from the masses of information heard or read.

Whichever method you find best for your purposes, your aim should be to make the notes really memorable. Visual impact is necessary both for clarity and memory. Make all the key words and ideas stand out well so that you can see at a glance the main points and the overall structure of the subject. Often it is useful to use the author's or lecturer's headings. Expand on brief headings, adding your own findings and conclusions. Look for the key sentences from books, technical reports and articles, and incorporate them in your notes, using your own words.

## How to set out outline notes

1.1 *Layout*
   Main headings: begin at the margin.
      Secondary headings: begin by indenting a short space.
      Tertiary headings: indent even further in.

   Try to make the relationship clear between different items (main and subordinate).

1.2 *Classification*
Use letters, numbers and brackets. For example:

Main headings: 1, 2, 3, 4, 5, etc.
  Secondary headings: A, B, C, D, E, etc.
    Tertiary headings: (a), (b), (c), (d), etc.

For further identification, use Roman numerals both in capitals and lower case.

<u>Underline</u> all headings that need emphasis.
(Note the way that this section has been classified.)

1.3 *Colour coding*
Colour is very useful as a distinguishing feature and as a memory aid. Important topics may be underlined in a selected colour. If the notes contain references to another related topic, use a separate colour to indicate this. Key words and concepts may be written in the appropriate colours. Experiment to see how you can use colour to make the notes more interesting and memorable.

1.4 *Symbols, capital letters, drawings, etc.*
Use these for extra emphasis, and to clarify points for yourself. Put important words within shapes. Arrows can be very helpful in linking ideas, and so can ***s and other symbols. Combine with colour for greater impact.

1.5 *Diagrams, graphs, tables, etc.*
A simple sketch is usually sufficient, but make sure it is accurate. Check that all numbering and labelling is clear and unambiguous. Use a ruler for straight lines and table divisions. You may know what it is all about as you make the notes, but several months later a muddled diagram will fill you with horror and confusion.

1.6 *Abbreviations*
Make certain that you are aware of the most common abbreviations. A good dictionary will help. Make your own list to suit the circs, but make sure that you always use the same abbv's otherwise you can get very c'fused. Most disciplines have special terms that can be contracted quite easily.

1.7 *References*
Make a note of all references to books, articles, reports, etc. Include page numbers of material that could be of particular use for an essay, project or seminar. You may well read a passage that is interesting but not absolutely essential to what you are doing, only to find in a few weeks that the information is vital for your latest assignment. If you have not made a note of all the material you read you can waste an immense amount of time searching for a passage. It is even more infuriating if you have actually taken notes, but do not remember where they came from originally.

Professional qualifications, management diplomas and degrees and other forms of higher and further education are all ingredients in the upward movement of those who are aiming high. The successful manager never stops learning and the skills and techniques described in this book should be of value when used for formal study or in everyday managerial situations.

*Margins are useful for adding notes and references*

**Figure 7.1**

1.8 *Handwriting*
If you are unable to read your notes after a few weeks you have been wasting a lot of valuable time. It *is* possible to improve your handwriting. Take it slowly, and form the letters and words carefully. If you still have trouble, even after practice, use a typewriter. Even a two-finger typist can produce good notes at reasonable speed. I have included some exercises on handwriting in Chapter Thirteen. A word processor is extremely useful both for doing an extended piece of writing and for note making. Make certain, however, that the 'mechanics' of it do not interfere with the need to make your notes memorable and colourful. Usually the discipline of turning the rough notes from a lecture or VCR into typed (or word-processed) notes will help to clarify your ideas and understanding of what you have heard. In any case, make your permanent or revision notes as soon as you can after taking them in rough form, and while the information is still fresh in your memory.

Finally, make sure that all the notes that you *make* are well planned and interesting to look at. They will then be much easier to understand and remember. By becoming involved with their preparation and by reworking them where necessary, you will absorb and integrate the material you want to learn as you progress through the course. From the ideas in this chapter, extract what is useful to you and make your notes to suit yourself. Your own personal note-making techniques and learning strategies are always more effective than those imposed from outside.

### Making scientific linear notes

Make sure you understand any scientific terms you have come across that are new to you. Memory and comprehension will be difficult unless you are completely sure of technical and scientific expressions. Possible sources of information include:

(a) scientific dictionaries. These are useful so long as not too much detail is required. Specialist technical and scientific terms rarely occur in standard dictionaries;

(b) specialists, tutors and lecturers;

(c) textbooks. Be careful here, as knowing which book to refer to is difficult. Many textbooks are very specialised and may use the expression in a very particular way. You must have a general idea of the area in which the word is being used. For example, to find out about protons and neutrons, it helps to know that they are part of an atom. In this case, a book dealing with atomic structure will be needed.

Make sure that you are clear about any mathematical terms, as many scientific papers contain graphs, equations, etc.

When drawing sketches or diagrams, make sure that they are not vague. Label them properly, and make accounts of experiments so clear that a lay person could follow and understand the general principles. Clear diagrams are important for effective revision.

When using abbreviations in notes or reports it is important to use the *correct* name at the start. It is a good idea to put the abbreviation in brackets after the full word has been written.

For example:

Electromagnetic (EM) waves are transverse waves; examples of EM waves are radio waves, light waves and X-rays.

Obviously it is essential that scientific notes, and especially formulae, are written out with great care and accuracy. If learning scientific and technical information is only one element in your course, you will need to take even more care than if it was part of your normal working life.

## Concept trees

An important skill of learning is to be able to classify and organise material logically. There may be times when it is not appropriate to make long, detailed notes. What is wanted instead is an outline of the concepts involved so that you can follow and analyse the way in which the subject is structured.

Key words are essential with this method, and the selection of the words to use in this type of diagrammatic note is all-important. By arranging the words in a logical way you construct the concept tree so that it may be followed through easily.

An example of a simple concept tree is shown in figure 7.2.

Of course, you could just write this out as outline notes, using

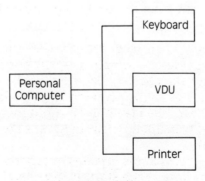

**Figure 7.2**

the words in the concept tree as headings. However, it is often easier to see the logic and organisation behind the subject if you break it up into stages. Some people find it easier to remember the material when it is arranged in this form.

A slightly more complex concept tree is illustrated by figure 7.3. When you have seen how this method works, practice making concept trees by using notes that you have already made on any subject.

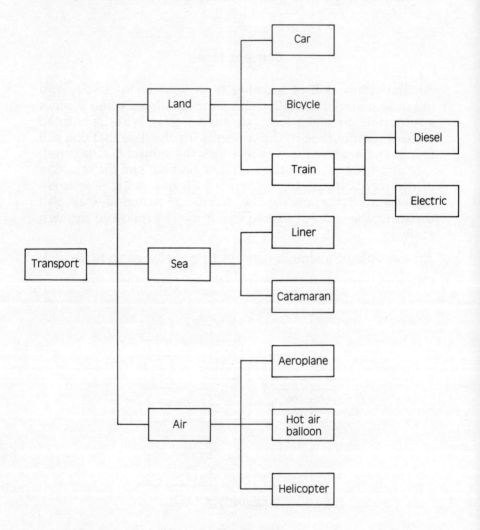

*Figure 7.3*

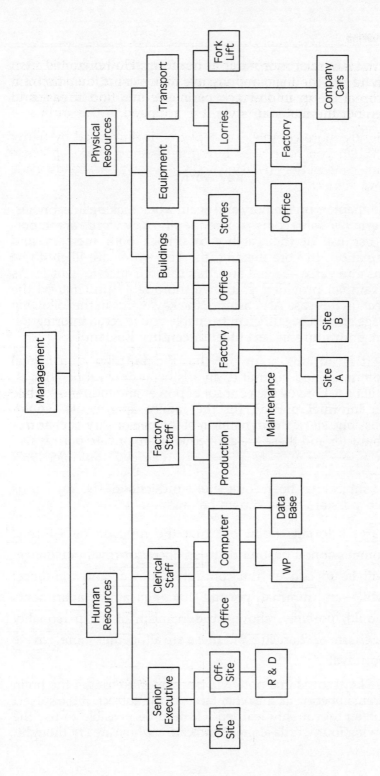

*Figure 7.4*

It is not essential to make it in the form of a horizontal tree. As in figure 7.4, it is quite possible to construct the note from the top of the page down. Experiment until you have found a way which suits your style.

### Key words

In the chapters on memory and again when making linear notes, the term *key words* comes up frequently. Key words are important because of their ability to unlock both memory and imagination. In note making, the key words are likely to be nouns and verbs — what are often called 'concrete' words. As an example, provided you have thoroughly understood the subject (in this case Art History), the key words in the following passage should be sufficient to enable you to recall information about portraiture in seventeenth century England.

> 'Art Historians point out that the function of a formal commissioned portrait of an aristocrat or royal personage, will be to convey the concept of power and influence: while an informal portrait for the family apartments would, possibly, show the dynamism of the personality or charm of character and these are altogether more private portrayals.'
> (*Derek E. Sutcliffe*, 1982)

If the subject has been completely understood, the key words would possibly be as shown below:

'Art Historians point out that the function of a formal commissioned portrait of an aristocrat or royal personage, will be to convey the concept of power and influence: while an informal portrait for the family apartments would, possibly, show the dynamism of the personality or charm of character and these are altogether more private portrayals.'

These key words in a note will be enough to trigger the brain into remembering all the other facets of the subject. If the subject had been thoroughly learned it would be possible to use the following four words alone to indicate a whole area of thought:

FORMAL    POWER    INFORMAL    PRIVATE

Remember the importance of word selection in note making. There is no point in writing long, involved sentences. You need to have the key points summed up by effective key words to help you to think through and recall essential information.

## Pattern note making

(These notes may also be called topic webs, spider diagrams, mind plans, etc.)

Pattern notes exploit your brain's ability to recognise and remember patterns and shapes more easily than blocks of text. Try to recall a familiar room. You will 'see' the room, the furniture, pictures, wallpaper, the colour of the curtains and so on in your imagination. You do *not* see a neatly-typed, sequential, written description of the room.

Pattern notes are not sequential and linear. They use the brain in a completely different way and have very definite advantages both for note taking and note making. Do not confuse them with concept tree notes, flow diagrams or algorithms. Pattern notes require a good deal of personal involvement and choice making as they are built up. This means that they have a very positive effect upon learning, retention and subsequent recall. They grow in an organic way as the mind becomes interested and involved with a problem (whether recording information or thinking through an idea). When you make pattern notes, both the left-hand side of the brain (used for logic, analysis, sequential thinking, etc.) and the right-hand side of the brain (used for synthesis, recognition, creativity, etc.) are working together.

Colours, patterns, shapes and symbols are all easier to recall than blocks of printed words. Printed key words, which may be emphasised with colour and decoration, stand out on the page and in the memory. Sometimes a drawing can be used instead of a word. It is possible to add new material as you come across it or as it occurs to you. This is very difficult with linear notes and impossible with taped notes. Do you remember the last time you tried to add something in the margin because there was not enough room on the page?

ELEM—H

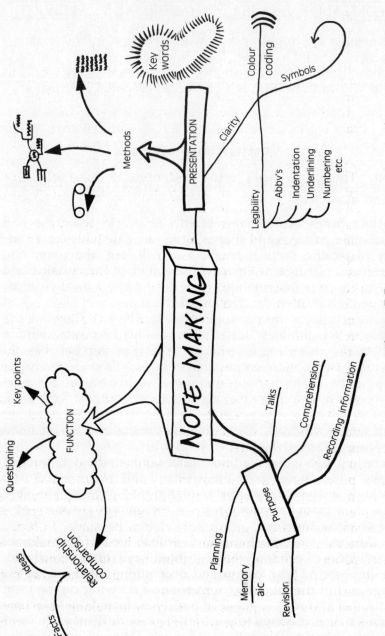

*Figure 7.5*

Figure 7.5 gives an example of a pattern note which shows some of the points already made in this chapter. You will see that, instead of beginning the note at the top of the page as with a linear note, the main heading is, in fact, in the centre of the page. It stands out because of the shape surrounding the words. Subheadings also appear, in shapes which are linked to the main title (in this case by arrows). Important points are highlighted with large lettering, and by symbols and shapes. The brain works associatively, whether with patterns or with words. All key words should bring to mind a host of associated words, concepts or images. In pattern noting we use key words only. There is no need to use sentences, as the combination of words will bring you the recall you need, through association. Of course, all words to some extent have associations for us but a well-chosen key word will encapsulate many concepts or details. In the chapters on memory we saw how a word and an image, together, can make retention and recall easy. The process of selecting a key word makes you more aware of the significance and meaning of the passage being studied, or the lecture being attended. You analyse, compare and select as well as form images and associations between the key words. Comprehension and recall are thus helped considerably.

As the pattern note grows, the relationship between the varying factors become obvious. It is easier to realise how an argument or fact fits into the overall idea when you can see it spread over the page. A good pattern note will enable you to see the topic from different angles. This is a definite advantage, especially when problem solving, or when planning reports and assignments.

You will find that each note will be quite individual. Indeed, other people's notes often look messy and unstructured. This is normal — after all your way of thinking and planning is unique. However, although a pattern note is very personal, it does not mean that a group note cannot be made. In fact, a brainstorming or planning session is enhanced by making a large pattern note from the contributions of different members of the group. It is an ideal way of noting all the stray but potentially valuable ideas which arise.

Some of the advantages of pattern note making have been mentioned. A comparison with linear notes shows that, with the linear method key words are often dissociated visually, especially over time. Thus, we find that with linear notes:

(a) comprehension and retention is weaker;
(b) attention wanders more easily;
(c) review takes longer and is more laborious.

As with most notes, the pattern variety may be informal, or structured carefully for a permanent record. Apart from using pattern notes for study and personal planning, consider some of the other uses to which they may be put:

(a) recording information;
(b) planning assignments, reports, etc.;
(c) taking notes in meetings (speakers often return to an earlier point during a talk or meeting; it is easier to record *all* that has been said with this method);
(d) brainstorming;
(e) forward planning;
(f) problem solving (association of ideas or words written in a 'random' fashion will often prompt you to the next logical step);
(g) summaries of books, chapters, articles, reports, etc.;
(h) creative thinking;
(i) examination revision;
(j) planning meetings, agendas, etc.
(k) notes for talks (it is much easier to talk from one piece of paper than to try to keep your place in a sheaf of closely written notes).

Once you have mastered the skill of pattern note making, you will find many other uses (planning do-it-yourself projects, holidays, career moves, forward planning, etc.). As with any other skill it is important to concentrate on learning the method, practising the skill and then adapting it to your own individual study and work preferences. Most people use a combination of note-making methods, choosing the appropriate method for the task in hand.

The key functions of good note making are to:

(a) bring out the main points;
(b) help the student to see the relationship between different concepts and facts;
(c) reinforce comprehension and aid memory;
(d) lead the student on to further learning.

## Pattern note-making method

As we have seen, both visual and word associations play an important role in the way our brains work. Picking out the key word in any idea should bring the overall meaning of the concept back to you.

Creative writing often depends on this association of key words:

'The Assyrian came down like a wolf on the fold, and his cohorts were gleaming in purple and gold.'

(Byron)

Key words that are 'concrete' generate images $1\frac{1}{2}$ seconds faster on average than abstract words, and they are also much richer in associations. For example, compare *tree* (concrete) and *freedom* (abstract).

Of course any word will lead you on to think of others. Consider one person's list of associations (based on experience, memory, imagination, etc.):

Sea
waves
white horses
Camargue
marsh lands
reeds
thatched roof
cottage
roses
greenfly, insecticide, pollution, etc.

Now try to note down your own associations, beginning with *trade unions*.

The brain always tries to bring order from chaos, and it will impose a structure wherever possible. This process of classification and organisation is used to the full when making a pattern note, since it occurs naturally as you proceed.

In figure 7.6 see how:

(a) the key concept (main heading) is in the centre of the page;
(b) subsidiary ideas (subheadings) radiate from the centre (note that two ways of labelling subheadings are shown);
(c) words and symbols radiate from the subheadings.

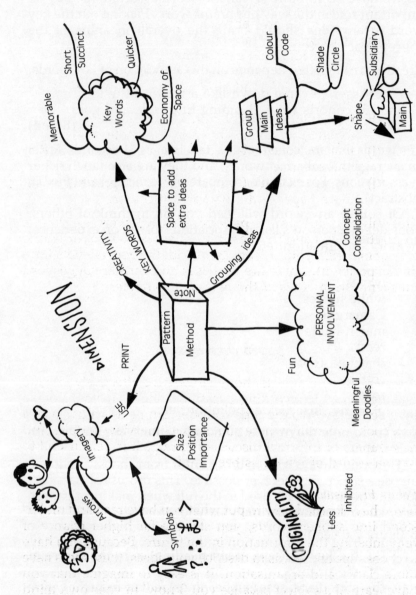

*Figure 7.6*

Points to remember:

(a) the title or main theme word (picture) is in the centre;
(b) ideas are grouped and classified (colour code?);
(c) key words and phrases are used;
(d) drawings illustrate points;
(e) colour coding is used to draw ideas together;
(f) arrows are used to connect ideas;
(g) symbols, signs and abbreviations are used to link and highlight;
(h) important groups of words can be shaded or drawn together by colour in a *completed* note;
(i) *print* words wherever possible — they are then easier to memorise;
(j) if you run out of paper there is no problem — get more paper and sellotape it together!

The only way to know if pattern notes will work for you, is to practise them and try them out. There is no right or wrong way of making a pattern note. Start with the general guidelines and experiment. There are exercises and further suggestions for using these notes at the end of the chapter.

## Taped note making

A tape recorder or a dictaphone can be used effectively for note making, and for recording occasional ideas. If your course involves fieldwork, the tape recorder can be as valuable as a notebook, especially where you need to interview people. And in seminars or informal discussion groups it is very useful to have a record of what has been said.

*Points to consider*
If you have learned how to put what you have read and understood into spoken words, you stand a far higher chance of remembering the information in the future. Because you have to choose specific words to describe your ideas, these ideas have more clarity and organisation. It is easy to imagine that you have learned a subject because you 'know' in your own mind what it is about. The test comes when you have to explain it to others. If you cannot put the information into words that can be understood easily, you have not really grasped the

content thoroughly. Explaining things in your own words helps to consolidate the material in your memory.

Concentrating on your own or on other people's spoken notes is not easy, and the extra effort required usually makes the information more meaningful when it is incorporated into your own scheme of learning.

When you play a taped note back, the concentration required helps to fix the facts or ideas firmly into your memory. As it is impossible to glance back at a previous word or phrase, you have to depend a great deal on your ability to memorise the material. The more practice you get in memorising, the easier recall will be when you need to use the material in examinations, or in work situations.

If you tape meetings, talks and lectures, you will be able to extract important information at a later date. (Of course, it is necessary and courteous to ask the speaker or lecturer if they object to the tape recorder being used.) You will be able to focus on particular areas that you found interesting — areas that were perhaps only glossed over in a few words during the spoken session. Making pattern or linear notes from a taped talk is a good way of sifting the relevant from the irrelevant.

We tend to get a great deal of our information from the television or video screen, and most people find it difficult to listen efficiently. Yet in all aspects of business, academic and personal life we constantly have to listen to other people's points of view. The tape recorder is a good training ground for those who want to practise effective listening skills.

An experienced manager can use the taped notes of colleagues to assess their contributions, and can then at leisure sift out the valid points for future reference. This demands a high level of skill and should not be undertaken lightly.

## Note taking

Taking notes implies that you are recording information as it happens, or in informal circumstances. To take notes you really do need to practise a good deal. There is a world of difference between sitting at your desk making clear, well-constructed notes from a book or from your own mind, and trying to capture the information, ideas and asides in a lecture or meeting.

Of course, many of the suggestions mentioned earlier will

apply to taking notes. You may find that a more extensive use of abbreviations will be needed. You should be able to listen more than you write, and to develop a personal shorthand if this is a skill that you have not mastered. Apart from the conventional abbreviations which you will find in any good dictionary, try abbreviating words that you use frequently. For example:

| ex | = *example* | wrt | = *write* |
|---|---|---|---|
| p | = *page* | b/4 | = *before* |
| diff | = *difference* | b/c | = *because* |
| w/ | = *with* | w/o | = *without* |
| Q | = *question* | lrn | = *learn* |

If you are rushed, you can abbreviate a word by omitting the vowels. Use the same abbreviations in all your rough notes, and make sure that you transcribe the notes as soon as possible after you have taken them.

If you are taking linear rather than pattern notes, it is sensible to spread yourself out over the pages. Leave room for the speaker's afterthoughts and for your own comments. If you note information that you realise is not essential, *never* black it out. The moment you erase the name of a book or reference to a topic, you will find that you need the information desperately. This is a natural law of study! Just draw a line through it or bracket it clearly.

If the lecturer makes a particular point that is obviously crucial, mark it in a recognisable way, with asterisks, or by underlining in colour, or in some other way that makes it stand out on the page.

You may have noticed that in Chapter Four I suggested a way of taking notes using columns. If you have not tried this before it could be worth experimenting with it. Practise from a discussion programme on television or radio.

## Case study

Mark Hollins works in an office in a large multi-national company. He is ambitious, but has only average educational qualifications. He is working for an Open University degree with the encouragement of his area manager. He has attended a study skills course run by the company's training department.

As a result of this he is able to choose the appropriate note-making methods for his course and revision strategy for his examinations. This planned efficiency spills over into his daily routine. Mark has learned how to listen well, and finds the occasional lecture and taped material easy to cope with. He can also be relied upon to listen to a phone call and act on the information swiftly and accurately. He has used pattern notes as a planning device to think through his career plans, and he also uses them when given responsibility for planning some of the office activities. The positive action he is taking to improve his career prospects has proved valuable to his company, and he is already marked as a young man with a future.

### Individual exercises

1  Before taking any notes for a course or project ask yourself:

    (a)  When do I need to take notes?
    (b)  Why do I need to take notes?
    (c)  How do I make the notes?

2  Go through any notes you have made in the past. They may not be for study, but could be perhaps notes for memos, reports, letters or projects. They may be on the back of an envelope or in an impressive folder. Try to analyse *how* you made the notes. Was it an effective method? Could you apply any other note-making method to future study or work situations?

3  Using the incomplete pattern note in figure 7.7, produce a comprehensive set of ideas that record your thoughts and knowledge about the subject.

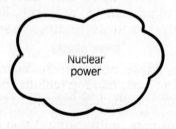

*Figure 7.7*

4 Make a pattern note to summarise all the chapters of this book you have read so far. Chapter headings could act as the key words for subheadings. The main central heading would be the title of this book. Figure 7.8 is a basis for this.

*Figure 7.8*

5 Take one topic from the pattern note you made in exercise 4 and develop it in more detail as in figure 7.9.

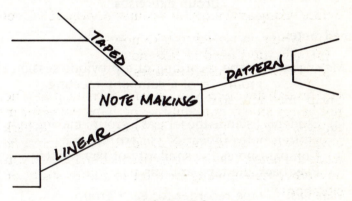

*Figure 7.9*

6 Using a tape recorder or dictaphone, make notes with it during the day. It will be of more value if you choose a day with a variety of problems to deal with. Rerun the tape, and try to record the key ideas, findings or solutions in written form.

7 Make a clear linear note which incorporates the ideas suggested about note making (colour coding, indentation, etc.). Take a subject which is relevant to your study or work.

8 Make a pattern note on the subject you know most about, namely, *yourself* (title: *myself*). How would you tackle it?

Would you choose a forward-planning exercise? A problem-solving exercise? A summary of your strengths and weaknesses? Or a note about your personality, interests, aspirations and character?

When you have completed the exercise, think of what you selected for inclusion, what you rejected, and why.

9 Practise taking notes from a radio talk or a television broadcast. Use linear notes, pattern notes or a combination of what seems appropriate. If you are able to record the broadcast, check to see that you have noted all the main points. This exercise is particularly useful if you often have to take notes in lectures or meetings. With practice you will gain confidence in your ability to extract the essential points.

## Group exercises

### Taped notes

1 *Materials:* a tape recording of a previous session of the group, or of a company meeting
  *Group size:* any size

(a) Students listen to the tape as a group, making individual written notes (linear or pattern) from it.
(b) Compare notes for similarity of key points.
(c) Play back the tape and discuss.

2 *Materials:* tape recorder for each group
  *Group size:* 3—4 people in each group

(a) Ask two or three students to discuss a topic of general interest for five minutes.
(b) All groups record the discussion. After the discussion has been heard and taped, each person recalls the main points and makes notes.
(c) The group compares the notes made by members, and makes a group note by combining the existing notes.
(d) Each group plays the tape back again and the final note is checked. Discuss these questions:
    — How accurate was it?
    — What points were left out?
    — Did individual notes differ greatly? Why?
    — Were the main points listed in sequence?

**Linear notes**

3 *Materials:* examples of badly written notes, photocopied and distributed

   *Group size:* any size of group, although it may be useful to divide very large groups

   (a) Each student rewrites the notes in an acceptable way, or notes down errors and makes suggestions.
   (b) The group discusses what constitutes an error, and what makes for clear, meaningful note making.

      Opinions will vary considerably. It should be emphasised that there are guidelines for successful note making, but that group members' preferences should be respected, especially when they work well for the individual.

4 Through group discussion, make a composite list of the basic elements of linear note making. Emphasise that good notes are important for all forms of communication in business, not only for study purposes. The following list may be of help:

   *What is the purpose of any note making?*
   (a) to understand content?
   (b) to record information?
   (c) to produce effective learning?
   (d) to act as a memory aid?
   (e) to help with revision and examinations?
   (f) to allow planning?
   (g) to allow assessment?

   *Common weaknesses in note taking:*
   (a) illegibility
   (b) word-for-word recording
   (c) bad organisation
   (d) non-sequentiality
   (e) untidyness

   *Good notes will contain:*
   (a) key points, highlighted
   (b) clearly-shown relationships between factors
   (c) clearly-expressed personal thoughts
   (d) well-labelled and recognisable diagrams, flow charts, etc.

(e) information recorded in one's own words
(f) adequate references

*Presentation:*
(a) spacing and layout should be well considered
(b) the notes should be legible
(c) the notes should be properly paginated
(d) there should be a good use of indentation, under-lining, colour coding, symbols, abbreviations, high-lighting, etc.
(e) the notes should be filed in an organised manner

## Pattern notes

5 Pattern notes may be used in a variety of ways.

Group notes can be made when thinking or planning. If possible, use the experience of the group to give examples of problems, examples of forward planning, and examples of the recording of information. Some further examples are given below.

*Materials:*   large sheets of paper
coloured markers or felt tipped pens
*Group size:*  3—5 people (if a good relationship has developed within the main group try mixing different grades if practicable)

*Examples*
(a) John Maynard is a well-qualified and efficient com-pany man. He is a creative and valuable member of the management team. Joan Bates is his assistant and she has the potential to be of equal value. John is however very abrasive and Joan feels he undervalues her contri-bution. She is looking for other openings and it is known that she has been approached by a rival organisation. The company is anxious to keep both members of staff. Relating this situation to your experiences, think through the problem, noting down any possible action (however trivial) or conclusion that you arrive at.
(b) You are members of the planning department in your local authority. As a sub-committee, you have been asked to recommend a course of action to deal with the

situation below. What will you do? Make a pattern note of your ideas, then expand your choice in another, more detailed note.

*The situation* Elderly Eliza Biggs has left £20,000 to your town. However, she has placed several restraints on the way it is to be spent:

- Once the money becomes available, it has to be spent (or allocated) within fourteen days or it will be forfeited.
- The money must directly benefit old people *or* handicapped children *or* The Crown and Anchor darts team.
- The name *Albert Biggs* has to be incorporated in some permanent way, so that her late husband will be remembered for at least fifty years.

(c) Using your company or organisation as the main title, make a pattern note which could be the basis of a detailed report. For example, you may have to consider some of the following factors: *location, function, market, personnel, government involvement*, etc.

6  Some of the individual exercises can be adapted easily for group work. For example, by using a video recording of a documentary (with permission!), you can ask the group to compare resulting notes with each other. This is a valuable exercise in discussing which key points individuals consider to be most important, and in exploring different (possibly equally effective) methods of working.

# EIGHT

# Reading strategies

Of all the skills needed for learning, and especially for study learning, reading is the most significant. In many subjects, over 80 per cent of a student's time is taken up with this activity. And at work, staff must read reports, financial columns, technical journals, user manuals and so on day in day out. We must consider how to approach different types of reading in such a way as to get the most out of each one. These strategies for reading will also include consideration of the rate of reading speed. This will be looked at in more detail in Chapter Nine.

There are many ways of studying a textbook or any other piece of technical material. (Throughout the chapter I will refer to a book, although it could apply equally to a report, an article in a journal, or any other piece of extended writing.)

The way in which many people approach the task is to read the book slowly and carefully, all the way through, conscientiously taking notes as they go along. This is very worthy and it is certainly what many teachers and lecturers have advised in the past. However, it is not a particularly efficient way in which to absorb and learn new material.

An advance on the practice of reading slowly and carefully is to:

(a) reread over and over again as time permits;
(b) read, underlining the main points as you do so; or
(c) read through and then make outline linear notes.

These three methods are all useful. But as with other study skills techniques, it is important to select the appropriate method, not only to fit your personal learning style, but also to suit the material you are working on. Much will depend on the relevance of the material to your ultimate goal. For example, background reading is important, but you would not necessarily need to take intensive revision notes from this type of reading.

It has been said, with justification, that reading a text ten times at speed is more valuable than reading it through once, slowly. The relationship between one aspect of a book and another is often crucial to the understanding of the author's meaning, and the faster you read the work the more the different aspects become unified in your own understanding and reasoning. The skill of speed reading is extremely useful and the next chapter will be concerned with this subject.

It is important to view the book as a whole, while at the same time keeping in mind the information that you need to extract. Starting at the beginning and slogging through to the end may sound sensible, but is in fact counterproductive. The way to get your shopping done is not to start at one end of the street, visiting every shop to see if they have got what you need. Normally, you make a shopping list and then go straight to the places where you know you will obtain exactly what you want. However, window shopping is often the preliminary to a bargain, so bear this in mind when studying a text for the first time.

Critical reading and personal involvement with the task are essential. You need to look for the structure and organisation of the book, to fit it into the overall scheme of knowledge that you already possess. Knowing the structure improves comprehension and, by implication, recall. You need to plan your work before you begin to read, so before starting, go through the following steps:

1 *Establish your objectives*
What do you need from the text? Is is pleasure? Many books being studied for English literature, for example, will be enjoyed for their own sake quite apart from any critical appraisal. Or is it for some practical application — perhaps to construct something or to carry out a scientific experiment? It may be that you require only one piece of specific information. But possibly you need to read the entire book to evaluate critically the content and ideas presented by the author.

Is it background understanding? Is it material for an assignment or seminar contribution? Is it to add to material already known and learned? Will the new material lead you on to the next stage of studying this particular subject? Is is absolutely essential, or is it peripheral?

If you begin to think about your objectives you will find that there are many different reasons for reading the book. If you

ELEM—I

have established just why you need to read the material (and you may have several different objectives in view) your task of reading will be easier, as your brain begins to classify and organise the material you are reading. You may also find that in some cases you do not need to read, but merely to skim over the content in order to extract one specific fact or figure.

### 2 Review your current knowledge of the subject

Think about the subject you plan to study, and dredge up from the depths of your mind all the information you already have about it. You will then have a nucleus to which you can add new material as you come across it.

### 3 Make a glossary of new words required for the subject

A working vocabulary is essential if you are to learn effectively. Spend some time going through the course syllabus, textbooks and any other relevant material (the index is a useful source of words). Even if the new words do not occur immediately in your studies, it is an advantage to recognise them as they appear and to have at least a superficial understanding of their meaning.

### 4 Ask yourself if you have the skills to read the book

On the surface this seems a silly question. If you can read and want to learn, this may seem sufficient. For many books this will be true, but ask yourself if you are able:

(a) to read a graph correctly;
(b) to understand a histogram;
(c) to read a table of statistics;
(d) to read a contour map properly;
(e) to interpret a plan or blueprint;
(f) to understand formulae;
(g) to evaluate a bar chart.

If these skills are important throughout your course, get some help in learning to cope with them. It is worth asking your tutor for help if some of them are unfamiliar. Do not be afraid to confess ignorance about material which you find difficult to read. Over the past few years, many different forms of graphics have come into use, and you must be able to interpret them.

Many graphics are not 'read', in the conventional sense of the word; they need to be looked at and studied carefully. For example, when reading a graph, apart from being able to interpret the trends within it, you should note that:

(a) the title will usually show the main points and relationships;
(b) the text near the graph often summarises the key points being made.

When you are studying an illustration or diagram, you should:

(a) look at it systematically, perhaps in a sequential way;
(b) draw it roughly from memory, adding labels;
(c) check your drawing against the original illustration;
(d) make a second attempt;
(e) check again.

Time spent on doing this exercise even superficially will be repaid later. For some subjects such as biology, anatomy and mechanics, this spatial understanding is vital.

Visual aids add to the interest of any book. Moreover, if studied properly, they can not only give information, but also aid retention of the general background of a specific topic.

No doubt you will think of many other areas that need specialised skills of reading and interpretation.

5 *Plan your reading session*
Select the area to be covered, and have a definite time for completing a certain amount of work. This topic is covered in more detail in Chapter Eleven, on *time organisation*.

## Selection of background material

Apart from required reading, you will obviously need to read widely so that you can thoroughly understand your chosen subject. But you must not waste your time in reading books which are going to be of little value to you on the course. You may wish to note them and read them at your leisure; but most people will have quite enough to do, coping with their studies, their job, and domestic chores. There will be no point in reading material which is not of immediate value.

Before you begin to look for suitable books, ask yourself why you feel you need to read more. What do you want to know? Write down specific questions you want answered. If you have any earlier notes, they will probably suggest areas you need to explore in more depth. So will the course syllabus.

Not all printed matter is worth looking at. If it is on a recommended book list or is required reading you will have to take it on trust. However, if you are looking for a book on your own, be very critical. A brief, 2—3 minute appraisal should be enough to tell you a good deal about the volume you have taken from the library or bookshop shelves.

Just looking at the cover of a book can tell you a considerable amount about the contents. For example, it will tell you the publisher. Most publishers have a certain area of interest and keep to this general field. Thus, Prentice Hall International publish mainly academic, 'serious' books. You would be able to rely on a Penguin book to be worth reading, while a book on a serious scientific subject is unlikely to be on the list of Mills and Boon. Get to know the firms which publish the best books in your subject.

The back of the cover will often advertise other books in the same series or by the same author. Press comments are often quoted, and these can be useful, although you will need to take some of them with a pinch of salt.

Inside you will find a good deal of information which will tell you whether the book is suitable for your purposes. Look at the date. A book on computer science will only have historic interest if it was published in 1962. It will not be of much use if you are embarking on a course concerning information technology in industry and commerce. However, a book published in 1977 on report and letter writing could still be of value.

Beware of the publisher who reissues a bestseller of yesteryear in a new cover. Check the date when it was first printed!

Note what edition the book is. If it has run into many editions this could mean that it is worth reading, since it has proved to be a successful textbook. Of course, it may mean simply that new ideas are slow in being accepted!

There should be a reasonable amount of information about the author, giving qualifications and possible reasons for writing. A book about Astrophysics by Marilyn Monroe would be rather suspect while a book entitled *The History of the British Labour Party* could be informative but possibly biased if the author was a leading member of the party. It is important to know from which angle any author is writing. Most people will take a very definite stand on certain basic ideas that they hold, and will write accordingly. A book on study methods by a well known nutrition expert could be interesting; but it would be necessary to realise that he or she would probably write it from the viewpoint of 'we are what we eat', and that they might have strong views about the effect various diets have on the learning process.

The title can usually give you an idea of the range of the book. *A Few Thoughts on Snails and their World* and *Snapshots for the Family Album* will be different in range from *Helix Aspersa, the Garden Snail, Behaviour and Habitat* or *Photography: History, Theory, and Darkroom Technique.*

Look at the table of contents. This will tell you how the book is constructed and what the author feels is important. It surprises many people to realise that books frequently have only one or two main themes. Most of the text will be taken up with the clarification, explanation and implication of these themes. The index will also give you a fair idea of the range and scope of the book. Is it easy to find your way around the book using the index? If the book has no index, ask yourself why not. Any reputable textbook will have a full and detailed index.

Look at the blurb, the press comments, the author's academic background or practical experience, and so on. Flick through the book briefly and decide then whether it is worth carrying on.

If the book looks useful but you are very short of time, a glance at the preface or first chapter, and the final chapter, will often tell you a good deal about the book and the author's reason for writing it.

If you decide that the book is relevant and that you are going to study it in some depth, look again at:

(a) the title and subtitle, to get the author's slant on the subject;

(b) the title page. Is the book American? British? A foreign translation? A book on negotiating skills will reflect different priorities, and a different background of labour relations, in different countries;

(c) the table of contents. Get a feel for the layout of the book. Which parts are going to be of most interest to you? Are there sections that you will not need to read? Looking at the overall structure of the book will aid comprehension and memory;

(d) the index. Follow up some cross references, looking

at points from different angles. Note what the author considers to be the key points of the book;

(e) appendices, glossaries and bibliographies. Check to see if these will be useful to you. Ask yourself for whom the book is intended and at what level the book is aimed;

(f) diagrams, illustrations, graphs, etc. Are they clear? Note that graphics are often only included when words are less clear; they are more expensive to print than ordinary text, so they have to justify their existence. If they are included, they are important, and must be studied. Remember that visual information is easier to recall than the written word;

(g) the preface. This is usually written last. The author will often sum up the main ideas of the book here, and may state the purpose of writing it;

(h) the style. Is it easy to follow? Can you understand the material and follow the arguments easily? Look at the end of each chapter. There may be exercises or summaries which will be useful. Very often the author will have phrased the questions or summed up the chapter, making use of the key points that she feels are the most important (useful for revision exercises).

As you read, actively try to link the knowledge you have already to what is new. How does it fit into the jigsaw of your existing understanding of the topic and allied subjects? As you read through quickly and see something that catches your eye, stop and look at it. Interest in something means that you will be motivated to learn, and will retain the information longer.

At the second or third reading, you could begin to note down (not take notes of) important passages. Consider using colour coding. 'Highlighters' are extremely useful here, or at least a pencil code so that you can identify the relative importance of the material. If you use colour, keep to the same colour code whenever you take notes on the same subject. Underline key passages, and perhaps summarise any part which you know will be vital for examinations or essays. This is an instance where pattern notes are extremely effective. Note down all references that you may need in the future.

It goes against the grain to many people to think of marking a book in any way. Of course, if the book is not yours you have no choice. However, if it is your book, think of it as a basic notebook to which you are adding new notes or information. Where it is impossible to mark the book, cut paper to the size of the pages and insert these in the appropriate places, using them for your preliminary noting. Remember to add the page number to each loose sheet. It is always the unmarked sheet that slips to the floor when you are moving your papers and books around.

Look out for what are often known as signal words. These are familiar words and phrases which are important for good reading because they signal what is going to come next in the text. Use these signals to help you read faster and better. A list of some of these signals is given below:

Words signalling that more of the same is to come:
*also; moreover; again; and; in addition; more than that; furthermore*
Words signalling that you should slow up, as a change of direction is indicated:
*but; nevertheless; despite; however; yet; although; rather*
Words signalling that a conclusion or a summary is about to be stated:
*thus; so; therefore; consequently; accordingly; to summarise*

When reading a chapter, try looking at the first paragraph and then the last one. These will often sum up the entire chapter, with the paragraphs between giving only supporting detail. Check to see whether there is a summary or list of key points at the end of the chapter or section. A bird's eye view of the material will help you understand it better as you go along.

It will help you to get the most out of each book if you become involved in the text, take positive steps to think about the structure and planning of the book, and then structure your own thinking and note making. This will also ensure that you really learn the material as opposed to just reading through it without completely understanding the content, or in such a way that you forget it soon afterwards.

As you read, ask yourself the following questions:

(a) are the facts correct?
(b) does the author distinguish between fact and opinion?
(c) do conclusions follow from facts?
(d) would other conclusions follow equally as well?
(e) do the author's conclusions agree with mine?
(f) what shall I learn from this book?

Argue, question, be critical, become involved. You must be on your guard against an author who wittingly or unwittingly uses language to influence the reader unduly. For example, as you read look out for:

(a) emotive words;
(b) lack of good references;
(c) attempts to prove a point by analogy;
(d) use of false premises;
(e) generalisations from a small number of particular cases;
(f) padding and waffle.

NB: You may have noticed that this book contains no footnotes or specific references. This was a conscious decision, however the bibliography contains all the books used for source material.

You should now be reading in some depth. Remember that your subconscious will be working away as you read. Questions that need resolving and concepts that are not quite clear could become obvious as you carry on through the text. If by the time you have attained an overview of the book you *still* have questions or material that you do not completely understand, now is the time to seek help from your tutor or to discuss it with a colleague.

When reading the book for the first time, if you come across an unfamiliar word, do not stop to check its meaning. If it is important, the meaning should become apparent as you read on. If it is not important, you can look it up afterwards. If it is jargon or a technical word you will be in a good position if you have previously made a glossary, as suggested earlier in the chapter. It is important not to stop the flow of the book during the first readings. During later readings you will be able to stop and think about specific points.

As you read, be prepared to reject as well as select the material you finally need for notes or background reading. Put a diagonal pencil line through sections which are irrelevant, repetitious, padding, or unnecessary examples. Then, when you read again and ultimately make your notes, you will not have to spend time on material which is of little value to you.

Finally, go through the book once more very quickly, concentrating on the parts you have selected as being important. Try to see the material as a whole, slotting in the knowledge that you already have and thinking about its relationship with other books and other subjects you are studying.

## Note taking from books

If you have done the preparatory work suggested above you will be in a good position to start taking effective and meaningful notes.

Go through the material fairly rapidly, taking notes as you go along. You will already have colour coded, made margin notes and eliminated irrelevant material, so the outline notes you need for revision work will only consist of essential material. The work will be much easier than if you had slogged through an unfamiliar book, not really knowing what was important or even what was coming next. Meaningful notes are essential if you are to revise properly and achieve examination success. You will also need good notes for future assignments.

When making notes from written material, make sure that you never copy anything out. There are two reasons for this. Firstly, if you write down other people's ideas in *their* speech patterns and rhythms, with their own idiosyncratic way of expressing themselves, you will never make the ideas and information part of your own experience. You must write the material in your own words (even if they are selected key words rather than sentences). Secondly, you may inadvertently use this material in an essay or assignment without remembering where it came from. This plagiarism could be at the very least embarrassing, and at worst could mean failure or disqualification. Always make sure that within your personal notes you put quotations of whatever length into inverted commas, and write down the reference details.

Number the pages of your notes as you make them. It is also a good idea to put the subject or topic in colour at the top of the page. This is very useful if you are revising, or need to select material for inclusion in an assignment.

Ask yourself whether your note-making methods are the best and most appropriate for what you are doing. For example, a short book or article may be more useful if it is noted on file cards, with key points only noted down.

If you are making fairly extensive linear notes it is often helpful to summarise a section with a pattern note or by means of a concept tree (see Chapter Seven).

Always review your notes when they are complete to make sure that they are legible, clear and meaningful. Then review them again after a few days, possibly with the book at hand. Close the book and your file of notes. Make a quick pattern note of the main points. Use one colour of pen for this. Then check with the book and notes, and add in a second colour any points you have missed. Keep a file of these summary notes for quick reference.

This method of reading, thinking and note making can also be used for daily reading, which you may have to do at work. Possibly you may have to read several reports and prepare an action plan. The same methods can apply. Read each report several times at speed, one after another. This will give you the overall view of what has been covered. Mark the information which is relevant to your department or section, and make brief notes on the important factors. This will give you the basis of an argument to put forward in a meeting, or in a written analysis.

As you read, you will notice that each paragraph has one basic idea. This idea will usually be contained in a *key sentence* (sometimes called the thesis sentence). All the other sentences should contain supporting detail or an expansion on the original thought. Practise identifying this sentence. Frequently it will be the first sentence, but not always. Within this key or thesis sentence there will also, naturally, be key words. This is a great help when note making, because these key words will be useful in memory work and when making notes.

If you can find the key sentence in a paragraph you will also be able to find the *key paragraphs* in a chapter. These will often be the first and the last paragraphs (the introduction to the theme of the chapter and the summary of the theme).

As well as key sentences and paragraphs, the first and last chapter of the book are sometimes *key chapters* (the preface may act as the initial key chapter). The key chapters can usually be recognised by looking at the table of contents. It is useful to know about all the levels from key words to key chapters; if you are in a hurry, it can cut down your time considerably when you are trying to assess a book quickly, or are looking for a piece of information that you know is contained somewhere in the volume. Of course, you will not then really be reading or studying, but there are times when the quick way is the only way.

Do not rely on any author writing in a completely systematic way, but keep a look out for the principal themes in sentences, paragraphs and chapters.

## Common errors

Some of the common errors to avoid in note making are listed below. Look at your own notes and decide if they could be improved. Go back to Chapter Seven again if you need to rethink your note-making methods. The errors are concerned with linear notes rather than pattern notes.

(a) It is harder to make efficient notes with a small notebook, if only because it becomes more difficult to compare points without turning backwards and forwards. Indentations, colour coding and categorisation of ideas are all made more confusing. A4 file paper is a good size, allowing you to spread yourself and your ideas. Naturally, you may need a small notepad for fieldwork or for making unobtrusive notes. Transfer these field notes to your regular note file as soon as possible.

(b) Do not have too many separate notebooks. There is always a time when you have to note down a useful piece of information on the back of an envelope or in your pocket notebook; but try to have only one place where these informal notes can be made, and transfer them as soon as possible.

(c) Do not have notes on a variety of topics which are not divided within a file. If you are using a ring binder it is essential to have a set of file dividers so that you can look up information easily. A different file for each aspect of the course is highly desirable. Colour code the files if possible, and label each one as clearly as possible.

(d) Do not have notes which are too detailed. The inexperienced student will try to amass pages and pages of notes, for fear of missing out essential material. This is counter-productive. Notes should be easy to read, and key points should stand out easily. It is far better to have clear, brief notes, and to use the original book to check for any extra detail required.

(e) Pages and sections must be numbered. Without clear marking you will find that it is impossible to find your way around your early notes. If you have the misfortune to drop your file, the frustration of trying to get your notes back into the correct order will make you realise that numbering and categorising is not an optional extra!

(f) Poor labelling is a common fault, both in respect of labels at the top of the page and headings. Make sure that all your headings and key points are in capitals or in colour. Wherever possible, stick to the headings that you find in the book you are noting from. This makes life far easier if you need to refer to the book at a later time.

(g) If you prefer to write in sentences rather than in key words, try not to be too wordy. It wastes time, both when you make the notes and when revising.

(h) Do not copy material directly from the book. It is better for retention, recall and comprehension if you write your own notes and not someone else's. This applies to using other student's notes as well. If you share any information-gathering or discussion notes with anyone else, do not file them as they stand; rewrite them in your own words.

### Other reading strategies

So far, we have concentrated on looking at specific books for specific purposes, either for note taking or background reading. There are many factors involved in improving your general reading ability. The person who reads widely and with intelligence will improve not only her or his chance of examination success, but also possibilities for career advancement. Apart from these practical aspects, the personal pleasure and profit to be had from reading is inestimable. You might not go as far as Logan Pearsall Smith who wrote: 'People say that life is the thing, but I prefer reading.' However, it is very valuable to look at the way in which you read for whatever purpose.

## Dealing with vocabulary

Have you got a good vocabulary? To comprehend and to explain any concept or device it is essential to have sufficient words to cover all ramifications, components, particulars, segments, divisions, branches, complexities, factors, divergencies, deployments, deviations, spread or breadth, catholicity, characteristic, entirety and comprehensive nature of whatever you are trying to describe, portray, delineate, depict, profile, recount, picture, detail, communicate, specify, represent, embody, evoke, personify, duplicate or illustrate.

It is not only when studying that an extensive vocabulary is of benefit. Anyone who has a good command of language is at an advantage both in business and in social life. If you are one of thousands who have never been able to cancel a *Reader's Digest* subscription, resign yourself to your fate and turn to the section which appears each month called 'It pays to improve your word power'. The chart at the end which gives your vocabulary rating is illuminating!

The educated reader will automatically make extensive use of a good dictionary and a thesaurus. Do not imagine that the dictionary you had at school will do. Words and their meanings change over the years and new words are constantly entering our language. A good dictionary will also act as a mini-encyclopedia. (Note that the word 'mini' would not have appeared thirty years ago in the sense in which it is used in this paragraph.)

A knowledge of the derivation of words and an understanding of the meanings of common prefixes and suffixes will enhance your reading skills considerably. Knowing the difference between *anti* and *ante* and what *mal* and *para* mean will help you to comprehend any words which begin in this way. Or consider the suffixes: -*itis* ('inflammation of'), -*ferous* ('producing') and -*able* ('fit for', 'capable of').

Many of our words are taken from Latin and Greek roots. Even a smattering of these languages, with a little knowledge of French, will help you to make an educated guess at the meaning of a word. An obvious example is *philo*. If you know that this is Greek for 'love of', and that *sophia* means 'wisdom', then

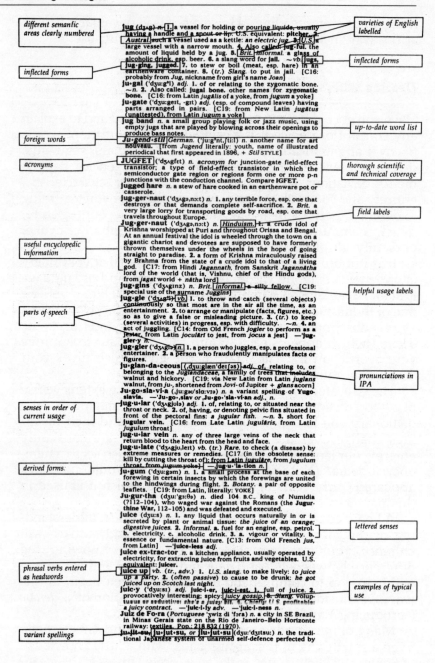

different semantic areas clearly numbered

inflected forms

foreign words

acronyms

useful encyclopedic information

parts of speech

senses in order of current usage

derived forms:

phrasal verbs entered as headwords

variant spellings

varieties of English labelled

inflected forms

up-to-date word list

thorough scientific and technical coverage

field labels

helpful usage labels

pronunciations in IPA

lettered senses

examples of typical use

**jug** (dʒʌg) *n.* **1.** a vessel for holding or pouring liquids, usually having a handle and a spout or lip. U.S. equivalent: **pitcher.** **2.** *Austral.* such a vessel used as a kettle: *an electric jug.* **3.** U.S. a large vessel with a narrow mouth. **4.** Also called: **jugful.** the amount of liquid held by a jug. **5.** *Brit. informal.* a glass of alcoholic drink, esp. beer. **6.** a slang word for **jail.** ~*vb.* **jugs, jug·ging, jugged. 7.** to stew or boil (meat, esp. hare) in an earthenware container. **8.** (*tr.*) *Slang.* to put in jail. [C16: probably from *Jug*, nickname from girl's name *Joan*]

**ju·gal** ('dʒuːgˈl) *adj.* **1.** of or relating to the zygomatic bone. ~*n.* **2.** Also called: **jugal bone.** other names for **zygomatic bone.** [C16: from Latin *jugālis* of a yoke, from *jugum* a yoke]

**ju·gate** ('dʒuːgeɪt, -gɪt) *adj.* (esp. of compound leaves) having parts arranged in pairs. [C19: from New Latin *jugātus* (unattested), from Latin *jugum* a yoke]

**jug band** *n.* a small group playing folk or jazz music, using empty jugs that are played by blowing across their openings to produce bass notes.

**Ju·gend·stil** *German.* ('juːgˈnt,ʃtiːl) *n.* another name for **art nouveau.** [from *Jugend* literally: youth, name of illustrated periodical that first appeared in 1896, + *Stil* STYLE]

**JUGFET** ('dʒʌgfet) *n. acronym for* junction-gate field-effect transistor; a type of field-effect transistor in which the semiconductor gate region or regions form one or more p-n junctions with the conduction channel. Compare IGFET.

**jugged hare** *n.* a stew of hare cooked in an earthenware pot or casserole.

**jug·ger·naut** ('dʒʌgə,nɔːt) *n.* **1.** any terrible force, esp. one that destroys or that demands complete self-sacrifice. **2.** *Brit.* a very large lorry for transporting goods by road, esp. one that travels throughout Europe.

**Jug·ger·naut** ('dʒʌgə,nɔːt) *n. Hinduism.* **1.** a crude idol of Krishna worshipped at Puri and throughout Orissa and Bengal. At an annual festival the idol is wheeled through the town on a gigantic chariot and devotees are supposed to have formerly thrown themselves under the wheels in the hope of going straight to paradise. **2.** a form of Krishna miraculously raised by Brahma from the state of a crude idol to that of a living god. [C17: from Hindi *Jagannath*, from Sanskrit *Jagannātha* lord of the world (that is, Vishnu, chief of the Hindu gods), from *jagat* world + *nātha* lord]

**jug·gins** ('dʒʌgɪnz) *n. Brit. informal.* a silly fellow. [C19: special use of the surname *Juggins*]

**jug·gle** ('dʒʌgˈl) *vb.* **1.** to throw and catch (several objects) continuously so that most are in the air all the time, as an entertainment. **2.** to arrange or manipulate (facts, figures, etc.) so as to give a false or misleading picture. **3.** (*tr.*) to keep (several activities) in progress, esp. with difficulty. ~*n.* **4.** an act of juggling. [C14: from Old French *jogler* to perform as a jester, from Latin *joculārī* to jest, from *jocus* a jest] —'**jug·gler·y** *n.*

**jug·gler** ('dʒʌglə) *n.* **1.** a person who juggles, esp. a professional entertainer. **2.** a person who fraudulently manipulates facts or figures.

**ju·glan·da·ceous** (,dʒuːglæn'deɪʃəs) *adj.* of, relating to, or belonging to the *Juglandaceae*, a family of trees that includes walnut and hickory. [C19: via New Latin from Latin *juglans* walnut, from *ju-*, shortened from *Jovi-* of Jupiter + *glans* acorn]

**Ju·go·sla·vi·a** (,juːgəʊ'slɑːvɪə) *n.* a variant spelling of Yugoslavia. —,**Ju·go·**,**slav** or ,**Ju·go·'sla·vi·an** *adj., n.*

**jug·u·lar** ('dʒʌgjʊlə) *adj.* **1.** of, relating to, or situated near the throat or neck. **2.** of, having, or denoting pelvic fins situated in front of the pectoral fins: *a jugular fish.* ~*n.* **3.** short for **jugular vein.** [C16: from Late Latin *jugulāris*, from Latin *jugulum* throat]

**jugular vein** *n.* any of three large veins of the neck that return blood to the heart from the head and face.

**jug·u·late** ('dʒʌgjʊ,leɪt) *vb.* (*tr.*) *Rare.* to check (a disease) by extreme measures or remedies. [C17 (in the obsolete sense: kill by cutting the throat of): from Latin *jugulāre*, from *jugulum* throat, from *jugum* yoke] —,**jug·u·'la·tion** *n.*

**ju·gum** ('dʒuːgəm) *n.* **1.** a small process at the base of each forewing in certain insects by which the forewings are united to the hindwings during flight. **2.** *Botany.* a pair of opposite leaflets. [C19: from Latin, literally: YOKE]

**Ju·gur·tha** (dʒuː'gɜːθə) *n.* died 104 B.C., king of Numidia (?112–104), who waged war against the Romans (the Jugurthine War, 112–105) and was defeated and executed.

**juice** (dʒuːs) *n.* **1.** any liquid that occurs naturally in or is secreted by plant or animal tissue: *the juice of an orange; digestive juices.* **2.** *Informal.* a. fuel for an engine, esp. petrol. b. electricity. c. alcoholic drink. **3.** a. vigour or vitality. b. essence or fundamental nature. [C13: from Old French *jus*, from Latin] —'**juice·less** *adj.*

**juice ex·trac·tor** *n.* a kitchen appliance, usually operated by electricity, for extracting juice from fruits and vegetables. U.S. equivalent: **juicer.**

**juice up** *vb.* (*tr., adv.*) **1.** *U.S. slang.* to make lively: *to juice up a party.* **2.** (*often passive*) to cause to be drunk: *he got juiced up on Scotch last night.*

**juic·y** ('dʒuːsɪ) *adj.* **juic·i·er, juic·i·est. 1.** full of juice. **2.** provocatively interesting; spicy: *juicy gossip.* **3.** *Slang.* voluptuous or seductive: *she's a juicy bit.* **4.** *Chiefly U.S.* profitable: *a juicy contract.* —'**juic·i·ly** *adv.* —'**juic·i·ness** *n.*

**Juiz de Fo·ra** (*Portuguese* 'ʒwiz di 'fɔrə) *n.* a city in SE Brazil, in Minas Gerais state on the Rio de Janeiro–Belo Horizonte railway: textiles. Pop.: 218 832 (1970).

**ju·jit·su, ju·jut·su,** or **jiu·jut·su** (dʒuː'dʒɪtsuː) *n.* the traditional Japanese system of unarmed self-defence perfected by

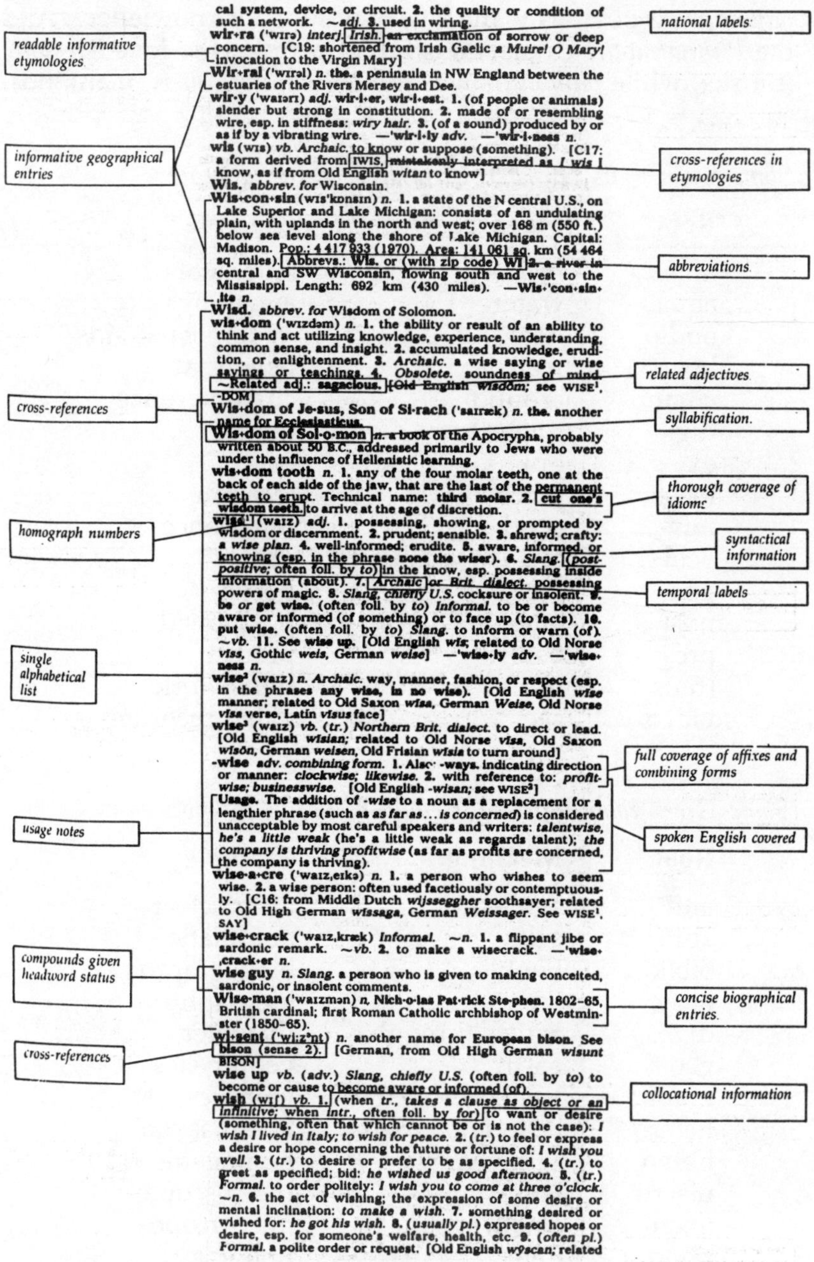
national labels
readable informative etymologies
informative geographical entries
cross-references in etymologies
abbreviations
related adjectives
cross-references
syllabification.
thorough coverage of idioms
homograph numbers
syntactical information
temporal labels
single alphabetical list
full coverage of affixes and combining forms
usage notes
spoken English covered
compounds given headword status
concise biographical entries.
cross-references
collocational information

cal system, device, or circuit. **2.** the quality or condition of such a network. ~*adj.* **3.** used in wiring.

**wir·ra** ('wɪrə) *interj. Irish.* an exclamation of sorrow or deep concern. [C19: shortened from Irish Gaelic *a Muire! O Mary!* invocation to the Virgin Mary]

**Wir·ral** ('wɪrəl) *n.* **the.** a peninsula in NW England between the estuaries of the Rivers Mersey and Dee.

**wir·y** ('waɪərɪ) *adj.* **wir·i·er, wir·i·est. 1.** (of people or animals) slender but strong in constitution. **2.** made of or resembling wire, esp. in stiffness: *wiry hair.* **3.** (of a sound) produced by or as if by a vibrating wire. —**'wir·i·ly** *adv.* —**'wir·i·ness** *n.*

**wis** (wɪs) *vb. Archaic.* to know or suppose (something). [C17: a form derived from IWIS, mistakenly interpreted as *I wis* I know, as if from Old English *witan* to know]

**Wis.** *abbrev. for* Wisconsin.

**Wis·con·sin** (wɪs'kɒnsɪn) *n.* **1.** a state of the N central U.S., on Lake Superior and Lake Michigan: consists of an undulating plain, with uplands in the north and west; over 168 m (550 ft.) below sea level along the shore of Lake Michigan. Capital: Madison. Pop.: 4 417 933 (1970). Area: 141 061 sq. km (54 464 sq. miles). Abbrevs.: **Wis.** or (with zip code) **WI 2.** a river in central and SW Wisconsin, flowing south and west to the Mississippi. Length: 692 km (430 miles). —**Wis·'con·sin·,ite** *n.*

**Wisd.** *abbrev. for* Wisdom of Solomon.

**wis·dom** ('wɪzdəm) *n.* **1.** the ability or result of an ability to think and act utilizing knowledge, experience, understanding, common sense, and insight. **2.** accumulated knowledge, erudition, or enlightenment. **3.** *Archaic.* a wise saying or wise sayings or teachings. **4.** *Obsolete.* soundness of mind. ~Related adj.: **sagacious.** [Old English *wīsdōm;* see WISE[1], -DOM]

**Wis·dom of Je·sus, Son of Si·rach** ('saɪræk) *n.* **the.** another name for **Ecclesiasticus.**

**Wis·dom of Sol·o·mon** *n.* a book of the Apocrypha, probably written about 50 B.C., addressed primarily to Jews who were under the influence of Hellenistic learning.

**wis·dom tooth** *n.* **1.** any of the four molar teeth, one at the back of each side of the jaw, that are the last of the permanent teeth to erupt. Technical name: **third molar. 2. cut one's wisdom teeth.** to arrive at the age of discretion.

**wise**[1] (waɪz) *adj.* **1.** possessing, showing, or prompted by wisdom or discernment. **2.** prudent; sensible. **3.** shrewd; crafty: *a wise plan.* **4.** well-informed; erudite. **5.** aware, informed, or knowing (esp. in the phrase **none the wiser**). **6.** *Slang.* (*postpositive;* often foll. by *to*) in the know, esp. possessing inside information (about). **7.** *Archaic or Brit. dialect.* possessing powers of magic. **8.** *Slang, chiefly U.S.* cocksure or insolent. **9. be** *or* **get wise.** (often foll. by *to*) *Informal.* to be or become aware or informed (of something) or to face up (to facts). **10. put wise.** (often foll. by *to*) *Slang.* to inform or warn (of). ~*vb.* **11.** See **wise up.** [Old English *wīs;* related to Old Norse *viss,* Gothic *weis,* German *weise*] —**'wise·ly** *adv.* —**'wise·ness** *n.*

**wise**[2] (waɪz) *n. Archaic.* way, manner, fashion, or respect (esp. in the phrases **any wise, in no wise**). [Old English *wīse* manner; related to Old Saxon *wīsa,* German *Weise,* Old Norse *vīsa* verse, Latin *vīsus* face]

**wise**[3] (waɪz) *vb.* (*tr.*) *Northern Brit. dialect.* to direct or lead. [Old English *wīsian;* related to Old Norse *vīsa,* Old Saxon *wīsōn,* German *weisen,* Old Frisian *wīsia* to turn around]

**-wise** *adv. combining form.* **1.** Also: **-ways.** indicating direction or manner: *clockwise; likewise.* **2.** with reference to: *profitwise; businesswise.* [Old English *-wīsan;* see WISE[2]]

**Usage.** The addition of *-wise* to a noun as a replacement for a lengthier phrase (such as *as far as . . . is concerned*) is considered unacceptable by most careful speakers and writers: *talentwise, he's a little weak* (he's a little weak as regards talent); *the company is thriving profitwise* (as far as profits are concerned, the company is thriving).

**wise·a·cre** ('waɪz,eɪkə) *n.* **1.** a person who wishes to seem wise. **2.** a wise person: often used facetiously or contemptuously. [C16: from Middle Dutch *wijsseggher* soothsayer; related to Old High German *wīssaga,* German *Weissager.* See WISE[1], SAY]

**wise·crack** ('waɪz,kræk) *Informal.* ~*n.* **1.** a flippant jibe or sardonic remark. ~*vb.* **2.** to make a wisecrack. —**'wise·,crack·er** *n.*

**wise guy** *n. Slang.* a person who is given to making conceited, sardonic, or insolent comments.

**Wise·man** ('waɪzmən) *n.* **Nich·o·las Pat·rick Ste·phen.** 1802–65, British cardinal; first Roman Catholic archbishop of Westminster (1850–65).

**wi·sent** ('wiːzənt) *n.* another name for **European bison.** See **bison** (sense 2). [German, from Old High German *wisunt* BISON]

**wise up** *vb.* (*adv.*) *Slang, chiefly U.S.* (often foll. by *to*) to become or cause to become aware or informed (of).

**wish** (wɪʃ) *vb.* **1.** (when *tr.,* takes a clause as object or an infinitive; when *intr.,* often foll. by *for*) to want or desire (something, often that which cannot be or is not the case): *I wish I lived in Italy; to wish for peace.* **2.** (*tr.*) to feel or express a desire or hope concerning the future or fortune of: *I wish you well.* **3.** (*tr.*) to desire or prefer to be as specified. **4.** (*tr.*) to greet as specified; bid: *he wished us good afternoon.* **5.** (*tr.*) *Formal.* to order politely: *I wish you to come at three o'clock.* ~*n.* **6.** the act of wishing; the expression of some desire or mental inclination: *to make a wish.* **7.** something desired or wished for: *he got his wish.* **8.** (*usually pl.*) expressed hopes or desire, esp. for someone's welfare, health, etc. **9.** (*often pl.*) *Formal.* a polite order or request. [Old English *wȳscan;* related

**Figure 8.1**

*These pages are typical of material contained in a dictionary. They are taken from (p. viii & ix) Collins Dictionary of the English Language (First Edition)*

*philosophy* is obviously 'the love of wisdom or knowledge'. And the *Philharmonic* Orchestra is full of people who love *harmony* (music), while *philanthropy* is the love of *anthropos* (mankind).

*Some Latin roots (affixes) it could be useful to know*

| Root | Meaning | Example |
|------|---------|---------|
| ante | before | antenatal |
| aqua | water | aqualung |
| audio | hear | audio-visual aids |
| bene | well | beneficial |
| circum | around | circumference |
| digit | finger/toe | digital |
| ex | out | exit |
| locus | place | location |
| mit | send | remittance |
| ocul | eye | oculist |
| port | carry | porter |
| post | after | postponed |
| pre | before | predict |
| trans | across | trans-world |
| video | see | video recorder |

*Some Greek roots (affixes) it could be useful to know*

| Root | Meaning | Example |
|------|---------|---------|
| anti | against | antinuclear |
| auto | self | automatic |
| biblio | book | bibliography |
| bio | life | biography |
| dia | across/through | diameter |
| geo | earth | geophysics |
| graph | write | graphics |
| hetero | different/varied | heterosexual |
| homo | same/equal | homogenised |
| macro | large | macroscopic |
| micro | small | microscope |
| philo | love | philology |
| phono | sound | telephone |
| poly | many | polytechnic |
| syn | together/with | synchronise |

The best way to achieve a good vocabulary is to read widely. You then get to know how words are used in context. Reading as a pleasure is sometimes thought to be on the decline. However, the sale of books (and their price) is increasing. Reading a book after you have seen it serialised on television or as a film can be a rewarding experience. Creative reading is where you read with all your mind, anticipating the outcome of the story, or arguing with the author's ideas. Read using your imagination in your leisure reading, and you will find that reading a report or a technical journal in a similar way will pay dividends. For example, putting yourself in the place of the person who wrote the report will help you to understand why it was written in that way, and could influence your understanding of the problems stated.

Do not neglect the advice in Chapter Three on the physical factors involved in any study. When you begin to read seriously, it is essential that you are in the right mental set and that you are unlikely to be disturbed. Unfortunately, there are always some people who, when seeing you reading, will assume that you are not doing anything important. You must make certain that you are in a place where you cannot be 'got at'.

The flexibility of your rate of reading is dealt with in Chapter Nine and it is a subject which you should consider. We read at different speeds for different purposes, and acquiring the skill of reading at speed is fundamental if you need to read a great deal at work, or for your studies. Beware of skimming through the material. Skimming is a useful device if you are looking for the name of a plumber, or searching for a particular piece of information, but by no stretch of the imagination can it be called proper reading. It is essential that you actually see *all* the words to get the full meaning of what the author is saying. There are, of course, times when skimming over a passage is necessary; but once you have learned the art of speed reading, this will only be used when you are looking in the telephone directory for that elusive plumber.

Finally, remember that whatever you are reading, your attitude of mind is crucial. Expect to be interested and stimulated and you will be. You may be reading material which you do not agree with, which is badly written or which you suspect to be incorrect. However, you will still get something out of it when you exercise your mind on it, and you will thus increase your own potential for creative thought.

Keep an open mind. Although you have the right to read

critically, acceptance of other people's points of view combined with a clear idea of your own standpoint will help you to approach any material creatively and sensibly. Motivation and involvement in what you are doing are necessary if you are to read all the books which are part of your course, and at the same time learn from them and enjoy them.

## Case study

Stephanie Diderot is a French-born junior buyer for a large department store in Manchester. Stephanie is taking an external business studies diploma to improve her career prospects. English is not her mother tongue, although she speaks it well. She therefore reads widely to try to overcome the language barrier. She frequently asks her fellow students and tutors to rephrase comments so that she can appreciate the implications of what has been said. When publicity material is sent to her department she is learning to read between the lines, and to discriminate between fact and fantasy. This skill is a direct result of the way in which she reads the set textbooks. She approaches them critically, selecting useful material and comparing one text with another. Stephanie reads modern British novels when she has time; she maintains that an understanding of how the British think and live is a good background to books on management studies written by British authors. For the same reason, Stephanie also listens to the way characters in American films use American English.

## Individual exercises

1 Start now to make a glossary of words required for your subject. Include definitions and background information if this could be of help. A small notebook can be used for the glossary, but some people find it helpful to use vocabulary cards. A good technique for overlearning words is to have a series of cards with the word printed on one side and the definition on the other. If you look at the cards every day, and make others as you come across new words, your vocabulary will increase. Your aim should be to know the

words so well that you can use them in conversation or in an essay without thinking.

2 Read the guide to the use of your dictionary (making certain that it is an up-to-date edition and includes words recently brought into the language). A good dictionary will give a great deal of information. Studying the dictionary will improve your vocabulary, but be sure to read *all* the information about each word including the derivation, part of speech, usage, etc.

3 Most textbooks have headings and subheadings. Use these as a basis for learning and note taking. Go back over a book or report and note these headings. At the same time, highlight key words and passages which are important. Compare these headings and key words with your own notes; they should be very similar.

4 Compare the notes you have taken after you have read a book with the list of errors included in this chapter. Can your notes be improved?

5 List the skills required for reading the material which you are studying. Make an honest appraisal of your ability. The time to learn the skills of map reading, statistical analysis, graph evaluation, etc. is the *beginning* of any course of study.

## Group exercises

1 *Materials:*   short company report
        newspaper articles relevant to your organisation
        articles from technical journals, etc.
 *Group size:*  small groups of 2—4 people (for discussion sessions)

Each person should have the opportunity to read a report, column or article provided, and to write a set of concise notes on the material.

An exchange of the written passages and notes within the group should lead to interesting comparisons and constructive criticism. But always remember that each person will employ an individual learning method. You may find it more helpful if all the members of the group are using the same report or article.

2   *Materials:*   a selection from all types of written communi-
                   cation within the company
    *Group size:*  small groups which report back, or a general
                   group of 10—15 people

Lead a general discussion about the skills needed to read
certain types of written material relevant to your company.
An attempt could be made to assist people who lack certain
skills with where to find help. It is unrealistic to expect an
office manager to have detailed scientific knowledge or a
background in statistics, for example. An explanation of how
graphs may be read or tables analysed is important. Very
often a self-help group can be formed, or expertise from
colleagues called on.

   This can be quite a sensitive area. Many people find it
difficult to admit that they do not have specific skills, and
a certain amount of tact and confidence building is called
for. An equal trade-off in information between different areas
of the organisation is called for here.

3   Exercise 1 in the individual exercises calls for a glossary of
    words to be made up. A valuable group activity is to compile
    several lists of words which are in current use in your
    organisation. This could also be useful to new members of
    staff; they are often unaware of the way in which certain
    words are used, in a colloquial sense or in specialist areas.
    Copies of these lists are also very useful for the secretarial
    staff.

   The categories will depend on the type of organisation you
   are in but could include jargon words, 'in' words and current
   slang, technical words, company word-usage, etc.

   *Definitions* of words are also useful. A *package* may mean
   one thing to a cleaner, another to the training officer, another
   to the advertising department and yet another to the finance
   director.

4   *Materials:*   documents — e.g., short articles, reports
                   brought by students
    *Group size:*  pairs

    (a) exchange documents with someone else, preferably
        from a different department;
    (b) each person notes key words or unfamiliar terms on flip
        chart paper;
    (c) put paper up on wall;

(d) the group then discusses:
common terms — are they clearly understood;
jargon;
abbreviations;
technical and scientific terms.

5  *Materials:*    short articles, reports, etc.
  *Group size:*   individual work

The group should read through the material provided and try to identify the key sentence in each paragraph. List these sentences.

The next stage is to extract the key words from each of the sentences and list them. Allow some time to elapse (coffee break!) and then ask the group to make a pattern note or a brief written (or verbal) summary of the original article.

Check with the article or report to make sure that the correct information has been recorded and recalled.

This exercise can also be carried out as a small group activity.

6  *Materials:*    report or article
  *Group size:*   pairs or individuals

Each student or pair of students should attempt to make a flow diagram or a concept tree of the written material you provide. If the content of the material is familiar the task should be comparatively easy. The following guidelines should help:

(a) extract the main themes or subjects;
(b) examine each main theme in turn, looking for specific facts and illustrated examples;
(c) analyse further for:
implications
applications
qualifications.

Where possible each student (or pair) should explain their diagram or concept tree to the rest of the group. This is a useful check on how well the material has been read and understood (or learned). If it is difficult to explain it is probable that the information has not been grasped thoroughly or that insufficient time and thought has been taken over the selection of the logical sequence of key points.

7 *Materials:*    a selection of non-fiction books of all types (one each)

  *Group size:*   10—15

Each member of the group should attempt to sum up a book by using the information on the cover, title page, contents page and index only. Then they should compare notes.

# NINE

# Speed reading

Reading is not merely a matter of recognising words; it is a complicated process which enables us to identify, assimilate, integrate and absorb the material we are reading. We do this on various mental levels from Agatha Christie to *War and Peace*, or from a brief company report to a detailed textbook on an advanced academic subject.

Effective reading does not mean being able to read the material very quickly. There are other skills involved. For example, it is essential to have a good vocabulary and a wide general knowledge. Also required is an understanding of how our language is structured, combined with a clear understanding of the passages read. We also need to be able to retain and recall the key ideas in the reading matter.

There are many different types of written material, and it is useful to consider the way in which we approach each type. The range is considerable: recipes, scientific treatises, road signs, computer languages, financial columns, and so on. We read for enjoyment and for vicarious experience. We also read for information, and sometimes we need to compare one piece of work with another, bringing critical skills into play. It may be that we must skim over an article to extract a few key points, or we may need to read our own written work to correct mistakes or add extra statements. Whatever our motive for reading, it is a good idea to take a flexible approach and vary the speed of reading according to the circumstances.

It is helpful to understand a little of the way in which we read. The main stages occur in the following order:

1  assimilation of visual data by the eye;
2  recognition of letters and words;
3  understanding words in context;

4   comprehension — relating the material to one's own knowledge;
5   storing the information in the memory;
6   recalling the information when it is required;
7   using the information; communicating it to ourselves or others.

Except for the blind or the partially-sighted, the first stage of the reading process is looking at the printed page. It is helpful to understand a little of the way in which the eye works.

### The eye

The eye is like a camera. The cornea and lens form a compound optical system which focuses images onto the retina. The lens is plastic. It alters in shape, enabling the eye to change its focus from distant objects to closer objects.

The retina is an extension of the brain, on which many millions (equivalent to the population of Europe) of light-sensitive nerves terminate.

The fovea is about 1/10th of a millimetre in diameter. Here is the highest concentration of nerve endings, all of which are cone-shaped. Cones are sensitive to minute variations of light intensity and colour tones. It is at the fovea that the image of the object of immediate regard falls.

When reading (for instance) we are not aware of eye movements as we switch attention from one word to the next. This is achieved by a finely balanced motor system of six external muscles working in harmony. However, eye movements are not smooth in reality, but jerky, shifting rapidly from one part of the object to another, in small jumps.

Looking at an object in a room you will be conscious of other things even though they are not clearly discerned. This is because their images fall on other parts of the retina, where there are fewer cones interspersed with rods. Rods are sensitive to the movement of objects. Because of them we can avoid things coming towards us which are not in the immediate line of sight. Rods are more sensitive than cones in conditions of poor illumination. That is why, to see a star properly at night, it is necessary to look slightly to one side of it.

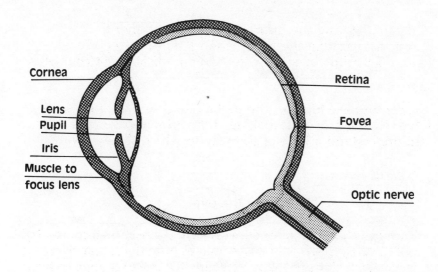

*Figure 9.1  The human eye*

## Eye movements

The eye is never still. It fixes on an object or word momentarily and only 'sees' in that instant. Movement creates a blur. People assume that their eyes move smoothly over whatever they are looking at, pausing briefly and then moving onwards in a continuous flowing motion. But in fact, the eye jumps from one 'fixation point' to the next; information is only absorbed during these pauses, which range from 0.25 to 1.5 seconds in length. Taking less time on each fixation will, obviously, increase reading speed.

Images are focused on the retina, and as we have seen, at the centre lies the fovea where the nerve endings are most densely concentrated. By practising, it is possible to make use of the area round the fovea, so extending the amount of print seen at each fixation. The combination of *extending the field of central vision* with *controlled eye movements* is the physiological basis for the method of speed reading advocated in this book.

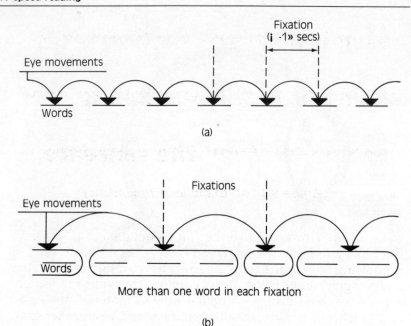

**Figure 9.2 Eye fixations: (a) the eye rests on each word; (b) the eye rests on more than one word**

Initially the eye and brain have to recognise shape and pattern. It is easy to recognise a letter or word once the basic pattern has been learned, even when it appears in different *angles,* sizes or **forms**. When you next walk down the High Street, look around at the number and variety of patterns associated with the same letter.

Consider this sentence:

We xan xroxs oxt exerx thxrd xetxer xnd xtixl rxax thx sextexce xrexty xelx.

and consider figure 9.3.

We are used to picking up small clues of pattern and shape in letters. In fact, much of our interpretation of what we read is due to our expectation that specific shapes will have particular significance. Verbal clues are also important, because in any language the grammatical constructions remain constant, and we know we can rely on the form of a sentence to remain the

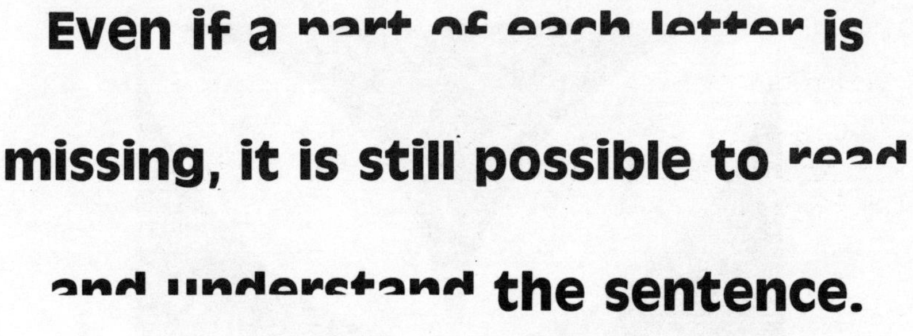

# Even if a part of each letter is

# missing, it is still possible to read

# and understand the sentence.

*Figure 9.3    An example of redundancy*

same. Many words 'go together'; for example *not only* is more than likely to be followed by *but also*. A large part of reading is knowing what these clues are likely to be, rather than reading and recognising the words out of context. The wider the reader's experience of reading a particular type of material, the easier and quicker it is to read with accuracy and comprehension.

Examples of how the eye and brain work together to make sense of visual clues are given by optical illusions. Look at the illustrations (figure 9.4). You will probably be able to 'see' a form straight away. But a longer look at the illustration will show that there is more than one way of seeing it. Once you have accepted one of the forms in your mind it is impossible to see the other form without a definite mental effort.

Luckily when attempting to speed read we are usually concerned only with the appearance of printed words on a page. If we have some idea of the subject and slant of the passage, we will be able to read it very much faster than if we were unsure of the pattern of each letter, and had to decipher each one separately. Letters are seen more easily if they are in a meaningful context. The ability to read and remember is helped by words and letters that mean something. Look at and try to remember the following characters:

*on*
*lyth*
*eg*
*ood*
*di*
*eyou*
*ng*

*Figure 9.4* **Note that in this diagram, either the light portion or the dark portion can be perceived as a pattern against a background, but not both**

Once you see the letters as forming a sentence, you can remember them easily. (The sentence is: *Only the good die young.*)

The more used you are to the style of writing of an author, the easier it is to read the material. As your eye travels over the page you are able to make predictions the words you expect to appear. In the last sentence there was a missing word after *predictions*. It could have been *of* or *about*. Did you notice the omission?

## Speed reading

The use of speed reading is often questioned by people who fear that real comprehension will suffer. And it is true that we need to adjust our rate of reading for the material being read. You may think that once the skill of speed reading has been acquired, everything has then to be read at a very fast rate —

indeed, you may imagine that a serious textbook must be devoured at the same speed as the lightest novel. However, the skilled reader will be able to select the appropriate speed for the task in hand.

Reading at speed is pointless unless you can understand and remember what has been read. Good comprehension is an essential ingredient in efficient speed reading. Reading faster needs to be approached with an alert awareness; as always, new material must be related to that which is already known.

Can you remember when you began to learn to read? Whichever method you learned by, at the beginning you mastered the ability to recognise a single word, then the words in context. As you started to read more fluently you stopped saying each word out loud, and after a while were able to read silently without your lips moving. From then on you were probably on your own. It is fairly unusual for any infant school teacher to suggest that you try to speed up your silent reading. In other words, this is probably where you got 'stuck'.

Most people do speed their reading up from where they were in the primary school. But unless you needed to read a good deal for school and examination purposes, or read a lot for pleasure, your normal rate of reading is probably well below the speed of which you are capable. Our brains function more efficiently and much faster than we usually give them credit for, and this activity of reading is a skill which frequently remains undeveloped.

There are several schools of thought about the best way to acquire the skill of speed reading. The method that I feel is most useful aims to re-educate the eye to move over the page more swiftly. To acquire this skill takes time and motivation, but it is easily learned with sufficient practice. It is quite possible to read at over 1,000 words a minute and at the same time have complete comprehension.

If you have decided that reading more quickly would be an advantage, it is sensible to choose a method which suits your requirements and particular style of learning. Various methods which people find useful are described below.

## The tachistoscope

This device displays a visual image or word for brief intervals, usually a fraction of a second. Originally it was used in experiments on perception and memory, but is has been adapted for use on some commercial speed reading courses.

*Advantages* The eye and brain learn very quickly to recognise and interpret known letters and words.

*Disadvantages* The context of the word within a sentence is not taken into consideration. Comprehension lags behind word recognition.

### Reading films (e.g. Harvard)

These films make the text visible in a series of blocks.

*Advantages* It is a controlled programme with group motivation and experienced tutors.

*Disadvantages* Only the words on one line at a time are usually visible, so the whole field of vision is restricted.

### Clockwork pacing machine

This device fits onto the edge of a book, and a controlled (clockwork) shield can be set for varying speeds as it moves down the page.

*Advantages* It can be set easily to the individual's needs, and is portable.

*Disadvantages* The pace does not vary during the reading session, therefore easily-understood and complex material on the same page are subject to the same restrictions. The shield prevents the eye from increasing its field of vision. It is expensive. Use a ruler instead!

### Flash window

This is a simple device, easily made at home. It consists of a piece of card with an oblong window cut into it, the width of the book. The card is then moved down the page as quickly as possible, at one's own speed.

*Advantages* It costs little and can be used at odd moments.

*Disadvantages* The field of vision is drastically reduced.

Other methods include:

## Reading exercises using comprehension tests

*Advantages* You can measure your progress in reading similar texts more and more quickly.
*Disadvantages* As you read, your mind is thinking of what the questions are likely to be rather than what the passage is really about. This can lead to you looking at the passage from a very limited viewpoint.

## Key word selection schemes

*Advantages* They are useful for looking up the plumber in a hurry!
*Disadvantages* This is not reading.

There are advantages and disadvantages with each method. However, I am certain myself that a broader approach is needed — one which is as concerned with comprehension as it is with speed. This brings us to the method, with exercises, which is explained in the next part of the chapter.

You will remember that eye movements are not smooth, as most people imagine, but jerky. Ask a friend to co-operate to illustrate this point. Get your friend to sit opposite you and to imagine a sheet of glass between the two of you. Drawn on the imaginary sheet of glass is a circle about 1 metre in diameter. Ask your partner to 'look' at the circle while you observe her or his eye movements. You will see that, although the looker thinks that the circle is smooth and accurate, the eyes are in fact moved in a jerky and rather erratic way. Now draw a circle in the air in front of your friend and ask your friend to follow your finger. This time the eye movements will be smooth. If you move your finger slowly at first and then increase the speed, you will see the eyes move more quickly in a smooth and seemingly effortless way as they follow your finger.

The basis, then, for this method of speed reading, is the use of a visual guide. You will be using either your finger or the end of a pen to help your eyes to move in a smooth and swift way across the printed page.

When you look at an object (or word) you are conscious of other things around it, even though you are not concentrating on them. Try looking at one particular word in the centre of this page. Concentrate on this word, but at the same time try to become aware of the words on either side. You may not see the whole of these words, but taken in context, the letter clues may help you to recognise the words. It stands to reason that if you can see two or three words together in a line (in one fixation), then you should also be able to see words *above* and *below* the line of print. Now try to see the words immediately above your central word. You may only be able to see part of the letters but these clues may be sufficient to help you to read the words.

We usually see what we expect to see. If you expect to see only one word at a time, this is what will happen. If you expect to see the surrounding letters and small words, both horizontally and vertically, this will also happen. How much you see will depend to a large extent on the physiological make-up of your own eyes. Some people will see far more than others. But by being aware of the possibilities, and by practising, you will begin to widen your field of vision.

To begin with, these are the two things you should be aiming for:

(a) being able to move your eyes more smoothly, using a visual guide;

(b) being able to widen the visual field by 'seeing' more of the page.

The practical exercises that follow will only be effective if you practise regularly. As with any new skill, frequent short practices are of more use than spasmodic, lengthy ones.

To begin with, you will find that the words are a blur. Even when you become more adept there will be times when your eyes will move quickly but you will not be able to remember all you have been reading. This is quite normal. Think of it in terms of learning to drive a car. When you start to drive, you find that it is extremely hard to do all the things required. It is not easy to change gear at the same time as looking in the mirror, signalling a movement and not knocking down the local constabulary. After a while, however, it all starts to come together. It will be the same process with speed reading. Remember also how difficult it was at first to co-ordinate the clutch and the accelerator. If you did not get it right you either stalled or kangaroo-jumped along the road. But once you had mastered the co-ordination, you moved away smoothly and were able to increase speed safely. With speed reading it is

similar. You need to be able to co-ordinate speed of eye movement with comprehension of material. To begin with, you will
either read very fast but not be able to understand or recall the
information, or else you will understand what you are reading
but your speed will drop. After a short time, with regular
practice, you will be able to balance speed and comprehension,
and your speed will start to increase to the point which is
suitable for your eyesight and your reading needs.

The first move is to establish your normal speed of reading.
I would suggest that you use a novel for practice sessions. Later
we will look at reading more serious material. Use a hardback
book (paperbacks are often difficult to lay flat). For timing
yourself, a stop watch is useful. Failing that, a kitchen 'pinger'
(which can be set in minutes) could be used. You will have
enough to do in learning to speed read without having to look
at your watch every few minutes, so get organised at the
beginning. Before you start to read, work out the average
number of words on each line; take about ten different lines,
counting the number of words and averaging them out.

You are now ready to begin reading. Try to read in a relaxed
and comfortable way, suited to the novel you have selected.
Read for five minutes. At the end of the time you will need
to do the following calculation:

$$\frac{\text{number of lines} \times \text{number of words on line}}{5 \text{ (minutes)}}$$

This will give you the number of words per minute. (You did
note at which line you began to read, didn't you?)

Record the results of the reading practice sessions on a sheet
of graph paper like that shown in figure 9.5 to monitor your
progress. Leave enough room to note details of each practice
session. The circumstances and timing of your practice session
can be interesting.

*Basic exercise 1*
For the first exercise, turn the book upside down. (Imagine that
it is a book in a foreign language with an alphabet that you are
not used to.) You will still be moving your eyes over the page
from left to right and turning over pages in the usual manner.
At this stage you are learning to use your eyes differently and
a 'book shape' is all that is needed. You are not attempting to
read upside down!

ELEM—K

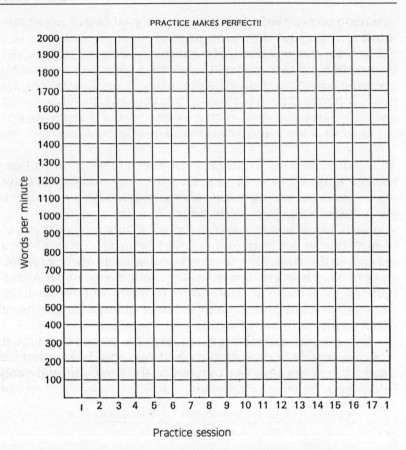

**PRACTICE MAKES PERFECT!!**

Words per minute

Practice session

***Figure 9.5    Speed reading progress chart.*** *Use this chart to record your progress. Record your 'normal' reading speed at 1. Remember, as with all new skills, you will find a sharp increase in speed to begin with and then possibly a flattening out of the graph until you go up to track your new speed of reading*

Using your finger (or a pen) as a guide, run your finger along and under each line (left to right in the normal way). As you move this visual guide along under every line, *watch the end of your finger.* Keep your eyes on the guide and get into an easy rhythm. Make certain that the guide moves from one end of the line to the other, and that your eye also travels the entire length of the line of print each time. As you find the rhythm, start to move your finger a little faster, still keeping your attention on the guide. Gradually move your finger quicker and quicker, over and down the page.

Initially, you will find that the print will blur as you get faster. You should be able to speed up so that your eyes are moving over the lines much faster than they have ever done before. It is very important that you move your eyes completely over the lines; you need to read *all* the material for real comprehension.

Your shoulders and head should be relaxed and still for this exercise (it is very easy to start moving your entire body as you look from one end of the line to another). Only your eyes and hand should be moving. (I admit that you must breathe and your heart may still beat, but otherwise the only things moving should be the eyes and the finger!)

Carry on with these movements for at least five minutes. You may find that your eyes ache, your neck is stiff and that you drop the book and get dizzy. All of this can be expected — after all, you are probably moving your eyes and hand more quickly and in a different way from normally. If you feel dizzy, slow down a little. You can gain speed again as your eyes get used to the new movements.

This exercise is the basis for most of the exercises to follow. You will need to practise frequently to gain speed. Once you feel that you will not be slowed up because you are unconsciously trying to read the words, you can practise with the book the correct way up.

*Basic exercise 2*
This exercise is designed to encourage the widening of your field of vision and to assist with your eye movements. It consists of placing the book in front of you, and *still following the visual guide*, making a series of large S shapes down the page. Again, you need to start by getting a good rhythm going and then speed your finger up as much as you can. Move your hand so fast in each exercise that your wrist begins to ache. This is no time to be ladylike; you need the fastest finger in the West, so to speak.

Each exercise should take a minimum of five minutes, and ten would be better. After a few practice sessions using both exercises in turn, turn to your book and read for understanding. Up until now, the words will have been blurred, and you will not have been reading properly. Now read for five minutes, consciously reading as fast as you can for comprehension but still having your finger running along under each line.

At the end of the time, do the calculations already mentioned (number of lines x number of words on the line, divided by the time in minutes). Record this on the graph.

A series of exercises follow. They will only be effective if you practise regularly. As with any new skill, motivation and constant practice are the things that will help you to achieve your ends.

### Practical exercises

1 Look at figure 9.6 and notice how your visual guide should go in a series of narrow, horizontal Vs from margin to margin. After practising these narrow Vs for a few minutes, change to wider Vs taking in roughly ten lines at a time.

This book is designed for those who want to acquire the skills and techniques of learning and who also want to be effective practical managers. Study skills are not used only when studying but are fundamental to everyday life. Using the memory, reading text books, planning and writing essays and researching projects are the same skills that are needed for remembering facts about clients, reading technical journals and finding and extracting information on which to base company decisions.
Most people enjoy the challenge of study and find it a stimulating activity. I hope that you will find this book enables you to acquire (or brush up) those learning methods needed for study and effective management.
Professional qualifications, management diplomas and degrees and other forms of higher and further education are all ingredients in the upward movement of those who are aiming high.

*Figure 9.6*

2 Still using the visual guide, move your eyes over the page in a series of vertical and horizontal movements. Consciously speed your eye movements up. Carry on for five minutes.

3 Select a word in the centre of a page, as suggested earlier in the chapter. *Expect* to see the letters of the surrounding words, above, below, and at either side.

Alternate these exercises with the two basic exercises (running the visual guide under every line at speed, and making a large S shape over the page, also at speed). After each session of practice, read for comprehension, but consciously read as fast as you can. Mark the results on the graph.

So far you have been using a novel. It is sensible to learn speed reading with this type of material. Once you have gained confidence in your ability to read very fast you can turn your attention to reading more serious matter. The skill will then be second nature and you will be able to concentrate on the material rather than on the mechanics of reading.

You may find that using your finger becomes irritating. Once you are quite sure that your eye does really move right across the page, taking in all the words, you could try running your finger down the centre of the page or down one margin. Experiment until you find a comfortable movement. However, do not do this unless you are absolutely sure that your eyes have become accustomed to sweeping along the line from margin to margin. To keep a high speed and a good rhythm it is necessary to use the guide whenever you want to read at a great rate. You will find that in any case your average reading speed will increase after you have acquired the skill, even without constant practice.

If you have not practiced for some time and suddenly find that it is necessary to read something very quickly, spend a few minutes on a conditioning exercise to regain the high speed of which you are capable.

For a few people, *subvocalisation* could be a problem. Subvocalising happens when we 'hear' the words in our mind as we read. Check whether or not you do this by reading a piece of dialogue, followed by straight prose. Very often we are aware of the voices in the dialogue, the emotional tone, the difference between a man's voice and that of a woman for instance. If you are reading a book and have seen a film or television programme on which it was based you may 'hear' the actors' voices in your head. If you still hear a voice when you turn from the conversation to, say, a description, you are subvocalising. This will slow your speed of reading considerably. Naturally, when reading for pleasure, subvocalisation can add to the enjoyment; but it is hampering if the same process occurs when reading a factual report.

It is possible to stop this inner voice with practice. Every time you become aware that you are subvocalising, try to bypass the imaginary sound, and concentrate only on the meaning of the passage rather than on the meaning of individual words. However, subvocalisation does sometimes have a positive side (apart from enhancing novel reading). By increasing the 'volume' and deliberately saying the words to yourself, it may help you to memorise certain facts or figures. Key words and phrases are often retained in this way.

## Reading more complex material

When you come to read material which requires thought and concentration, inevitably your speed will drop slightly. However, it should still be very many times faster than your original speed; moreover, you will find that by reading a passage several times at speed you have a far greater understanding of it than if you had read it slowly and carefully. You will become aware of the overall meaning of the material, and as you read it through for the third or fourth time, the pieces of the jigsaw will slot into place with surprising ease. This repetition helps you to retain and recall the content.

With confidence, you will be able to get a far deeper comprehension than you once believed possible. Use common sense, however; do not expect to read scientific material which contains formulae or tables of statistics as fast as you would a straight piece of text. The formulae have already been shortened to condense the information, and tables are spaced in a different way from lines of text. You will certainly read them faster, but not at the same rate as regular printed sentences.

As with any new skill of learning, a certain pattern will emerge. When motivation and interest are high your speed of reading will show a swift upward trend of words per minute. This may drop off slightly as you reach a plateau. This is quite usual. After a while, regular practice will begin to tell, and the results will show a permanent rise which levels off at your personal optimum speed. The rise on the graph begins to occur when you are able to balance full comprehension with greater speed, and when you gain confidence.

## Case study

Mary Farrington is a local government officer whose job involves collecting information about future planning decisions in her borough. After a course on speed reading and on different methods of recording information, Mary is finding that she can easily absorb reports from surveyors, engineers and other government departments in addition to checking through archives. Her reading speed is 950 words a minute, and at this speed she can read and comprehend fully all the material she needs to collate. Her full reports are essential to those taking vital planning decisions in the borough. As she has learned to make good patterned notes, her summaries are appreciated by the senior staff; they get a comprehensive overview of the information and can easily see the relationship between varying factors. This enables them to make their decisions with a greater understanding of the issues at stake.

## Group exercises

As speed reading is a very personal skill, the main value in group activity is to encourage students to practise frequently. It may be necessary to emphasise that it is not a competitive skill, and that people vary so much in their reactions and physical ability that any comparisons are valueless.

Comprehension passages have not been included as they are of doubtful benefit. Where they are used, the reader usually concentrates her or his thoughts on trying to anticipate the questions, rather than on reading for full understanding. If you feel that comprehension exercises would be useful in your particular circumstances there are several books on the market which include them, although the speed reading methods will not be those suggested here.

1  *Column exercise*

*Materials:*  a newspaper passage or an article from a journal that has been printed in columns for each student.

The students should read the passage at speed (using the visual guide), consciously adjusting their eyes to the shorter span. You will find that most people prefer to run the finger down the centre of the column, or to one side. This is fine, so long as they are reading all the words. It is important to practise with different spacing and printing once a reasonable speed has been attained (*at least* two to three times the original speed).

2  *Materials:*  different types of reading matter. Try to obtain different kinds of print, paper (shiny or matt) and type (heavy or light). Include newsprint, small posters, handouts, etc.

Using this material, assess and discuss the way in which the speed of reading can be affected quite considerably by the print, paper, and so on.

3  Ask the group to read some non-book material (magazines, newspapers, reports, etc.) at speed. While reading, students should jot down the key points. Afterwards, they should check these points against the passage, to make sure that what they 'understood' was in fact in the material.

4  *Pyramid exercise*

*Materials:*  a photocopy of the pyramid (see figure 9.7) for each student

Ask the members of the group to try to take in a whole line of print in one or two fixations. How far can they progress with one fixation per line?

Finally, those people who have mastered the art of speed reading and know that their understanding is enhanced rather than diminished, should try this last exercise. It can only be done successfully when students are confident of their own brain's ability to work at speed.

Still using a visual guide, run the finger in the usual manner along under the words of the first line. Then, instead of flicking the finger and the eyes back to the start of the next line, take the finger *back* along line 2. Carry on in this way so that the eyes are moving over the page with a continuous movement and rhythm. At speed, it is perfectly possible to 'read backwards'. The deep knowledge that everyone has of the construction and meaning of their own language will ensure that the brain reverses the words instantaneously and that comprehension does not suffer. If you try to think about what you are doing or how the process works, the words will seem meaningless.

```
                  A
                 cat
                makes
               most of
              us  think
             of soft fur
            and a  gentle
           purring  sound.
          A scientist  will
         probably  think  in
        terms of teeth.  Cats
       have  fewer  teeth than
      any other carnivore, only
     about thirty.  When they hunt
    they use  their  large canines
   for seizing and holding prey.  To
  cut off gobbits of flesh  and bone
 the short premolars  are used.  Their
rough tongues  rasp the meat  from the
bone.  Their acute  hearing, large eyes,
 long  whiskers and  retractable claws  are
feline characteristics for efficient hunting
```

**Figure 9.7**

Have sufficient confidence in your brain's ability to cope, and your reading will be even faster, and considerably greater comprehension will be attained. Remember that the brain processes information 'automatically'. For example, the eyes 'see' objects upside down, as in the screen of a simple camera; but this is reversed instantly by the brain so that all objects are perceived 'the right way up'!

# TEN

# Information retrieval

Knowing how and where to find information is almost as important as learning itself. You need to be aware of all the different sources of information needed for your studies. These can range from the library service to on-line data. Of course, other sources of information exist apart from libraries and computer systems, and it is useful to be familiar with them.

There are many informal, but valuable sources of information. These can range from a conversation with a colleague to an article in a colour supplement, a detailed advertisement, a television or radio documentary, notes you may have made for a talk, asides in meetings, and so on. The person who keeps an alert and interested mind will store away pieces of useful data like a squirrel hoarding nuts for later use. Managers who are oblivious to anything other than the conventional, and whose minds and eyes are blinkered, are unlikely to reach the level of senior management — well perhaps some do — but in an organisation which is efficient and worthwhile the likelihood is remote. The point is that *all* information is useful, and extra pieces of relevant material enhance your studies and your career.

## Printed sources

Books, technical journals and other written material are the basic tools of study. Most people will use a library service, but you may also need to buy some books. A good bookseller, or your local library, will be able to show you a copy of the current *Books in Print* which will tell you what is available.

## Public libraries

Your local branch library will help when you want to order a book either from the county stock or through the inter-library lending scheme. The services of the British Library Lending Division are also available through the public library. Most large towns have a central reference library and this merits a visit at the start of any course. Apart from the books which will be of use as you study, you will come across commercial reference material, scientific journals, newspapers, financial records and many other sources of information which are essential for the development and growth of a company.

To know what books are available on any subject you may need to consult a bibliography. Your librarian will be able to tell you if there is a bibliography available by consulting the Library Association's *Guide to Reference Material* or the *World Bibliography of Bibliographies*. There are many other basic bibliographic reference works which your librarian will be able to show you.

Most of the central reference libraries throughout Great Britain have a large selection of periodicals and journals. Often the current copies will be on show, but it is usually possible to obtain permission to look at stored earlier editions. This also applies to newspapers and leisure periodicals.

Any student embarking on a thesis or dissertation as part of their degree course should be aware of work already done in their chosen field. The larger libraries will be able to show you several lists — for example, the *Index to Theses accepted for Higher Degrees in the Universities of Great Britain and Ireland*. Of course, the theses are also an excellent source for study purposes and management information.

Most British official publications are available from a central library. Such publications include government statistics, *Hansard, London Gazette*, and many HMSO publications. All of these may be important to the running of any business.

Maps, street guides, telephone directories, commercial information and book information services are all to be found at the central reference libraries. Much of the material may be borrowed by requesting a student's library card. Not all library services have this facility, but it is useful, as it means you may have a book out on extended loan without risking fines for not returning the books within a specified period.

Most public libraries now have non-book material on their

shelves, including audio and video cassettes. While many of these are primarily for leisure purposes, it is worth keeping your eyes open to what is available, since training and information films are sometimes kept. These could be of use on your course.

## Copyright libraries

A few libraries are entitled to receive one free copy of every book published in the United Kingdom. These are:

> British Library (Great Russell Street, London, WC1B 3DG, tel. 01-636-1544);
> Bodleian Library (Oxford, OX1 3BG, tel. Oxford (0865) 44675);
> University Library (West Road, Cambridge, tel. Cambridge (0223) 61441);
> National Library of Wales (Aberystwyth, SY23 3BU, tel. Aberystwyth (0970) 3816);
> National Library of Scotland (George IV Bridge, Edinburgh, EH1 1EW, tel. Edinburgh (031) 226-4531); and Trinity College Library (Dublin).

## Public records

The Public Record Office, now based at Kew (Ruskin Avenue, Kew, Richmond, Surrey, TW9 4DU, tel. 01-876-3444) is one of the most modern records offices in the world. Information is arranged by government departments or ministries, and qualified staff are available to guide the enquirer to whatever is wanted. The *Guide to the Contents of the Public Record Office* will be found in most reference libraries.

## Library systems

As the written word is still the most usual way to obtain information, the first section of the chapter will deal with library systems in common use. If you are putting into practice the advice given in the chapter on reading strategies, you will realise, after reading through this chapter at speed, that much of the information will be for reference and will not prove exciting reading. However, an understanding of how the library systems work can substantially cut down the time you take searching for specific books or subjects.

Most libraries in Great Britain use the Dewey Decimal System to arrange reference and information books. This was devised by an American, Melvil Dewey, and first put into use in 1873. In the USA this is being superseded by the Library of Congress system. You may find the Library of Congress system in use in some other libraries, so details are also included.

## Dewey decimal classification

The basic structure of the Dewey classification is that all knowledge can be divided and numbered under ten main subject headings called *classes*. These ten are divided into ten subclasses and each subclass is again divided. If a further division is needed it is shown by using a decimal point.

Main classes

| | |
|---|---|
| General works | 000—099 |
| Philosophy/Psychology | 100—199 |
| Religion | 200—299 |
| Sociology | 300—399 |
| Languages | 400—499 |
| Pure Sciences | 500—599 |
| Technology (Applied Science) | 600—699 |
| Arts and Recreation | 700—799 |
| Literature | 800—899 |
| Geography/History/Biography | 900—999 |

Each main class is subdivided. For example:

Sociology          300—399

| | |
|---|---|
| Statistics | 310—319 |
| Political Science | 320—329 |
| Economics | 330—339 |
| Law | 340—349 |
| Public Administration | 350—359 |
| Social Services | 360—369 |
| Education | 370—379 |
| Commerce | 380—389 |
| Customs/Folklore | 390—399 |

Each subclass is also divided. For example:

Education        370—379

| | |
|---|---|
| The School | 371 |
| Elementary Education | 372 |
| Secondary Education | 373 |
| Adult Education | 374 |
| Curriculum | 375 |
| Women's Education (!!) | 376 |
| Schools' Religion | 377 |
| Higher Education | 378 |
| Education and State | 379 |

If a further subdivision is needed it is shown decimally. For example:

Higher Education        378

| | |
|---|---|
| Institutions of Higher Education | 378.1 |
| Academic Degrees | 378.2 |
| Student Finances | 378.3 |
| and so on ... | |

*Problems with this classification system*
As this system was devised in 1873, and our knowledge and technology have grown rapidly in so many areas, the problem of classifying new subjects has caused some difficulties. A committee revises the system regularly, but sometimes many new subjects have to be classified under existing headings. Thus, new and important subjects may have very long classification numbers. For example, Computer Design and Engineering is numbered 620.0042502854.

Another problem is that many subjects once thought of as requiring only one main area may now have different aspects that have to be catalogued. For example:

| | |
|---|---|
| World Geography | 910—919 |
| Human Geography | 301.3 |
| Geomorphology | 551.4 |
| Economic Geography | 330 |

Thus, books on cars could be listed under *Transport* or under *Engineering*. Animals could be found under *Agriculture, Pets, Industry, Entertainment, Science*, etc.

It is very important to be aware of this, as you could miss

an entire section of useful material because you were looking in too restricted an area.

Get to know the classification numbers for books which are either directly or indirectly connected with your subject. Knowing the general classification numbers can save you a good deal of time. For instance, if you were studying optics, an important book would be *Introduction to Visual Optics* by A Tunnacliffe. This will be found in the Pure Science (500—599) section, and the book will be classified under 535.8. A glance along the shelves near 535 could produce other books which might be of value in your course.

*The catalogue*
The library catalogue is a complete list of books held in that particular library or library system. Very often the information will be stored on cards in a card index. Many libraries use a microfiche, and a very few have the books listed in a series of volumes. In most public library systems the microfiche will also contain books held in other libraries in the district. The microfiche is a transparency, usually the size of a filing card, on which details of books (sometimes journals, documents, newspapers, etc.) are recorded in miniaturised form, and which can be read using a microfiche reader. The use of computers has revolutionised library cataloguing systems.

Most larger libraries will have newspapers, journals and periodicals on microfilm, with a booth and equipment for viewing this material. Much reference material is now stored on microfilm because of the obvious advantages in storage space.

Computer-aided catalogues will be in use in some libraries, and a great deal of information about printed sources will be available through the librarian.

Novels will always have entries in an author catalogue and sometimes in a title index.

Most catalogues for non-fiction books are divided into at least three sections, as follows:

*Author index*
This section contains the names of the authors, with the surname of the author first, and initials second. This index will, of course, be in alphabetical order. Books with no obvious

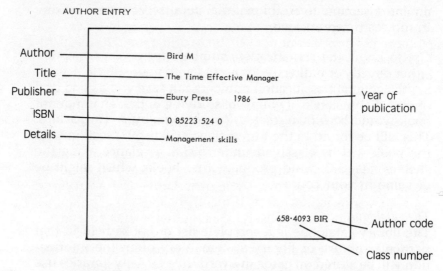

AUTHOR ENTRY

Author ——————— Bird M
Title ——————— The Time Effective Manager
Publisher ——————— Ebury Press    1986 ——————— Year of publication
ISBN ——————— 0 85223 524 0
Details ——————— Management skills

658·4093 BIR ——— Author code
Class number

**Figure 10.1  Example of an author index card**

author will probably be entered by the title. Books written by more than one author will be listed under all these names, or by title. Collections of articles may only have the editor's name in the author catalogue.

*Subject index*
This holds the card or entry that gives the correct, detailed classification number of the subject. More than one number may be listed if the subject has different aspects (e.g. geography). If there appears to be no entry, look for an alternative term, or a more general heading. For example, suppose you want to look up the Cabbage White Butterfly. If there is no entry under *Cabbage White*, you would look up *Butterflies*; if this fails you would try *Insects*.

*Classified index*
This index carries the details of the individual books held in the library. When you have found the subject classification number, look in the classified index, where details of all books on that subject will appear.

The index will be in numerical order, and this will correspond to the books on the shelves. The index will give details of author, publisher and date of publication for every non-fiction book in the library.

SUBJECT ENTRY

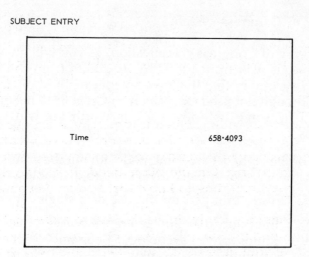

Time                              658·4093

**Figure 10.2   Example of a subject index card**

There are some public branch libraries in Great Britain which have what is known as a *leisure reading* or *browsing* system. The library will then put all its books together under very general headings, for example, *Sport, Gardening, Humour, Computers*, etc. This can be very confusing, and it is not worth spending time looking for a particular book. Ask the librarian for what you require, and let her or him point you in the right direction.

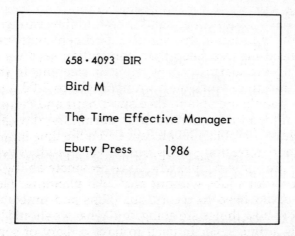

658 · 4093   BIR

Bird M

The Time Effective Manager

Ebury Press      1986

**Figure 10.3   Example of a classified entry card**

## Library of Congress system

The Library of Congress classification, as you will guess from the name, is also from the USA. It differs from the Dewey Decimal system in that it allows a wider method of classification. Although not used extensively in Great Britain it has been adopted by some libraries, so it is worth knowing how it operates.

Letters of the alphabet are combined with numbers; this means that, in theory, 676 subject divisions are available.

Main classes are grouped by the use of a single letter:

| | |
|---|---|
| A | Encyclopedias and reference books |
| B | Philosophy, Psychology, Religion |
| C | Antiquities, Biography |
| D | History |
| E/F | American History |
| G | Geography, Anthropology, Recreation |
| H | Social Sciences, Economics, Sociology |
| J | Political Science |
| K | Law |
| L | Education |
| M | Music and books on music |
| N | Fine Arts |
| P | Language and Literature |
| Q | Science |
| R | Medicine |
| S | Agriculture |
| T | Technology |
| U | Military Science |
| V | Naval Science |
| Z | Books, Bibliographies and Libraries |

The letters I, O, W, X and Y have not been used yet but are available for future expansion of the system.

Within the existing classes, the principle subdivisions are shown by an additional letter. For example:

Q = Science

| | |
|---|---|
| QA | Mathematics |
| QB | Astronomy |
| QC | Physics |

QD   Chemistry
QE   Geology
QH   Natural History
QK   Botany
QL   Zoology
QM   Anatomy
QP   Physiology
QR   Bacteriology

Further subdivisions are made by using numerals in sequence in each of the main divisions (starting with 1, and going as high as 9,999 in some cases). For example:

PN    Literal History and Collections
PN1   International Periodicals
PN2   American and English Periodicals
PN3   French Periodicals

Decimal letters and numbers are also used to subdivide a subject alphabetically.

As with the Dewey Decimal system the books are arranged on the shelves according to the classification number and then within each class by author.

**Other systems**

Occasionally an organisation will devise its own cataloguing system for the convenience of its members. For instance, a nursing library classification has been used for student nurses in their own very specialised library. Each book is assigned to a particular subject area and is then given a classification number. For example:

Aa   Anatomy and Physiology
Ab   Anaesthetics
Bb   Biology
Ca   Communicable diseases
Cb   Community and Social Services
       etc.

The Universal Decimal System (UDC), also known as the Brussels Classification uses symbols and numbers. It was first published in 1905. It is fundamentally the same as the Dewey Decimal base and hierarchy, but uses a colon to link class numbers. So, for example, 621.785 (heat treatment) combined with 669.14 (steel) would read 621.685:669.14 — the heat treatment of steel.

## Sources of information

### The librarian

Your most effective information-retrieval device may be the librarian of the library you use most frequently. Librarians are not merely there to reshelve books and to complain if your books are overdue; they are professionals with a great deal of knowledge and expertise in the art of retrieving information. They are concerned not only with books, but also with a wide range of non-book material. They will often be able to give you help in tracking down information from sources which you would never have thought about. Get the librarian on your side and the whole library system of Great Britain (including university libraries) will be yours.

If you are spending time in a university or college library, get to know and value your tutor librarian. He or she will have a great deal of knowledge about the subjects you are studying and will help you to find information which will enrich and enhance individual assignments and projects.

When you are working with library staff, bear in mind the following points:

(a) Be clear about what you want to know.
(b) Always ask for *exactly* what you want — don't ask for a book on management when you actually want a book about leadership.
(c) Do not assume that all the counter staff are qualified librarians; some will only be assistants.
(d) Be prepared to wait — most of the stock you see in a library is only the tip of the iceberg. The rest will be out on loan or stored.
(e) Find out the level of stock coverage by asking the librarian. A small branch library may only carry light recreational books.
(f) Ask yourself if you really need the *particular* book you

are ordering — would an alternative still provide the same information?

(g) If you need a particular book, have as many details available as possible. These details include:
   — *minimum information:* author and title
   — *best information:* author, title, date of publication, publisher, ISBN (International Standard Book Number)
   If the book has to come from somewhere else or be ordered, and you have not got these details, then the library staff will have to find them. This takes time.

(h) Expect a delay of at least three to six weeks between your request and the book arriving. It might be sooner, but do not rely on this being the case.

(i) *Anticipate what you will want and order it in good time.*

## Specialist libraries

Many large organisations have their own specialist libraries which contain material of particular relevance to them (BBC, ICI, BMA, etc.). It is sometimes possible to get permission to use these larger libraries. Universities and colleges of further and higher education will have a wide range of information as will research establishments and professional bodies. There are also libraries for smaller organisations, which are run for the benefit of members. These can range from a local photographic society's shelf of books and journals to the collection of a prestigious society which has amassed a wealth of information about its members' exploits and activities. The librarians of these specialist libraries will usually be able to give you a good deal of help.

## Aslib directory

The Aslib directory is in two volumes. Volume 1 is a subject guide arranged according to the decimal classification, and it also contains an alphabetical subject index. This is useful for cross-referencing. Volume 2 contains details about libraries and information services throughout the United Kingdom. The arrangement is by town, and there is also a regional index listing libraries under counties. Over 3,000 entries occur and they include information about national, hospital, company, cathedral and embassy libraries, among many others.

## Abstracting services

For a fee, it is possible to join an abstracting service such as ANBAR. The fee is too high for most individuals to use this service, but the organisation to which they belong might have a subscription. Included in the package will be:

— a monthly briefing of abstracted materials,
— a cumulative index,
— access to the service's own library,
— loan service of photocopied material.

Such services are particularly useful when you want up-to-date information which is usually only contained in magazine articles.

Below you will find some further books which could help you in your studies. It is not a complete list and your librarian will give you more comprehensive advice if you need it.

## Information on books

*Reference books*
Useful lists of reference books can be found in:

*Guide to Reference Books*, Constance Winchell
*Guide to Reference Material*, A.J. Walford
*How to Find Out*, G. Chandler

Most libraries will have a reference section. This brief list gives a few useful reference books:

*Shorter Oxford Dictionary*
*Collins Dictionary of the English Language*
*Roget's Thesaurus* (synonyms)
*RAC Handbook* (travel, distance between towns, hotels, etc.)
*Keesing's Contemporary Archives* (political, economic and social events)
*Whitaker's Almanac* (current events in government, national and local)

*Kelly's Dictionary of Towns* (business details localised)
*Oxford Book of Quotations* (quotations old and new)
*Dictionary of British Associations* (addresses)
*British Standards Yearbook* (information about standards)
*Willing's Press Guide*
*Encyclopedia Britannica*

## Bibliographies

Useful bibliographies include:

*A World Bibliography of Bibliographies*
*British National Bibliography* (published weekly)

The BNB, as the *British National Bibliography* is called, contains material not found in other places, e.g. government publications, pamphlet material, books published by organisations which are not regular book publishers.

## Books in print

There may be occasions when you will want to obtain details of books which are not stocked in the local library, or that you want to buy. These may be books by a particular author about a particular subject, or they may be new books. A number of periodicals are published to enable you to trace details of books published in Britain and at least one of these will be available in your local library:

*The Bookseller* (published weekly)
*Whitaker's Cumulative Booklist* (published quarterly)
*British Books in Print* (published annually)
*Paperbacks in Print* (published annually)

## Biographies

These include:

*Dictionary of National Biography* (from earliest times to the twentieth century)
*Who's Who* (issued annually, covers persons still living)
*Who Was Who* (biographies of people once in *Who's Who* but now dead)

You will also find books with biographical information relating to individual countries, professions, industries, periods in history, and so on.

*Periodical articles*
These are listed in specialist publications to be found in central reference libraries. For example:

> *Social Science and Humanities Index*
> *British Technology Index*

*Encyclopedias and dictionaries*
Every library provides a selection of encyclopedias ranging from multi-volume sets to single-subject volumes. Encyclopedias are usually arranged in alphabetical order of subject. The index of a multi-volumed encyclopedia should always be consulted to obtain maximum information on the subject; it will give cross-references to subjects as well as showing the main entry. Encyclopedias include:

> *Encyclopedia Britannica*
> *Chambers Encyclopedia*

Single-volume encyclopedias are often quicker and easier to use for checking a single fact, and many specialist 'dictionaries' are really small encyclopedias. For example:

> *Dictionary of Modern History* (Penguin)
> *Dictionary of Computers* (Penguin)

There are also true dictionaries in many subjects which allow for the checking of definitions and spellings. Such dictionaries range from the various language dictionaries to dictionaries of quotations, surnames and place names.

*Other sources of material*
In addition to local, university and copyright libraries, the following may be useful:

> Public Record Office (Ruskin Avenue, Kew, Richmond, Surrey, TW9 4DU, tel. 01-876-3444)
> General Register Offices (St. Catherine's House, 10 Kingsway, London, WC2B 6JP, tel. 01-242-0262)
> Bank of England Information Services Department (Threadneedle Street, London, EC2R 8AH, tel. 01-601-4411)
> BBC Written Archives Centre (Caversham Park, Reading, RG4 8TZ, tel. 0734 472427 ext. 281/2)
> Business Archives Council (Dominion House, 37—45 Tooley Street, London Bridge, London, SE1 2QF, tel. 01-407-6110)

City Business Library (Gillet House, 55 Basinghall Street, London, EC2V 5BX, tel. 01-638-8215)
Lincoln's Inn Library (Lincoln's Inn, London, WC2A 3TN, tel. 01-242-4371)
House of Lords Record Office (House of Lords, Westminster, London, SW1A 0AA, tel. 01-219-3074)
British Library of Political and Economic Science (10 Portugal Street, London, WC2A 2HD, tel. 01-405-7686 ext. 205/6)
British Library Science Reference Library (25 Southampton Buildings, Chancery Lane, London, WC2A 1AW, tel. 01-405-8721)
United Nations Information Centre (14/15 Stratford Place, London, W1N 9AF, tel. 01-629-3816)
British Library Newspaper Library (Colindale Avenue, London, NW9 5HE, tel. 01-200-5515)
Advertising Association Library (Abford House, 15 Wilton Road, London, SW1V 1NJ, tel. 01-828-2771)

The British Institute of Management is a professional institute and representational body providing practical assistance, short courses and advice to those who need it. They can be found at Management House, Parker Street, London, WC2B 5PT.


### Information on non-book material

*Picture research*
Sources of information include:

> *Directory of British Photographic Collections* (Heinemann)
> *The Picture Researcher's Handbook* (David and Charles)

*Weather*
Information can be obtained from:

> The Meteorological Office (Bracknell, Berks.)

*Film*
Information can be obtained from:

> National Film Archive (London)

*Maps*
Maps, or information on maps can be obtained from:

> HMSO, The London Map Centre
> Catalogue of the National Maritime Museum Library

## Computer-based information retrieval

On-line public access to information is changing the way in which the general public will be able to obtain material from libraries. Readers should soon be able to get the information they require with only a small amount of basic knowledge, such as a word from a title, the author's surname, or a key word from the table of contents. OPAC (On-line Public Access) means a major change in the way a library will operate. Gone will be the single central catalogue. The student or manager will be able to tap into the library system from the home or office. The cost of this operation is enormous and it will be some time before all libraries can use it, but it is surely the information-retrieval method for the future.

Many reference libraries now have access to at least one on-line data base, and they will carry out searches for you, either free or for a small fee. Taking advantage of this service will enhance the quality of your research and reduce the time taken to carry out a literature search.

Many commercial data bases will supply information needed to run an efficient business. Financial and credit information is available, as are the latest scientific and technical findings. You may need forecasts and figures found in published company reports, or information about leading world companies. Many of these items will be stored on a computer data base. Statistics on a wide variety of topics are easily accessed, provided the organisation can arrange the appropriate linkage. Investigate what can be obtained through your own organisation's computer department, and seek advice from those members of staff who know where to access information.

Many universities and colleges have computer links with others at home or abroad. If you are taking a course based at a centre of higher education, information could be available through the college computer.

If you have a television which will pick up the appropriate signal, the BBC's CEEFAX, IBA's ORACLE and the British Telecom's PRESTEL could be useful sources of information.

## Group exercises

There are no individual student exercises for this chapter. Individuals should make certain that they are familiar with their own local library and have a good idea where they can obtain the information they need for their course.

Training officers may feel that work could be done on the retrieval of information from within the company. Do you have company archives? Or a company library? Is it computerised? What facilities do you have? Where are the company reports stored? To whom are they available?

A group session on where and how to get local, company, national and international information relevant to your organisation can be valuable. Often information could readily be found within an organisation, yet it is at present only known to a few people. Listing the whereabouts and type of information used in the company is a useful project both for the student group and for use in the organisation.

Encourage the group to build up files of material that may be of use in their studies or working life. This may not only come from printed sources. For example, information can be obtained from conversations with colleagues, brochures and prospectuses, television programmes, professional organisations, newspaper articles, specialised libraries, government publications, etc.

# ELEVEN

# Time

Management is all about planning the many tasks that go towards running a successful business. Time is one of the most valuable elements that both managers and students have at their disposal. Books on the art of managing time roll off the presses constantly. In an ideal world, each person would be able to plan their time in such a way that every hour of the day was organised and productive. However, life is not like that, and perhaps it would not be so ideal after all. Humans need time to sit and think, and to enjoy the occasional lazy time. A tightly-planned schedule which inhibits the person using it is much less valuable than a more relaxed system which allows the user to work effectively.

To manage any business successfully it is important to set the right goals for that business. In the same way, a manager who has planned a career and has set realistic long-term goals will find the detailed planning of study time easier than someone who is just drifting from job to job. Your own career plans and long-term goals will include the study course that you are now taking. These long-term goals are the framework in which shorter-term goals are set. Goal-setting implies arranging short-term goals into priority areas, and this skill is essential if you are to make good use of your study time.

If you are taking a distance-learning or open-learning course, it is sensible to organise your time well so that you may fit in work, study and leisure. If you are in the habit of thinking through your tasks at work and setting goals, you will already have a fairly clear idea of how to utilise the time you have available. Goal-setting, delegation and assessment of time is an important part of a manager's role. These skills are also needed when planning a study timetable. Learning at school or college is simple compared with working on your own, especially when you have family and work responsibilities.

If you want to be successful in your studies you will need to think through how to use your time efficiently. It may mean that you are going to have to change your routine, and although this may only be for the time you are on the course, it is still quite a difficult thing to do (easy enough to plan on paper, but very much harder to put into operation). The key will be motivation and organisation. With some thought, plus supportive family and friends, you should be able to plan your workload so that you can cover all your study requirements and still retain some sanity.

Most students enjoy their studies. By planning time effectively, this enjoyment will not be clouded by feelings of guilt about using time for study that should perhaps be given to other activities. Do not fall into the trap of believing that you can only study or work when you are 'in the mood' or 'feeling creative'. The successful senior executive in any organisation will tell you that it is hard work and attention to detail which is the key to success. Flair and imagination play their part, but getting priorities right plus hard work are the cornerstones of success. And planning a timetable which takes into account your other commitments and your own study preferences is an important preparation for any course of study, whatever the length of the course.

If you intend to plan a working timetable, it is usually better to make a series of weekly timetable sheets. You will probably alter them as you get into your stride, but they are a starting point for longer-term planning. Begin by filling in your essential activities — eating, travelling, shopping, business commitments, regular sporting and leisure interests, and so on. Then fill in (try another colour) the time you feel you need for study. It should be possible for you to assess the approximate time you will need quite early on in the course. Ask your tutor for advice also. Her or his experience will give you guidelines. You may see that it is necessary to curtail some of your leisure activities for a while and to replan some of your business responsibilities. Do not stop all of the things that you enjoy doing, though. Relaxation and physical well-being are as essential for productive and effective study as they are for productive and effective management.

A chart similar to the one illustrated in figure 11.1 can be used to plan out your weekly timetable. If you have been involved in a time-management course run for the staff in your organisa-

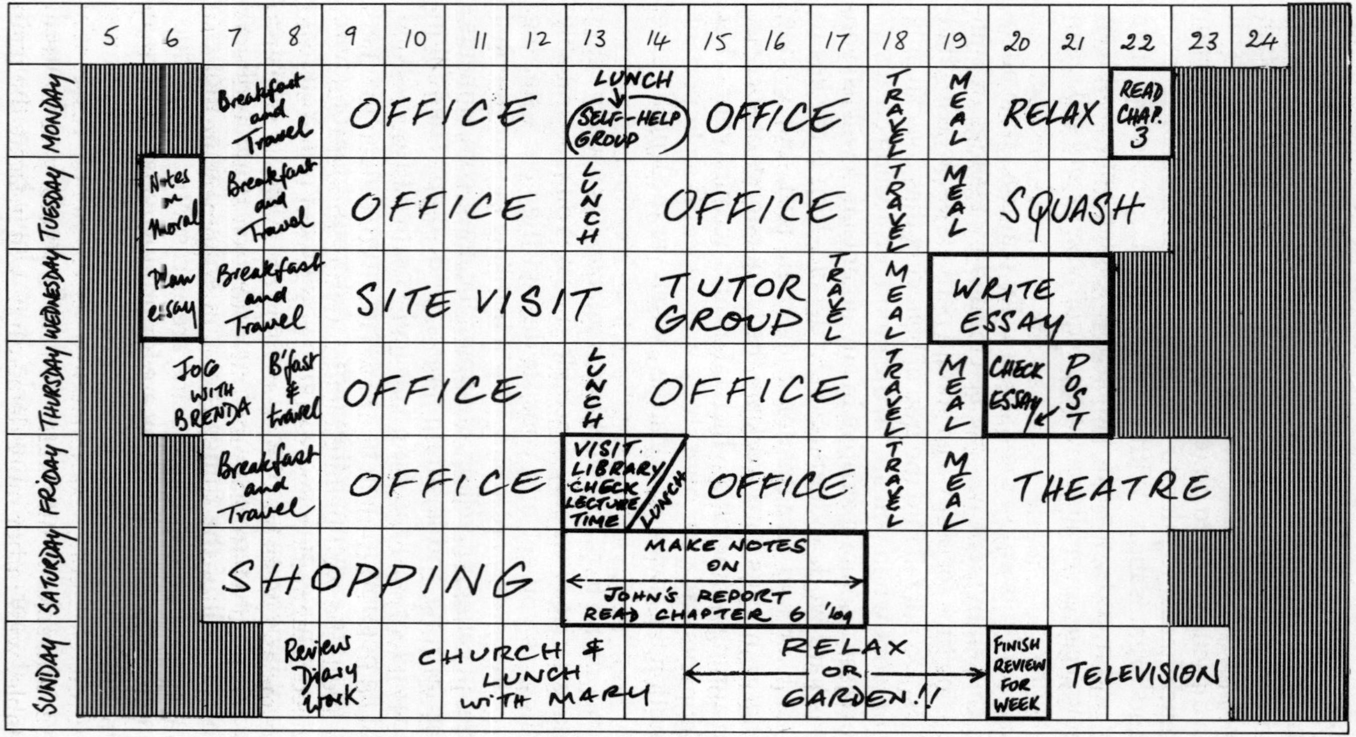

| Day | 5 | 6 | 7 | 8 | 9 | 10 | 11 | 12 | 13 | 14 | 15 | 16 | 17 | 18 | 19 | 20 | 21 | 22 | 23 | 24 |
|---|---|---|---|---|---|---|---|---|---|---|---|---|---|---|---|---|---|---|---|---|
| MONDAY | | Hotel in Hurrel | Breakfast and Travel | | OFFICE | | | | LUNCH (SELF-HELP GROUP) | | OFFICE | | | TRAVEL | MEAL | RELAX | | READ CHAP. 3 | | |
| TUESDAY | | Plan essay | Breakfast and Travel | | OFFICE | | | | LUNCH | | OFFICE | | | TRAVEL | MEAL | SQUASH | | | | |
| WEDNESDAY | | | Breakfast and Travel | | SITE VISIT | | | | LUNCH | | TUTOR GROUP | | | MEAL | | WRITE ESSAY | | | | |
| THURSDAY | | Job with BRENDA | B'fast & travel | | OFFICE | | | | LUNCH | | OFFICE | | | TRAVEL | MEAL | CHECK P OS ESSAY/JT | | | | |
| FRIDAY | | | Breakfast and Travel | | OFFICE | | | | | VISIT LIBRARY CHECK LECTURE TIME | OFFICE | | | TRAVEL | MEAL | THEATRE | | | | |
| SATURDAY | | | | SHOPPING | | | | CHURCH & LUNCH WITH MARY | | MAKE NOTES ON JOHN'S REPORT READ CHAPTER 6 | | | | RELAX OR GARDEN!! | | | | | | |
| SUNDAY | | | | Reviews Diary work | | | | CHURCH & LUNCH WITH MARY | | | | | | | | FINISH REVIEW FOR WEEK | TELEVISION | | | |

Figure 11.1

tion, you may already log your working time as a matter of course. This more detailed planning could be useful now. But however you decide to plan out your time, think through the implications of the plan and any extra duties or responsibilities that could occur over the period of time when you will be studying.

Make sure that you know when assignments and projects have to be submitted; if you have occasional assessment tests, note the date of the test and make certain you leave enough time for revision. If you have examinations to cope with, check when they are. You may be attending a residential session or summer school. Make sure that these are also noted down so that you can arrange study, work and social commitments well in advance.

At this stage it will be obvious that a weekly planner is not sufficient and that you will need a longer-term chart. A planner diary is useful, but a wall-planner is better because there will be more room to write down all the information. These are quite easily obtained, or they can be made fairly easily using a large sheet of thin card.

You will also find that a wall-planner chart is more useful than a book diary, as you will be able to see the comparative time factors very clearly. By seeing the units of time in visual form it is easier to assess them than by trying to organise the time structure mentally. This overview of the course helps you to space and organise your daily work and study load. You should find that there are fewer periods when chaos threatens to overwhelm you. You might find that to complete everything properly it will be necessary to delegate. To do this successfully, you need to be efficient in your own life. Work given to others will have to be well planned and carefully thought out. You will need imagination and careful preparation to foresee and overcome any problems. These managerial skills are similar to those required when planning out your own study and work time. Communication skills and time management are essential for study and management.

If you have got a good overview of your course, you may find it helpful to make a brief outline timetable of the most important elements, examinations, assessments, residential courses and so on. This might even cover several years. A term timetable, with rather more detail on it, will indicate the main tasks for those few months, and a very detailed weekly timetable can help you use the smaller units of time most effectively. Be careful not to spend so much time on planning time that you have no time in which to get on with your life and study. It can be very tempting to work out a really good-looking chart and then sit back and assume that this is all that is needed. The timetable is only a tool to help you to get to grips with your real aims.

It is worth spending time on time; if you are the sort of person who works well under pressure, the knowledge that assignments and work targets have to be completed on a certain date is stimulating. On the other hand, if you work more steadily, it is comforting to know that you are keeping up to schedule.

When planning study timetables, try to assess your most productive working time, the time when you are mentally and physically at your best. People tend to fall into two categories: those who are more alert in the morning and who flag by the middle of the afternoon, and those who get up late, drag through the morning and only come alive by lunchtime. Exploit your own characteristic where you can. This is not to say that it is impossible to work at other times, but you may find it better to save your routine chores for the less productive hours of your day.

If you wake up early, full of energy, harness this energy for study sessions. Could you get up a little earlier and have an hour of work before breakfast? If you find that your best time is later in the day, could you work after the family have gone to bed? There are those who come home from work, relax, perhaps have a short sleep, and then find they can work very well in the middle of the night. Experiment with time. We usually need far less sleep than convention says we should. Try setting the alarm for 5.30 a.m. or sleeping in the early evening and then working from midnight to 2.00 a.m.

Some people are able to take short naps and can sleep for the odd fifteen or twenty minutes during the day. Take full advantage of this ability if you can. Often the time immediately after a short refreshing sleep can be very productive.

There are some people who have an innate ability to carry out their various jobs without any such planning. However, most of us do need to record our plans and timetables as a reminder of how things are going, and what we should be doing next. It is a time saver in itself to have a diary of some sort, however simple.

Once you have planned an overall timetable which is flexible enough to allow for the unexpected, it is a good idea to think through your study tasks to see where you can use your time most profitably. An earlier section in the book, on reading strategies, suggests that you should learn to read at speed. Although you will need time in which to practise, this time will be amply repaid. So also will time spent in arranging your notes and material in such a way that you can easily lay your hands on information needed for a seminar or essay.

If you plan your study times well you will have spread the load over a period of days, weeks, or months, with achievable goals along the way. And realistic goals make your study time more effective and less tiring.

### Time-planning checklist

A course planner should include:

      dates when assignments are due;
      dates of residential courses;
      dates of examinations;
      details of business commitments;
      study seminars and self-help groups;
      examination revision sessions, if appropriate.

A weekly timetable should include:

      commitments, including work, travel, domestic responsibilities, etc.;
      assignment postal dates;
      study times;
      seminars and self-help groups;
      review diary sessions.

If you use a Filofax or similar planner-diary you will be able to enter your study times into the system. One great advantage is that it is easy to compare the study timetable with other work and leisure commitments. These extended planner-diaries are very useful for those of us who need to write down the details of our lives. Problems only arise when the 'fax' are 'filed' so efficiently and take so long to record that the diary becomes a substitute for the real activity!

Remember also to spend a little time in planning out what is required for each assignment. Subdivide main tasks into

ELEM—M

smaller ones, for example, *reading, working problems, fieldwork, memorising, planning, writing,* etc.

### An alternative course planner

Pattern notes can also be helpful in course planning. Look at the example in figure 11.2.

## Planning a single study session

Organising study periods in the abstract or the long term is fine; but what is equally (if not more) important is knowing what to do when confronted with a desk, a blank piece of paper and a pile of books. Any single session needs to be planned as carefully as any longer unit of time. The correlation between comprehension, memory and understanding in study is the main factor to take into account.

The word 'study' covers a variety of different things. Essay writing, project planning, information retrieval, working through a mathematical problem, reading, memorising, thinking, note making, revising — these are all study activities. Each will need concentration and hard work. By organising your study time effectively you can work hard, memorise more, learn the material more efficiently, and get greater satisfaction from doing it.

Start to work before you even sit down at your desk. Getting into the right 'mental set' or frame of mind is vital. Try to collect all the material you will want: papers, calculator, books and so on. As you gather them together start collecting your thoughts as well. Start by recalling what you already know about the subject. Decide how you are going to spend the time. Try to bring to mind the overall view of the course and see how the material you are about to study fits into that overall scheme. If you prepare yourself in this way, you will go straight into your studying with no delay and few distracting thoughts.

It is important to break your study period into reasonable 'concentration' spans. Most adults can work for between thirty and fifty minutes without losing much concentration, although each individual will vary. Decide what your normal concentration span seems to be, and use this when planning your session.

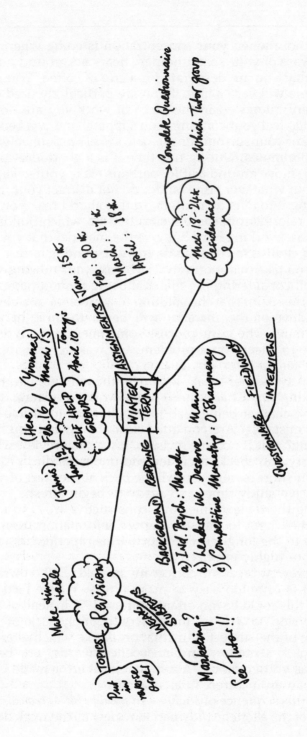

Figure 11.2

You will know when your concentration is going when you become aware of your surroundings, hear background noises or realise that you are desperate for a cup of coffee. You may find the time will vary a little if you are particularly tired or if you are very interested in the piece of work you are doing. When you do feel your concentration slipping, and you become very aware of your surroundings, have a *brief* break of between one or two minutes. During this time it is a good idea to get up, stretch, move around a little, perhaps make yourself a cup of coffee; but whatever else you do, do not distract your mind by switching it to outside matters. In this short break you not only get a release from the physical tension which builds up when you are working hard but give the material that you are studying a chance to consolidate in your mind.

While you take this short physical break, your subconscious mind is still considering the material being thought about. It is often at this point that the solution to a problem or a clearer understanding of the material will begin to form in your conscious mind. The same process sometimes happens when you decide to 'sleep' on a problem. On waking, the answer to the problem is often obvious.

After taking a brief break, look over the material you have been working on. Check the written work for errors; skim through the chapter being read for the key points. Have you found any mistakes? Are you quite clear about what you have been reading? This is not true revision, just a short review which aids memory and checks accuracy and understanding. At the end of each short review you will be back at the start of your next intensive study time, and ready to begin afresh.

By using the review times in a constructive way, you will find that they help to transfer learned information from the short-term to the long-term memory. This repetition is fairly painless, but highly effective.

Use the review breaks to correct any mistakes. When writing at speed it is only too easy to make errors. Where facts are concerned this could be important; putting 1957 instead of 1975 when referring to a legal matter could imply lack of real knowledge of the subject. Punctuation marks which alter the meaning of a sentence, and misspelled words, are better corrected as you go along. A mathematical error made early on can mean an incorrect final solution.

Repeat this sequence of *study — physical break — review*, and at the end of the allotted study period review all the work done.

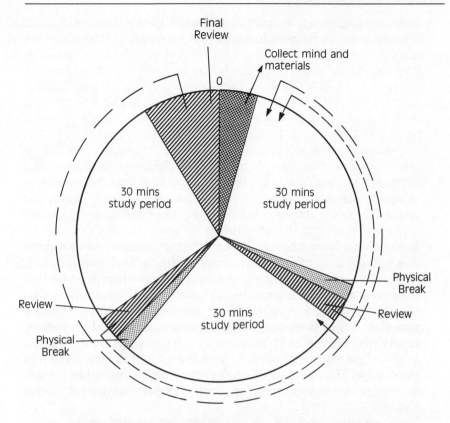

*Figure 11.3  Time division during a 1 hour, 55
minute study session. Study includes: essay writing,
reading, making notes, revising, planning,
reviewing, thinking*

Decide how long you are going to work, and stick to it, whether
it is thirty minutes or three hours. In a thirty minute session
a physical break will probably be unnecessary, but a review will
still be useful. In a three hour session you will probably have
about five intensive study periods with four short physical
breaks and review times, plus a final longer review session
when you go over all the work you have done. Most of the
material will have been looked at several times and this
repetition will help to impress it on the mind and in the
memory.

     If your course ends with an examination, these constant,
if brief, review sessions will make the final revision more

effective and much easier to cope with. Below, we will look at a more formalised revision and review method — the *revision diary*.

## A revision diary

We have seen that by reviewing work done during a single study session the learned material will be more likely to be retained and understood. It is then linked into the memory, where it can be retrieved when required. A more structured approach to the entire course takes a short while to organise, but once working it will pay dividends in terms of material learned and remembered. Although it is called a revision diary it is equally as useful for those not taking a final examination.

Subjects covered at the beginning of any course may be half forgotten after a few months. Where this information can be kept to the forefront of the mind, it is easier to integrate new material. A firm basis of learned material is important for linking in any new information. Sometimes it happens that information is absorbed and learned only to have to be relearned later in the course. This occurs especially when an examination looms, or when an assignment or project refers to these earlier elements.

By reviewing course material at specific intervals it is possible to stop the decay of memory. It also makes it far easier to recall early topics and to slot them into the jigsaw of understanding and knowledge that you are building up.

Figure 11.4 indicates how the decay of memory can be halted.

A revision diary uses the correlation between time and memory in a practical way. It enables the student to memorise material properly. It also helps to make the current subjects more relevant, as it becomes simpler to relate various factors to each other.

A small notebook or conventional diary (one day to a page preferably) will be needed. If you are using a printed diary it will be necessary to go through it and block out times which you cannot use for study: holidays, travelling, business commitments and so on.

It will be necessary to number the pages of your notes and keep a record of any books and journals that contain important

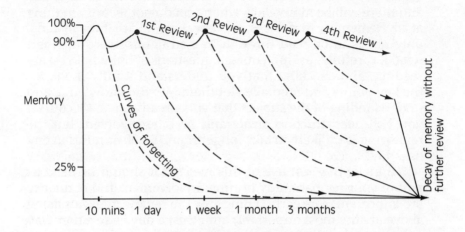

*Figure 11.4*

passages. Recording the details and page numbers of sources of information should be automatic. It is unlikely that you will be able to recall the precise details of a source of information several months after it has been first used. A separate small notebook is useful to record this type of information.

## Making and using the diary

After each study session, where new or relevant material has been learned or noted, the details must be recorded in the diary at the following intervals:

> next day;
> one week later;
> one month later;
> three months later;
> six months later.

The last two recordings can be combined if necessary; the length of the course will determine this.

Keeping within a 3—6 month period will take you through the usual academic year. For a two or three year course you could refer to your earlier diaries every three or four months as the course progresses.

The constant pattern of review will build up, and you will find that you will be reviewing material fairly frequently.

However, there will never be more than five items on a day and there will be many days when you do not record anything at all. Remember that this is a review diary and that the material only needs to be read through in a straightforward manner. Read it carefully, asking yourself questions about what you are reading, and checking that you understand it fully. Look for the key points and mentally slot them into the knowledge and understanding of the subject that you already have. Of course, you will need to concentrate and become involved, but the reviewing is unlikely to take longer than 15—30 minutes in any one day.

To make the best use of this method it should be used as part of your regular study routine. Involvement and regularity are important. The early timings for the review intervals listed above are the most important; after this, a day or so either way will not make all that much difference.

The brief record of review material will cover all aspects of your work. For example, you may include a particular chapter in a textbook, a page or two of your own notes, a table from which you have extracted information, an essay you (or someone else) has written, and so on.

Thus, if on September 10th you read a chapter on industrial psychology and made some notes on decision making, you might make the following entries:

| | | |
|---|---|---|
| September 11th | (next day) | Chapter 5 Indust. Psych. Moody Psych/M'gt notes pp. 4—8 |
| September 18th | (1 week later) | (the same entry, repeated) |
| October 18th | (1 month later) | (the same entry, repeated) |
| January 18th | (3 months later) | (the same entry, repeated) |
| April 18th | (6 months later) | (the same entry, repeated) |

The last two entries could be combined, and entered on any date around the 18th of any month between January and April.

If the next study session is on September 17th and you have been investigating the essential concepts of the Expectancy Theory, the entries could be as follows:

September 18th (next day)   Expt. Th'ry notes pp. 6—10
(esp. Fayol/Maslow)
Th'ry of M'gt structure
p. 56ff
Mary's essay on
McGregor (X&Y)

These items would then be entered again on September 25th (next week). October 25th (1 month later), January 25th (3 months later), and April 25th (6 months later).

Suppose that during your study time on September 18th you are planning and writing an essay on the economic policies of the government. The reviews (on September 19th, September 27th, January 27th, April 27th) will probably consist of rereading the essay and thinking in a positive manner about the views expressed in it. On the first and second review your ideas will probably be the same as when you wrote the essay. But are they still the same on the third, fourth and fifth review? Questioning is a good review and revision strategy, and it will help you to see how your ideas have developed.

A rule of thumb is to spend at least five minutes of review time for every hour of study.

Thinking about your use of time, and planning a flexible but realistic timetable, can help you to organise the time you have at your disposal. Some of the ideas in this chapter may appeal to you and you may use all or some of them in your own life. The important thing to remember is that no single way is the 'right' way. Worrying about how to plan your time and spending hours in making lists and timetables will be fruitless if you have not got the motivation to carry them through. Unfortunately, there are some of us who believe earnestly that by making a tight timetable we have actually got the work done!

You are an individual, and there is little profit in comparing with other people the way in which you work and the time you take over a task. Some students feel guilty if they manage to complete an essay in three hours when they know that a colleague has been burning the midnight oil for nearly a week. But the proof of the pudding, as they say, is in the eating.

Time spent in background reading, listening to others, and thinking, are areas where it is possible to feel you are 'wasting' time. But using your mind as opposed to recording with your hands is a worthwhile study activity. A long walk without a

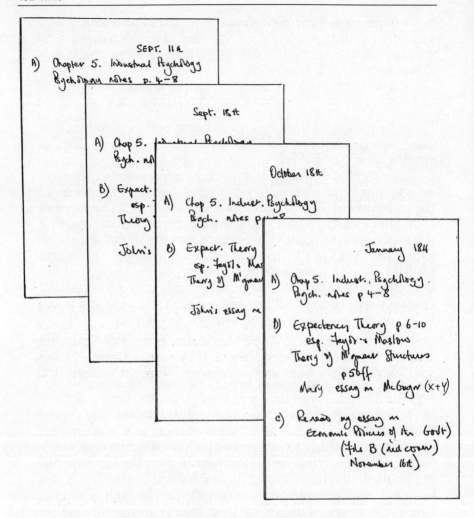

*Figure 11.5   Pages from a revision diary*

book in sight will often enable you to produce a better action plan for your factory or a more thought-provoking assignment than the same amount of time taken in sitting at a desk making notes and plans. Each study strategy has its value and it is important to use your time in such a way that it works for you. Try noticing how long it takes you to write an essay or make a set of notes. This can be useful when you are planning a particular exercise. Most of us have very little idea of how long we actually spend on various activities. Time often flies or drags according to the way we feel about what we are doing. A rough estimate of task time is as useful for study as it is for writing a report or dictating a letter.

A few lucky people seem to be able to do all the things required of them in a spontaneous way. If you are one of these people there will be little use in worrying your way through a set timetable. Each person needs to construct a way of working that is effective for them. You may prefer to follow a formal timetable, or to write out simple lists of tasks in priority order. Take whichever path you feel happiest with, but never believe those who say that the road to instant academic (or any other) success will happen purely because you have organised and planned life down to the last detail. Having said that, it is also true that by thinking and planning, many managers do get better results both in their own work and that of their staff. Anxiety and stress will slow you down. If feelings of stress persist, it is essential that you take steps to deal with the problem. The major causes of ill health and lost working time in the country are stress-related illnesses. It is fairly easy to get information about how to cope with stress, and many companies run courses on stress management. If you are not sure whether you are suffering from stress, here are some of the physical symptoms you can look out for.

| | |
|---|---|
| insomnia; | aching muscles; |
| tiredness; | ulcers; |
| lack of energy; | high blood pressure; |
| indigestion; | allergies; |
| headaches; | asthma. |

These are all warning signs; if you recognise several of them as symptoms that occur frequently it is sensible to seek advice from your doctor. Taking steps straight away will enable you to cope better.

## Case study

Kim Harding came from a happy-go-lucky family which was cheerful but disorganised. Meals were often late, trains rarely caught and punctuality unheard of. At school Kim found that getting homework done on time was very difficult. He was a bright boy and wanted to do well, but had little self-discipline. He would have liked to go on to further education after the sixth form but panicked at the thought of coping with a degree course. Kim started work in a large chemical works where he soon found that he was regarded as a high-flier. It was obvious that to gain promotion he would have to study for a business diploma. He was extremely apprehensive about this because he was not sure how he would be able to balance work, study and family commitments. After a difficult first year where he rarely got an assignment in on time and when his colleagues found that they often had to cover for him, Kim decided to take a crash course in time management. He did not learn anything particularly new, but he did find that he was forced to analyse his own pattern of work and study. Taking the time to think through his difficulties led him to change his routine slightly, getting the support of his wife and colleagues and making sure that he thought through all his priorities.

After some trial and error, Kim managed to organise his study well and eventually gained his diploma with honours. A rigid timetable would have been counterproductive, so Kim adapted his workload to fit into his life. He estimated as accurately as possible how long each of the short-term goals he set himself would take to complete. This helped his motivation and his confidence. Learning how to discipline himself has been of value in his managerial career, and because he is learning to manage his own time, he finds it far easier to delegate work to junior staff.

## Individual exercises

1  Time planning is about setting priorities. What are yours?

2  List all the things you need to do over the next week, both in your personal and business life. Put them in order of priority. You may want to set a target date for each one. Take the first six items and *tomorrow* try to complete (or at least start) them. Repeat this exercise tomorrow evening, and begin the following day with a new list of six essential things that you must deal with. Some of the six will inevitably carry over from one day to another until they are finished.

3  Plan out the next few weeks of study. This will include

assignment dates, reading time, fieldwork, etc. Make a formal timetable as a trial, even if you do not think that this method is for you.

4 Begin a revision diary.

5 Look at your own routine with a clear eye. Could your schedules be more flexible, more organised, more efficient? Have you achieved a good balance between work, leisure and study?

6 Log all your activities for a complete day. Look at the results. Is some of your time spent unproductively? Remember that an interruption from a colleague could count as (a) a waste of precious time, (b) welcome relief and a much-needed break, (c) an effective communication episode which will help the organisation run more smoothly.
Use the type of chart shown in figure 11.6.

7 Ask yourself if filling in timetables is taking up more time than getting down to study. Are you getting the right balance?

8 Use the checklist below to think about the way you use time. There are no right or wrong answers. The questions are intended to help you to analyse your daily routine and habits. The questions are in no particular order.

*Time and organisation*

1 Do you plan and think ahead?
2 Have you made a study/work timetable?
3 Do you do most things with a definite purpose in mind?
4 Can you say no?
5 Do you spend so much time in making lists that you waste time?
6 Do you find 'filler' jobs to do instead of getting down to the main task?
7 Can you use the occasional extra half hour productively?
8 Have you thought about how long various tasks take for future reference?
9 How punctual are you? Do you make an effort to start on time?
10 Do you consciously think about a task before you begin?

| START TIME | ACTIVITY | MINS |
|---|---|---|
| 8.30 | Arrive - Coffee | 5 |
| 8.35 | Sort out post | 15 |
| 8.50 | Mary 'phones | 3 |
| 8.53 | See MD about Clanmore site | 32 |
| 9.25 | Paul - chat | 4 |
| 9.29 | Planning meeting | 96 |
| 10.35 | Mary comes for files | 6 |
| 10.43 | 'phone - Johnson Bros (Mike) | 17 |
| 11.03 | Take new price lists to Jo | 20 |
| 11.15 | Coffee | 12 |
| 11.27 | Dictate letter re Clanmore Site | 9 |
| | | |

*Figure 11.6*

11 Can you resist the urge to watch just one more programme on TV?
12 Do you procrastinate?
13 Have you learned how to delegate?
14 Do you put off making decisions?
15 Are you a morning or an evening person? Do you exploit this?
16 Do you actively look for a quicker, more efficient way of working?
17 Is your desk cluttered, or is it tidy? Does it matter?
18 Do you prioritise your jobs and then carry them out?
19 Have you accepted the fact that it is you alone who are responsible for your own use of time?

20 Have you time for leisure and friends?
21 Have you learned to read faster?
22 Do you have an up-to-date diary?
23 Do you read, plan and think when travelling?
24 Do you keep and file your more creative ideas?
25 Do you avoid personality clashes wherever possible?
26 Can you cope with anxiety and stress?
27 Are you motivated to change your use of time when it seems important?
28 Do you enjoy what you are doing?
29 Do you complete one task before going on to the next?
30 Do you feel you spend too much time on study?

## Group exercises

1 *Materials:* copies of the checklist on time and organisation

*Group size:* any size

(a) Use the checklist as a basis for discussion.
(b) Ask each person to go through the list. They may want to alter some of the questions to suit their own circumstances.
(c) Discuss in small groups how members have responded to the questions. Points that could be raised include the following:
— When you have responded differently from the others, why do you think this is?
— What problems do the group have in common?
— Is is important or even necessary to have a clear timetable?
— How do others cope with organisation and time planning?
— What interesting ideas emerge from the discussion?
— What is the most important point to emerge?

2 *Materials:* none

*Group size:* small groups of three to four

Discussion on the general use of time within a department or organisation can have far-reaching effects and may lead to new working structures.

Consider the topics below for improving effective use. A group pattern note may be useful here.

(a) meetings;
(b) coping with paperwork;
(c) communicating with staff;
(d) decision making;
(e) forward planning;
(f) personal life and career planning.

3 *Materials:* none
*Group size:* small groups of 4—6

It may be appropriate to discuss personal and career goals within the group, looking at the following areas:

(a) What are group members' short-term and long-term goals?
(b) What opportunities are there within the company for personal development and training?
(c) What opportunities are there outside the company for personal growth and career development?

4 *Materials:* paper and coloured pens or markers
*Group size:* 10—15

There are definite advantages in actually writing down what your short-term goals are, and the effort needed to make a list will often clarify what is or is not a real priority.

Ask the group to make a list of what they have to do in the next few days. Then they should add to the list what they want to do. Use coloured pens to highlight priorities. For example, a red star could indicate items that must be achieved within a set time. A yellow star could show what the person would really like to achieve. A blue star can be marked beside items that it would be good to complete, but are not vitally important. When using the list, proceed as follows:

(a) cross a task off when it is completed;
(b) add new items to the list, and colour code them;
(c) carry the list with you (in your diary preferably);
(d) ask yourself if you are spending too much time on the yellow or blue items;
(e) decide if there is a sensible balance between the essential items and the things you want to do (especially

things you want to do for your personal benefit; do not neglect your own needs);
(f) check the list frequently — are you doing what you planned to do?

Some diaries have provision for this type of planning, and they can be very useful in helping to plan time effectively.

5 *Materials:*    flip chart
 *Group size:*    10—15

A group discussion on the ways in which individuals save time can be productive (and entertaining). List the ideas from this brainstorm session on the flip chart.

It is helpful to have a few ideas to start the group off. Any aspect of life can be covered. Here are a few ideas which may be useful:

(a) Carry a notebook with you so that you can jot down good ideas when waiting for a train, appointment or delivery. Time spent waiting for others can be used to plan out a piece of work, think about a decision to be made or check a priority list — in addition to enjoying the sunshine or remembering a friend.
(b) Set short-term goals; enter them immediately in your diary.
(c) Use a planner-diary to compare 'blocks' of work, study or leisure time.
(d) Think onto paper (perhaps using pattern notes).
(e) Organise your desk in the office. Can you lay your hands on basic essentials like pens, paper clips and sellotape? Have you got a small set of reference books: a dictionary, thesaurus, technical data, trade journals, and so on?
(f) Decide the previous night what you are going to wear the next day.
(g) Have a good personal filing system.
(h) Use travel time for thinking or reading.
(i) Use car travelling time to listen to taped notes or to make taped notes — so long as this is consistent with safety.

# TWELVE

# Writing skills

When your course tutor suggests, firmly, that your written assignment should be in on a certain date, the dreaded 'blank page panic' tends to strike. A similar feeling is created when the boss says, 'Could you get a report out by the week after next?'. Even quite rational, happy people shudder at the thought of committing themselves to paper, especially when there is a deadline.

As with all study techniques, organisation is the key to eliminating panic. You need to acquire the habit of approaching the assignment one stage at a time. In this chapter we will be looking at the four main stages used when producing a piece of written work. Chapter Thirteen will deal with the presentation and format of the material.

Before you begin, make sure what form the assignment is to take. Is it to be an essay in the conventional sense, a series of findings backed up by diagrams, graphs and statistics, or will you be expected to complete the work in the form of a company report? It is important that you are quite clear about the format before you start. Once you know this, you can adapt the planning techniques to any situation.

To plan and write effectively, you must have something to say. There will be certain ideas and facts in your mind which you want to communicate; these ideas must be properly organised so that the completed piece of writing will convey to the reader exactly what you intend. If you are to communicate well, you must consider who is going to read your writing. It is far easier to write for a specific person (or group of people) than it is to write in a vacuum.

Once you begin to write, the well-known advice of following the ABC should be remembered — *A* for *Accuracy*, *B* for *Brevity* and *C* for *Clarity*. If in addition you have good planning and skilful presentation, your work will be admirably clear and intelligible.

## Using your time well

It is unlikely that you will have the luxury of unlimited time in which to complete your work. It is vital that you plan your time well so that you do not neglect any of the four main stages, which are:

(a) overview and research;
(b) detailed planning;
(c) writing the assignment;
(d) checking the completed work.

As a rough rule of thumb, your preparation, research and planning should take up 50 per cent of the time available, writing the assignment 30 per cent, and reviewing and checking 20 per cent. If you have researched well and have a competent plan, the writing itself should take less time. Whatever amount of time you set aside it will never be sufficient; but if you cut short any of the time allocated to the different stages you will not achieve a satisfactory piece of work.

## Overview and research

Before you start, ask yourself the following questions:

(a) Am I clear about what is required?
(b) How much do I know about the subject?
(c) How extensive are the notes I have already made?
(d) Will I need to do any background reading?
(e) What other sources of information should I investigate?

Let us consider the implications of these questions, below.

### Being clear about what is required

Before starting any piece of writing, you must be absolutely clear about what is asked for. As with examination questions, the wrong interpretation will send you off on a false trail. Establish the scope and limitations of the work. Who will the reader be? The simple answer might be your tutor. However, many business and management courses require assignments to be written in the form of a company report, in which case your reader will probably be the managing director of an imaginary firm.

### Existing knowledge of the subject

Jotting down a few notes about what you already know and understand about the topic is important. You may have many ideas and details which will eventually be rejected, but this process will help you to begin to structure the assignment in a coherent manner. At this point you will begin to realise the gaps in your knowledge, which is an immense help. Once you know what is wanted you can start filling in these gaps. Pattern notes are particularly useful for this.

### Your own notes

Read through all the notes you have made on the subject. Do not neglect notes you made earlier in the course. Useful information, quotations or statistics may have been noted which could be very useful for this assignment. (A secondary benefit is that you are assisting your memory as you review these earlier notes.)

### Background reading

You may need to do some background reading. Books and articles which are important for your course will usually appear on a reading list supplied by your tutor, but you may need to consult the library catalogue for extra or more specific reading matter. If you are wise, you will already have given yourself an overview of your entire course, and you may have clippings, articles and references filed away. Speed reading comes into its own in these circumstances; you can use it to get through a good deal of material, selecting and rejecting items very quickly. If you have read the chapter on reading strategies, this is the time to put those ideas into practice.

### Investigating other sources of information

Apart from written material, you may need to do some research into other sources of information. Correspondence, personal observation, company reports, fieldwork results, the press and many other places could yield results. All this will take time but it is important. Material stored on a computer data base may need time for extraction, and to get a print-out. Statistics and diagrams need time to be photocopied. Questionnaires need time to be prepared, printed, distributed and collected as well as interpreted. Research of any kind tends to take far more time than one expects. When time is at a premium it is tempting to abandon the search for extra material which will really enhance your work. But organise yourself so that you get as much information as you can. You may not use all of it in this particular assignment, but the knowledge you will acquire, and the ideas it will generate in your mind, will be worthwhile. One source of informal information, often neglected, is the expertise and skill of fellow students and colleagues.

Note that there is a section on research skills later in this chapter.

## Detailed planning

A straightforward essay needs an introduction, a middle and a conclusion. You will need to think about what should appear in each of these sections. Irrelevant material must be discarded and the details must be sorted into a clear, logical sequence.

*Introduction* This will usually state briefly what your theme is to be, the various aspects of it and possibly the significance of any findings.

*Body of the assignment* Here you will develop your ideas, support them with facts wherever possible and deal with any objections. Your aim should be to present a well-balanced piece of work. You may prefer to deal with the material in sections, writing about each aspect in turn. Another way would be to write sequentially, with one point leading to another. Much will depend on the case you wish to make, the structure most suitable for the material and your own preferences.

*Conclusion* If you have postulated a theory, now is the time to write with confidence. A brief summary which will include the implications and conclusions is correct here. No new material or arguments should be included in this final stage.

It is important to separate planning from writing, and once you have decided on the overall structure of the assignment you should be thinking of planning each section out in detail. Always keep in mind the question you are answering or the statement you are making. Dividing the work into the smallest possible units really pays off when you come to do the actual writing. It is less daunting to write a good paragraph which fits into a well-ordered scheme than it is to embark on a 3,000 word essay with only a vague idea of where it is leading.

Much of the information that you will be using will be unco-ordinated, and on various different types of paper as well as disks, tapes, and so on. It is helpful to attempt to group the material under headings. Once you have the material which you intend to use in the assignment you are ready to start the initial planning.

Planning techniques are many and various; there are no 'correct' methods, only the ways which you find right for you. Be aware of how other people plan out their work, as it may contain elements which you can incorporate in your own working method. Below, I have included some techniques which may be helpful.

**Outline linear notes**

These notes are made sequentially, taking each section in turn. Leave yourself plenty of room on the page so that you can include late ideas and material which come to light after you have started.

*Advantages* This is a good method for a straightforward piece of writing which has a natural progression and where the sequence is obvious.

*Disadvantages* It is easy to get too narrow a picture of different sections and to lose the overall view. This could lead to an unbalanced piece of work. It may also mean that you leave out valuable material because you cannot see how to fit it in.

# Two-column planning

Divide the planning page into two. The main headings appear in the left-hand column and supporting detail relating to those headings in the right-hand column.

*Advantages*   The main headings and sections have to be thought out at an early stage. This leads to clarity of thought and purpose. Details can be added as they emerge.

*Disadvantages*   It may be necessary to use another method to organise lengthy or outwardly confusing detail.

# Cut and stick

Headings, paragraphs and even sentences are written down as they come to you. These are then arranged in the desired order for the main draft, using scissors and paste.

*Advantages*   This method saves you writing and rewriting good material over and over again.

*Disadvantages*   There is a temptation to insert a well-turned phrase at all costs. More importantly, this method makes it very difficult to keep the overall pattern in mind.

# Paper shuffling

This is a simplified version of the cut-and-stick method. In this case the pieces of paper with your notes on are rearranged until you have the information as you want it. Highlighters and coloured pens can be used to indicate order.

*Advantages*   The order can be changed easily without rewriting too often, and extra material can be inserted with ease.

*Disadvantages*   If you lose one piece of paper you are in trouble. As with similar methods, it is not always easy to keep the overall plan in sight.

# Verbal organisation

For those who can clarify their thoughts more easily when thinking aloud, this method is very effective. A small tape recorder or dictaphone is an obvious requirement.

*Advantages*   Stray thoughts can be captured easily. If you can put information into the spoken word, it usually means that you have grasped the essentials of the subject; you will therefore be able to communicate your understanding to others in the completed assignment.

*Disadvantages*   The material can take longer to process than when you sit down with pen and paper.

## Pattern notes

This method uses word association and the selection of key words to organise the material and make the overall structure. Chapter Seven gives you more details of this method.

*Advantages*   The planner can immediately see the relationships between various factors. Items can be noted down as they spring to mind, or as they are collected. When all the key points are included, go through the note and mark it with a coloured pen, to show the order in which you intend to write up the material.

*Disadvantages*   None, once you have got used to the method.

Figure 12.1 shows one of the initial pattern notes made when planning this book out.

There are, of course, other ways of collecting and arranging material. Each person will choose a method which is suitable for their own manner of working. It is worth giving some thought to planning techniques: experiment a little, combine several ways, until you find a method which suits your style of thinking and the writing tasks you have. And bear in mind that the writing skills that are being considered here will be of use throughout your working life, not just when you are studying.

If you need to include illustrations, graphs, maps or diagrams, you will need to decide at the planning stage where they are to appear in the text. Inserting this type of material as an afterthought is always a mistake. If an illustration of whatever kind is important, it must be an integral part of the finished product. Your aim should be to make the reader's task as simple as possible, and illustrations should be planned as a means of doing this.

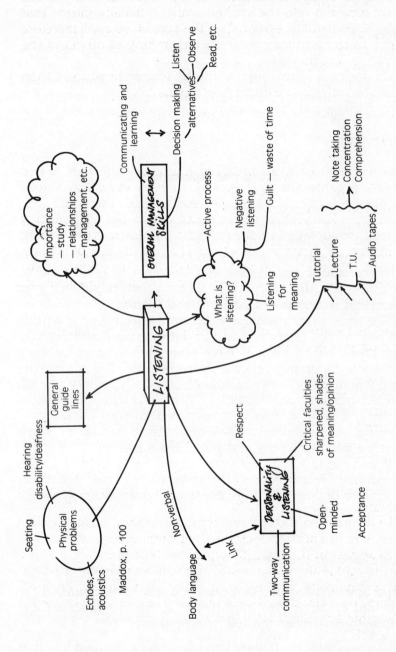

*Figure 12.1*

## A word on word processors

If you can beg, borrow or steal a word processor, your work will be reduced considerably. The initial planning of the assignment will probably still have to be done on paper. But with its ability to insert paragraphs in different places, change erratic spelling and alter sentences, a dedicated word processor is extremely valuable when you get to the writing stage.

## Writing the assignment

When you have researched and planned your work thoroughly and are sure that your arguments and conclusions are logical, then and only then should you begin to write.

The language you use, the grammatical structure and the style you adopt are all essential elements in good writing. Remember the ABC of writing — *Accuracy* (beyond doubt if your material is well planned), *Brevity* and *Clarity*.

The wider your vocabulary the more effective your writing will be, and the easier you will find it to explain and describe your ideas. No two words have precisely the same meaning and so it is important to choose the correct one. The appropriate word will mean not only accuracy but usually brevity as well. You can improve your vocabulary by reading widely and listening well. If your writing is to benefit from your reading and listening, you will need to look carefully at the way in which other people use words and put them together.

If you are to write well you will have to master the rules of grammar. This is beyond the scope of this book, but if you are unsure of yourself, there are many books available which will give you help.

## Guidelines for concise writing

If you have made a detailed plan you will have identified the facts and opinions you want to put across. To express them concisely, remember the following points:

(a)  A paragraph contains several sentences grouped together because they follow a main theme. Each paragraph should present a clear-cut set of ideas dealing with this theme. Most paragraphs will contain a key or topic sentence which states the main idea contained in it.

(b) Keep your sentences short and to the point. Sentences should:

- — make complete sense,
- — contain a verb and subject,
- — be clear and simple,
- — use appropriate words.

Sentence length should be governed by paragraph length. Complex sentences may be inevitable in a long paragraph, but are out of place where the paragraph is less involved. A reasonable length for a sentence is 20—25 words.

(c) Choose your words with care. Reject approximate words, and search for the one word which exactly encapsulates your meaning. Express simple ideas in simple language.

(d) Make sure that you are familiar with conventional punctuation and that your spelling is accurate.

## Beginning to write

Write the whole assignment through fairly quickly, following your plan. If you have a problem in getting started, write the last paragraph first. This will usually get you in the right 'mental set' and is less difficult than searching for the one, good, opening sentence.

Having written this first draft at speed, read it through and alter it where necessary. The first draft is rarely the final one. Rewrite it as soon as you can. Then reread it, and check that the alterations have not changed the meaning and structure of what you intended to say.

## Quotations and references

*Quotations* can lend interest to your writing, but remember the best quotations are the shortest. Very short quotes can be introduced in one of the following ways and incorporated within the text:

As James says, 'Management is no career for a nice young person.'

James says: 'Management is no career for a nice young person.'

Enclose longer quotations in single quotation marks and indent about 20 mm.

All quotations must, of course, be completely accurate.

*References* can be given in several ways, as follows:

(a) If your assignment is fairly long, you may want to put a bracketed reference number in the text, for example (1). You would then list the full details at the end of the section or the end of the assignment itself. For example:

> (1) G Chandler, *How to Find Out: A Guide to the Sources of Information for All Arranged by the Dewey Decimal Classification*, 3rd edition (London, 1967)

(b) You may prefer to put the complete reference as a footnote. For example:

> * C A Moser, *Survey Methods in Social Investigation*, Heinemann (London, 1958)

(c) A brief reference in the text, or as a footnote, can be linked with a bibliography at the end of the assignment, where the complete reference will appear. For example:

> (Lawton, 1968, p. 65)

Whichever method you choose, make sure that you are consistent throughout. It is sensible to check with your tutors to see if they have any preference. It has been known for universities to fail postgraduate students for inaccuracies in citing reference material, so it is as well to be very careful on this point.

However you deal with reference material, the most important thing to remember is that you must *always acknowledge your sources*. Passing other people's work off as your own is not only dishonest but stupid as well. Tutors are familiar with all the texts students are likely to find, and are perfectly capable of detecting material written in a different style or taken from another source. Evidence of wide reading and statements backed by extensive research will impress, so long as you record the reference details accurately.

## Checking the final draft

Once you are satisfied with your final draft, thorough checking is essential. It is better to leave the assignment for a while before revision, if you possibly can. A fresh look at the writing will help you to be more objective and to note inaccuracies which may otherwise pass you by. Make your own checklist of particular points which your subject (and your capabilities) demand. The ideas below may be adapted to suit your own circumstances.

Do spend enough time in reviewing your work. It is impossible to reread your work and check all aspects at the same time. Read separately for:

clarity and meaning;
style;
punctuation and spelling;
references and footnotes;
layout and illustrations.

It takes less time to check each aspect separately, and it is more effective than trying to keep everything in mind at one time.

### Clarity and meaning

Ask yourself:

Have I kept to the main themes?
Are all the sections complete?
Are my headings meaningful?
Is the sequence sensible?
Are all facts and figures correct?
Are there any glaring omissions?
Have I padded and waffled?
Are facts and opinions differentiated?

Are my conclusions:
(a) clearly stated?
(b) too exaggerated?
(c) biased?
(d) indiscreet or libellous?

Are my recommendations:
(a) clear?
(b) itemised?

    (c)  justified; and if there are alternatives, have reasons been stated for the choice?

Is it the correct length?

## Style

The style in which you write is very individual of course, but it is important to write in such a way that the reader is not hampered by an uneasy way of expressing oneself so that he or she loses track of what is being stated.

The last paragraph is an example of bad style.

Ask yourself:

Is my writing dull or turgid?
Have I avoided vague and meaningless phrases?
Have I used short, simple, precise words?
Are the sentences short, complete, unambiguous? (Yes there is a five syllable word here, sometimes the only 'correct' word is not always the shortest or even the simplest!)
Are the paragraphs a suitable length?
Could I eliminate any surplus adjectives or adverbs?
Are there too many qualifying phrases in one sentence?
Is the transition from one topic to another too abrupt?
Is my style too informal?
Is my style too pompous?
Have I generally used the active rather than the passive voice? Compare:
    *The girl ate the apple* (active), and
    *The apple was eaten by the girl* (passive).
Am I guilty of writing in clichés?

When you are expressing an opinion, do you write in the first person? Some people are rather hesitant about doing this. If your ideas are well thought out then they are as valid as those of anyone else, and it is reasonable to say firmly: 'I think that . . .'

An 'essay' type of presentation may not always be the best way of arranging your material. If your points are made more clearly by using headings or making lists, then use your own sense of what is suitable.

## Punctuation and spelling

Try reading the assignment aloud. Errors in punctuation will then be easily detected. The omission or addition of punctuation marks may change the meaning of a sentence, so it is essential to check for mistakes.

Punctuation is necessary so that the reader can interpret the text correctly. If the reader is confused it could be because your punctuation marks are incorrectly placed or wrongly chosen.

If you are a poor speller, acknowledge the fact and have a list of words that crop up frequently. Make sure that you have a correctly spelled list of technical words that apply to your particular subject. Do not take any chances; consult a dictionary if in doubt. If you are an exceptionally bad speller, get someone to check the work for you.

## References and footnotes

Ask yourself:

> Have I been consistent with any references?
> Are they in the correct place?
> Is the information accurate?
> Are they punctuated correctly?

## Layout and illustrations

The general appearance of the assignment will also need revision. A suggested checklist will be found in Chapter Thirteen, where we look in more detail at general presentation, layout and the use of illustrations.

## Research skills

Every student, at some time or another, has to do research. Gathering information is also an essential managerial function, as informed decisions can only be undertaken if a wide range of options are available. In Chapter Ten we looked at different methods of information retrieval. In this section we will look at some practical ways of organising collected information for future reference.

Do not leave all information gathering until it is required. If you have got a good overall view of the course you should be aware of topics which will be coming up in the future. Try to note down any relevant information as you come across it rather than waiting until you need it. Collect articles, reports, correspondence and other material as and when you can. Sometimes you can combine forces with another student and share photocopying costs and background information. This is no substitute for doing your own research; but there will be times when the same material has to be used by more than one person, although each person will interpret it in a different way.

Perhaps the most valuable advice is to urge you to note down accurately and in detail where information comes from. It is incredibly easy to forget which book contains a vital statistic or which library houses an important volume relevant to your subject. Have a small notebook which lists items such as these:

> libraries (and their telephone numbers);
> important reference books;
> details of computer-based data;
> reports, articles, files, etc. stored within your organisation.

Every time you record a piece of information, make sure of its *accuracy*, and its *source*. If there is any doubt about the reliability of the source make certain that you double-check the facts, where possible.

There is little point in accumulating information unless you have devised a system whereby you can pull it out reasonably quickly when it is wanted. Methods will differ from person to person but tend to fall into three categories. These are *the card index*, *loose file paper* and *bound notebooks*.

### Card indexing

The advantage of a card index is its flexibility. Record cards can be bought in several sizes, the 5″ × 3″ or the 6″ × 4″ being the most usual. You may need two different types of record: a source card and a note card. It might be more convenient to keep to different sizes, or at least use different colours.

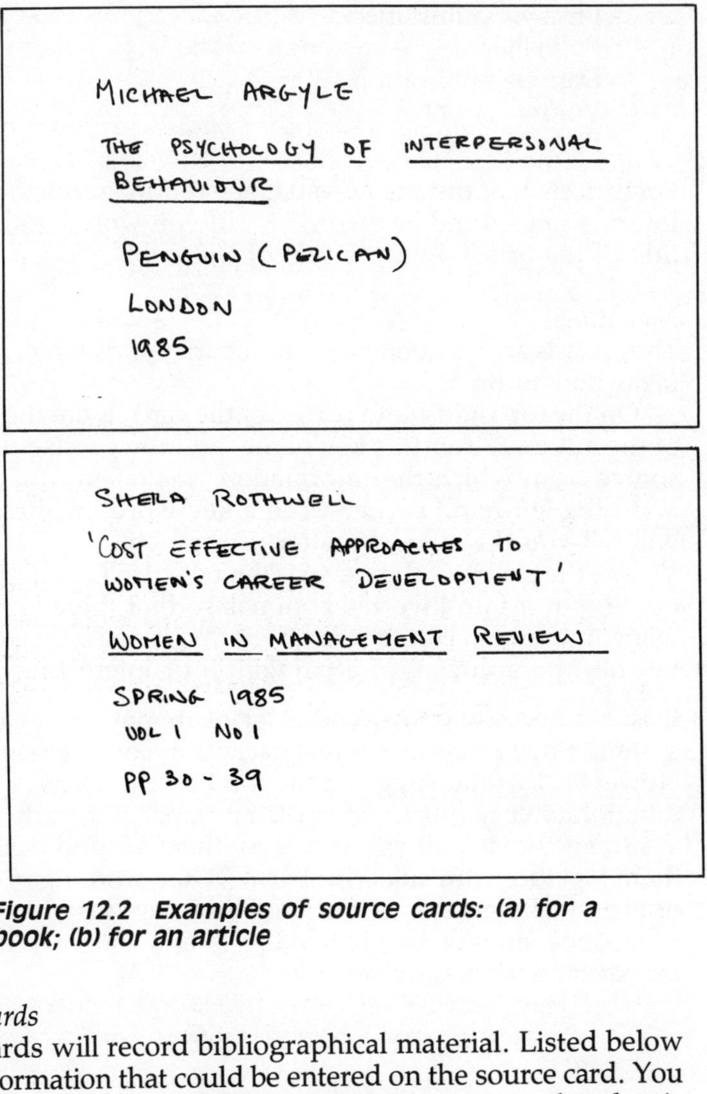

MICHAEL ARGYLE

THE PSYCHOLOGY OF INTERPERSONAL
BEHAVIOUR

PENGUIN (PELICAN)

LONDON

1985

---

SHEILA ROTHWELL

'COST EFFECTIVE APPROACHES TO
WOMEN'S CAREER DEVELOPMENT'

WOMEN IN MANAGEMENT REVIEW

SPRING 1985
VOL 1 No 1

PP 30 - 39

**Figure 12.2  Examples of source cards: (a) for a
book; (b) for an article**

*Source cards*
These cards will record bibliographical material. Listed below
is the information that could be entered on the source card. You
may not require such detail, in which case note only what is
useful for your own purposes.

> Name of author(s) or issuing body
> Title
> Editor/Translator
> Edition
> Volume

Place of publication
Publisher
Date of publication
Volume number
Page numbers

For articles in journals, newspapers and magazines, the same information should be recorded, but you would add both the title of the article and the title of the publication.

*Note cards*
These cards are for quotations, summaries of material, important ideas and so on.

On the top right-hand corner of the card, write the surname of the author. After this key name, add the precise part of the source from which the information was taken.

In the left-hand corner write a key word or phrase which will tell you the subject matter of the note.

Use the centre of the card for the note itself. If this is a direct quote, put it into inverted commas so that there is no risk of using it without acknowledgement. Most notes, however, will be short paraphrases of a paragraph or interesting passage.

It is not necessary to spend a lot of money on a card index system. Shoe boxes and cereal packets make excellent holders. However, I would suggest that you buy the cards as they can deteriorate very quickly if cut from paper. One advantage of a card system is that you can carry them around easily. Keep them together with an elastic band. When working in a library, or even making notes in the field, cards are easier to use than notebooks and A4 file paper. Cards are also very useful for preparing a bibliography.

**File paper**

It is best to record each piece of information on a separate sheet and to use one side of the paper only. It is very frustrating to file and eventually use the notes without realising that there is further information on the back. Try to file away all the information as soon as you have returned from the library or any fact-finding expedition. Material can get misplaced all too easily, especially if you are working from home and have small children with a strong desire to express themselves on paper!

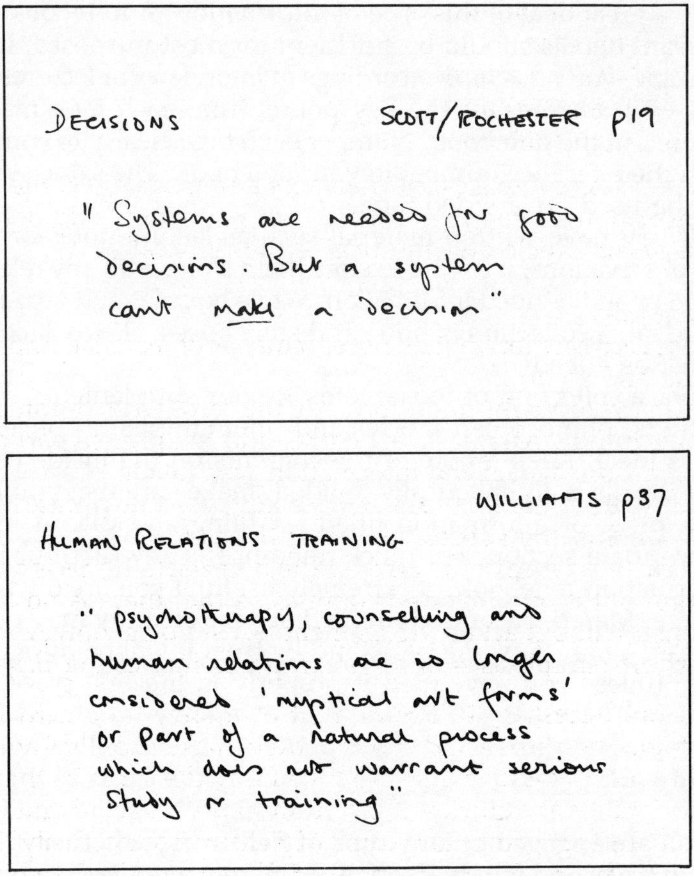

*DECISIONS          SCOTT/ROCHESTER p19*

*" Systems are needed for good decisions. But a system can't make a decision "*

*WILLIAMS p37*

*HUMAN RELATIONS TRAINING*

*" psychotherapy, counselling and human relations are no longer considered 'mystical art forms' or part of a natural process which does not warrant serious study or training "*

**Figure 12.3   Examples of note cards: (a) for a book; (b) for an article**

## Notebooks and files

If you prefer to use a bound notebook, make sure that it is a reasonable size. A pocket book is useful for brief notes in the field but is of little use when writing lengthy notes. Number the pages, and have a page at the front for an informal table of contents.

There is no standard way in which to record non-written material, and you will need to devise your own system if you have a great deal of this type of information. A notebook with relevant details should be sufficient for most purposes. If, for example, you have tape recordings of interviews or lectures that you wish to refer to, the key points from each tape may be entered in the notebook. Number each tape clearly to coincide with the reference number in your notebook. The same system can be used for a video tape.

If you have written material such as lecture notes or field trip observations, it is wise to store them along with any relevant video or audio-taped information. While box files and tape racks are ideal, a collection of shoe and shirt boxes, clearly labelled, is just as effective.

For a collection of loose notes, colour supplements, press cuttings, photocopied articles and photographs, a concertina file is ideal. Keep a note of the contents on the inside cover; or if the file is alphabetically divided, make sure that you have each piece of information titled for filing and placed in the appropriate section. For quick reference, a key (in your basic information notebook) is extremely useful if you are on a long course. Material acquired in the first year of study may not be needed again for some time, and by then it will be difficult to trace unless you have filed it properly in the first place.

**Fieldwork**

If you are engaged on any type of fieldwork, whether it is on site in a wet and windy location, or merely interviewing people in the warmth of an office, you will still need to record your findings carefully for future use.

The method of investigation will be a matter for you and your tutor, but it will be important to keep accurate notes. Often some kind of form or questionnaire will be used and these will be interpreted in a variety of ways. If you have a field book for recording findings while you are actually outside, it is wise to transfer this information to a more permanent form as soon as possible. In the weeks to come you may need not just the findings, but also your impressions, together with any extra notes. These should be added before you forget them.

Personal observations are not very reliable, and if it is possible to back up your written notes with tape recordings or photographs, make sure that these are all kept together. Wherever possible it is sensible to check any interview notes with the people you interviewed.

## Case study

Annette Agboola is a young manager who was recently asked to carry out a fact-finding exercise within her company. This involved visiting various factory sites and asking pertinent questions.

At first she used a tape recorder and wrote up the findings in the evenings. This proved unsuccessful, as the interviewees were rather inhibited by the recorder. She then used a small notebook to record the key words of the information gained, making fuller notes whenever she had a break. As well as this type of information, she also collected material about working conditions and the areas in which the factories were sited. In addition, she listened to throwaway comments from people on the staff and from local officials, noting their reactions.

She placed the mass of papers, brochures, cuttings and reports in a concertina file, taking care to classify all entries for easy access. She spent considerable time in organising and planning the final report. When it was completed, she thoroughly checked it for errors against her written and taped material before asking her immediate boss to read it through and give comments.

The final report was submitted, and she was congratulated on the thorough way in which it presented the facts and came to realistic conclusions. Annette had shown that she was not only capable of assembling relevant material but could also present it to senior management in a straightforward and effective manner.

## Individual exercises

The only reliable way to assess your skill at writing is to produce written material for analysis. Your tutor should be able to give you guidance and advice on any course assignments. The exercises below are intended to be 'thought provokers', especially for those people who have not yet started their courses.

1 Using the checklists in this chapter, make a review or checklist to suit your course. An honest appraisal of your strengths and weaknesses is important. You will want to add items of particular relevance to the subject you are studying.

2 Make a glossary (with correct spellings!) of technical words. If your spelling is suspect, make a list of the words you always have trouble with, and try to make some mnemonics to help you. Go through the list of the most commonly misspelled words at the end of this chapter and check your own performance.

3 Establish an 'ideas' notebook. Assignments are often known some time before they have to be submitted. Use the notebook to jot down ideas that may be of use, references that you come across, information that colleagues mention, media reports, etc.

4 Make a detailed bibliography (at the back of your ideas notebook, perhaps) of books, journals, reports etc. that are relevant to your work.

5 If you get the opportunity, discuss essay titles with other students and colleagues. There may be more than one way to approach the subject. Discussion often leads to new perspectives on the subject.

6 Make a detailed plan for an essay or report. If you have not started your course yet you could use some of the following subjects:

   (a) What are the arguments for and against abortion? Is abortion a moral and social evil?
   (b) How do you become a millionaire?
   (c) What are the main aims of the government's economic policy?
   (d) Explain the apparent reasons for the rising crime rate.
   (e) *The renewal of urban waterways makes economic and ecological sense.* Discuss.
   (f) *The entrepreneur has no place in a structured society.* Discuss.
   (g) Industry gets the managers it deserves.

7 Organise an effective recording system for any research you may be doing now or in the future.

## Group exercises

1 *Materials:*    reports, articles or passages from a textbook
  *Group size:*   not more than 10—12

Some of the practical exercises designed for individual use can be adapted for group work. The discussion about essay/assignment/report titles is usually very fruitful. Writing a succinct title is another possible test. Use company reports, or articles from technical journals with the titles removed.

Light relief can be had by taking passages from the more popular newspapers and requiring the group to come up with pithy headlines.

2 *Materials:*    a badly written report (have a copy for each person)
   *Group size:*    10—12 or less

It is usually possible to obtain badly written company reports (names should be altered to protect the guilty).

Give each member of the group a copy of the 'bad report' and ask for constructive comments, or require them to rewrite it.

It would be useful to have a 'good' report written by someone who can write well, as an example of how the material could have been written and presented.

3 For those people who find writing very difficult, it may be worth running classes with an English teacher present. Note also that local colleges often run short 'remedial' courses in written English for business studies.

4 *Materials:*    a folder of material on a particular theme (including office memos, brochures, letters, etc.)
   *Group size:*    individuals or small groups

Present the material to the group. Ask them to write a report on the content.

One possible theme would be 'setting up a conference'. Brochures could be obtained from hotels and conference centres. There could also be timetables, letters, memos from the managing director, maps, department comments, etc.

### English words most commonly misspelled

There are some rules for spelling, but also many exceptions. You will have to learn to spell the words as they are. The real secret of spelling correctly is to be observant, looking at the words carefully and trying to spot possible danger points. Making mnemonics to help with particular words is helpful.

Bear in mind, also, that there are many differences between British English and American English, in both usage and spelling. It is particularly important to remember this when taking notes from books written in American English.

| | | |
|---|---|---|
| absence | disappear | judge |
| access | disappoint | judgement |
| accessible | describe | |
| accommodation | description | knowledge |
| achieve | discriminate | knowledgeable |
| address | dissatisfied | |
| advantageous | development | leisure |
| analyse | | library |
| appoint | eligible | likeable |
| argue | embarrass | |
| arguing | exaggerate | maintain |
| argument | exceed | maintenance |
| auxiliary | excessive | managerial |
| awkward | except | manageable |
| | | miscellaneous |
| beautiful | February | mistake |
| business | forty | |
| build | four | necessary |
| benefit | | necessarily |
| benefited | | noticeable |
| beginning | gauge | neighbour |
| | grammar | ninety |
| category | guard | |
| ceiling | | occur |
| changeable | height | occurring |
| commit | humour | occurred |
| committing | heir | occurence |
| comparative | | organiser |
| comparison | immediately | |
| corroborate | incidentally | parallel |
| condemn | independent | paralleled |
| conscientious | indispensable | |
| conscious | insistent | persistent |
| | installed | possess |
| deceive | instalment | possession |
| definitely | irrelevant | predecessor |

predictable
preliminary
privilege
procedure

queue
queueing

receive
receipt
recommend
repetition
restaurant
rhyme
rhythm

ridiculous

secretary
secretarial
seize
separate
similar
sincerely
succeed
success
supersede

thorough
transfer
transference

transferred
transferring
truly

umbrella
uncontrollable
unilateral

view
veracity

Wednesday
whole
wholly

yield

# THIRTEEN

# Presentation techniques

In the previous chapter on planning and writing skills, little was said about the layout and presentation. This is an important area and should be taken seriously. We all know the person who maintains that appearance is nothing and that it is ideas that matter. However, to convince people that they should listen to your ideas you first have to convince them that you are worth listening to. Personnel officers maintain that in most cases the first three minutes of an interview decides whether or not the candidate has got the job, as first impressions are a very strong factor. It is therefore important to present your written material in such a way that the first impression is a good one. Different types of material will require appropriate language and a suitable format. Leaving aside fiction and personal letters, there are many areas in which the skills of writing and presentation become necessary for the smooth running of an organisation. Note the following areas:

*Communication with yourself* This includes your diary (personal or office), notes and reminders, incredible ideas that will gain you instant fame in your field, etc. They are usually in handwritten note form with abbreviations and cryptic remarks. Can you read your own handwriting?

*Memos* These are internal office communications, often written in a similar, informal manner, with recognised abbreviations and in-jokes. They can be ambiguous when not worded carefully. Do newly appointed staff understand them?

*Letters* Sometimes these are formalised to such an extent that they become meaningless. The format may need to be reviewed periodically.

*Reports* This is an important area and one which causes more panic than many other forms of writing. A good report should be informative, meaningful, and a true record of an organisation's progress. Too often they are badly planned and presented, and are full of waffle.

*Advertising and press releases* This area is usually best left to the experts, although a clear written statement of what is required is helpful to the advertising department.

*Training manuals and instruction leaflets* However informal they are, written instructions and information must have clarity and purpose. Trainees, at whatever level, need to be able to understand and learn from the material provided. It may be necessary to cut the information into clear stages. The background knowledge of a trainee should not be overestimated.

*Essays and assignments for study purposes* The information in the assignment is not merely an indication of how well the student has grasped the concepts he or she is studying; it is also important for the student as a summary of knowledge acquired, and it could be needed for future revision. The way in which the essay is structured and presented will show if the student has clarified and evaluated the material effectively.

Each of the above categories will require a different use of language and a different format. A personal diary or notebook may be untidy and apparently disorganised, but this is unimportant if the writer knows where and what has been noted down. An internal memo may be on a simple, standard form; the only requirement is that the message should be clear.

The structure and layout of a business letter can tell a client a good deal about the company that sent it out. A badly organised letter with an outdated layout could indicate a lack of drive and commitment, and this could reflect the quality of the service the company offers.

The company report should have a clear format. As many students are expected to write their assignments in the form of a report, the way in which a conventional report is presented is detailed below. Look at a selection of reports from within your own organisation, and elsewhere if possible; compare them and decide which way is the most effective. You may be in a position to restructure the overall look of your company's reports if they are not as effective as they could be. A report on company reports is a useful exercise.

As with reports, study assignments are often lengthy. Although they may not be as formalised as a report, the basic formula of a report can be adapted to them.

A thesis, dissertation or research project is an important element in many diploma and degree courses. The essential planning techniques will be the same in every case, but it is vital to find out how the examining body wants the work to be submitted, as requirements can vary considerably.

The written English for reports, essays and theses will be more formal than for an internal memo, but it should never become cliché-ridden (that combination of words being a cliché in itself!), wordy or pompous. The choice of appropriate language will depend on the audience for which the work is intended.

The conventional format of a report or essay is designed to make it simple for the reader to grasp the ideas being presented. The language, structure and format help to fulfil this purpose.

The physical presentation will involve the layout, placing of illustrations, numbering of pages and use of handwriting or typescript, among other considerations. Once the work has been planned thoroughly and diagrams, graphs, etc. have been worked out, it is time to look at each of these carefully.

## The report layout

Double spacing for typed material is advisable, with wide left-hand margins so that it is easy to bind the finished document.

### Title page

The title (where not supplied for you) should convey the subject and the contents. Its purpose is identification not description. The title page should also include the following information:

(a) the date;
(b) the reference number (for filing);
(c) the classification (*secret*, *confidential*, etc.);
(d) the author's name, position, qualifications, etc. (where appropriate);
(e) the authority for the report (*produced at the request of . . .*);
(f) the distribution list.

## Summary

This is only necessary for very long reports. It should incorporate:

(a) the intention of the report;
(b) the outline of what has been done or observed;
(c) findings;
(d) conclusions;
(e) recommendations.

## Contents list

This should be a separate page, carefully laid out. It indicates the structure and organisation. Main sections will be listed (with an identifying number or symbol). The headings must correspond with those in the main text and should include page numbers.

## Page numbering

Start numbering with the report proper. The title page (together with any acknowledgements, etc.) may have Roman numerals. The position of the number on each page must be consistent.

## Introduction

This can also be called *Matter for consideration*. It can include:

(a) terms of reference;
(b) a short account of the subject;
(c) the reasons for writing the report;
(d) name of person or body requesting the report;
(e) scope of the report;
(f) limitations of the report;
(g) any special considerations.

## The body of the report

This will give the facts and findings, and any inferences which can be drawn from them. Some reports, especially scientific reports, will have standard headings.

## Conclusions

This section gathers up the threads of the case and comes to a conclusion. Nothing new must appear here. The conclusions must be:

(a) consistent with what has gone before;
(b) reasonable and unbiased;
(c) clear;
(d) concise, and possibly itemised.

## Recommendations

Sometimes different courses of action are suggested, so the various possibilities should be defined clearly. Any possible consequences must be stated, or costed where appropriate.

## Appendices

Any material too bulky or detailed to put in the body of the report can go in appendices. You will have to decide whether it is easier for the reader to have this type of material inserted in the main text or whether it would cause less trouble to put it into an appendix.

## Bibliography

This is a list of works consulted by the writer. If it is for a study assignment it could be very important. Your tutor will want to know where you have found the material and the extent of your background research.

The usual way of setting out an entry follows the order *author, title, edition, publisher, place of publication, date of publication, volume* (if applicable). For example:

P Russell, *The Brain Book*, Routledge & Kegan Paul (London, 1979)

## Glossary

This is included if the report is to be read by those not expert in the field.

## References and footnotes

These should be placed at the foot of the page, at the end of the section, or at the end of the report. Common sense will dictate which is most suitable.

## Numbering

Consistency is important. Either use a numerical system where the first section is labelled **1** and subsections appear as **1.1**, **1.2**, **1.3**, etc., or use the consecutive system where each section or subsection is **1**, **2**, **3**, **4**, **5**, etc.

For lengthy reports it is important to consider which method the reader will find most helpful.

## The essay or assignment layout

The detailed presentation of a report may be far too formal for an essay; nevertheless, the imposed structure is a useful guide. A suggested format is listed below. As with a report, a wide margin (on either side) is a necessary space for your tutor to add comments. Double spacing both for written or typed work is helpful for the same reasons. Writing on every other line will seem odd at first, but think of how much easier it will be for your tutor to read. An easily-read essay is more likely to attract good marks than a badly-presented one.

> Title Page, will include the Title or Question
> Student's name/reference number
> Approximate number of words

Summary: only necessary for an exceptionally long essay. Contents list: useful for scientific or very factual assignments. Page numbering: essential as your tutor is bound to drop the thing on the study floor at least twice!

Main essay/assignment text: this will include the introduction, conclusions and possibly recommendations.

Appendices: if required. Bibliography: make certain you give detailed references if you are not making footnotes or section references. Your tutor will need to know exactly where you got your information if it is not included in the text (e.g. 'As Martin

says in his book on Fishing Rights in Polynesia (1923)' ...).
A list of non-written sources can also be included in the
bibliography.

N.B. When referring to another writer in your text make
certain you *always acknowledge* your sources. Failure to do this
can lead to accusations of plagiarism.

*Look back at the last section. Is it easy to read? Can you pick out the
required information easily? If you have difficulty, you will appreciate
the importance of spacing and layout.*

## Layout for theses or dissertations

While the layout will be similar to that of an ordinary essay it
is essential to find out in what form the work is to be submitted.
Most universities and colleges issue instructions about their
requirements. Some places expect the work to be bound. This,
with the typing, takes far longer than one would expect; it is
vital to leave sufficient time for typing, checking, collating and
binding. It is, of course, your responsibility, not the typist's,
to proof-read the final work.

### General information

*Paper*   Use good quality A4 size. Write or type on one side only.
*Margins*   30—35 mm for the left-hand margin
             20 mm for the right margin, and at the top and bottom
             of the page
*Spacing*   Have double-spaced typing and handwriting, with
             quotations and footnotes single spaced and indented.

If you are not typing the assignment yourself, give the typist
clear instructions. For example:

(a) Give the material to the typist in the correct order
    and properly numbered.
(b) Give precise instructions about margins, spacing,
    layout, etc.
(c) Indicate where abbreviations may be used. Do not
    rely on the typist to understand where you are

writing in a hurry and where you actually want the typed word to be abbreviated.

(d) Tell the typist exactly how much space to leave for any illustrations.

(e) Give a definite deadline for completion.

### Diagrams, graphs, tables, etc.

Any illustration included must justify its inclusion. You will have to decide on the best placing by considering the following factors:

(a) Illustrations should go in the main body of the text if they are important for a clear understanding of the material.

(b) If the illustrations are lengthy, they should be placed in the appendices. If more than one page is involved the reader can find it confusing if these pages are included in the main text.

(c) If the illustration, although not large, is to be referred to frequently throughout the essay, it should appear at the beginning of any appendices.

Always consider the convenience of the reader. Unless it is impossible, place the illustrations the same way up as the rest of the text. If they have to be at right angles to the text, ensure that the page numbers are in the same place as those preceding them. The title must, however, be the same way up as the illustration so that it can be read easily.

If you are including maps or plans give the scale used. Include the north point in any map. When including graphs, specify the axes.

When you are putting illustrations in the main body of the assignment think about their size and scale. Place them on the page so that they produce a well-balanced and pleasing effect. The visual aspect of presentation is important. Look at a well-produced illustrated book; note how the text is balanced with illustration and how the illustrations, whether they are graphics, diagrams, tables or graphs, enhance the text.

### Handwriting

With word processors and all the wonders of modern

technology around it may seem superfluous to include a section on handwriting; nevertheless, many people still present their work in this form.

Most tutors and examiners will say that they are influenced by good presentation and in particular by legible handwriting. Experiments have been done whereby a paper which had already attracted good marks in a previous examination was copied out by a variety of people with handwriting ranging from clear to near-illegible. These papers were then sent out with a normal set of scripts, to be marked by outside examiners. These examiners were, of course, unaware that they had been included. Marks awarded were compared with those for the original paper; it was found that all the papers written clearly and legibly had consistently high marks, while the poorly-written papers, although exactly the same, had been marked very much lower. In some cases this meant that the paper had dropped a grade.

Many adults lapse into a scrawl that only their nearest and dearest can decipher. This is a real disadvantage in cases where your notes are important, or when you have to submit handwritten essays to your tutor.

Contrary to popular opinion, it *is* possible to improve your handwriting although it needs practice. If you can spare ten minutes a day and are prepared to write slowly and with care, you will soon be able to write more legibly. Most people have evolved a distinctive hand; and while the practical exercises below will change this, it is usually only a temporary thing. Once you have relearned how to form the letters in a legible way, the individuality of your style will re-emerge.

*What pen to use*
Experiment with fine, medium and thick ball-point pens and fibre-tip pens, as well as different types of nibs in fountain pens. Sometimes changing your pen can have a dramatic effect on legibility. For some people an italic nib works well, and for left-handers it is possible to buy a special left-handed nib (Osmiroid and Platignum).

*Positioning the paper*
The paper should be a little to the right of your body, and with a slight slope to the left (the opposite if you are left-handed). See illustration below.

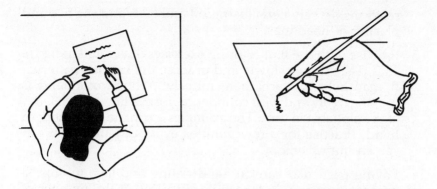

**Figure 13.1** *(a) positioning the paper; (b) holding the pen*

*Pen grip*
It is best to hold the pen between the thumb and first finger, about 3—4 cm from the tip. The end of the pen should be pointing over the right shoulder (the left shoulder if you are left-handed). See figure 13.1.

## Posture

We have already discussed the sensible height for a table. The correct height for your own comfort is important for the legibility of your handwriting. It will also make your arm and wrist less tired when you are writing a long essay or taking lengthy notes.

### Individual exercises

1 Collect together various different pieces of written material (reports, recipes, articles, newspapers, children's books, etc.). Make notes on the characteristics of each. Note the differences in language, vocabulary, formality, etc.

2 Collect together a variety of books, reports, brochures, manuals, newspapers, etc. Concentrate on the layout and design for each one. Note how they differ and ask yourself why some are more successful than others. Look at the

relationship between illustration and text, and the use and placing of headlines.

3  Practise with the handwriting exercises illustrated in figure 13.2. Take things slowly and practise the various patterns. It may help to trace them initially. When your hand is moving freely and with confidence, form a line of each letter of the alphabet in turn. The examples are in the basic modern hand. Practise for a few minutes every day until you can see an improvement.

4  Paying particular care to handwriting and layout, copy a passage or poem. You may be surprised at the number of layout and design problems you have to resolve in this simple exercise.

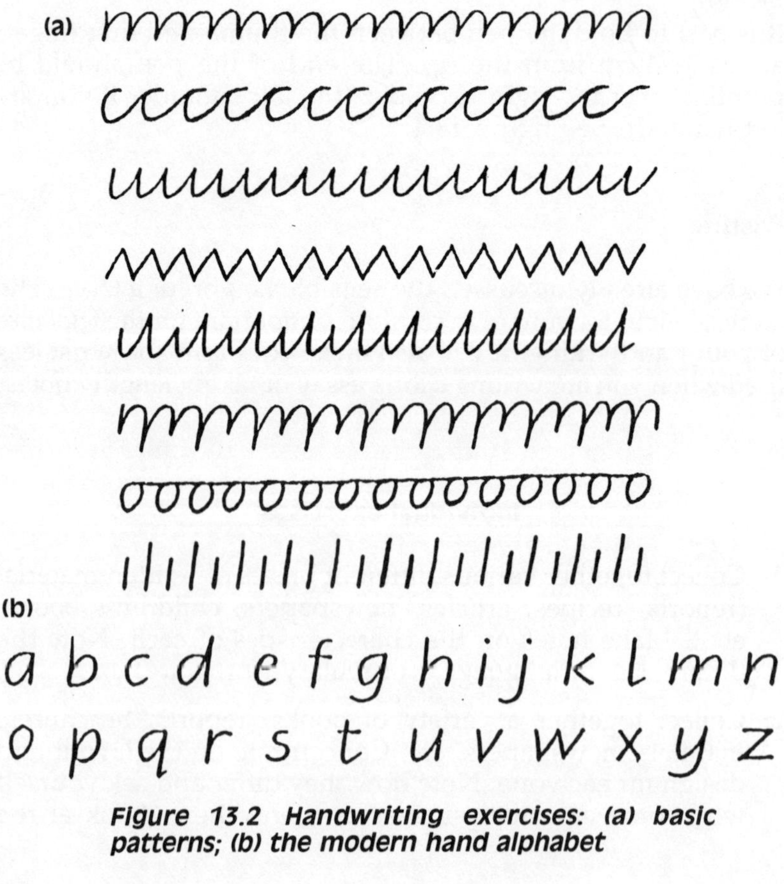

**Figure 13.2 Handwriting exercises: (a) basic patterns; (b) the modern hand alphabet**

5   Look critically at any writing you did recently. It may be an essay or a letter. How did you use space? Is your writing easy to understand? Are illustrations well placed on the page, and close to the words to which they refer?

# FOURTEEN

# Revision and examinations

When you begin any course the first few weeks are taken up with finding your way around the material and coping with having to fit study times into your life. The last thing on your mind will be thinking about revising for an examination which could well be in two or even three years' time. This is a pity, since a little planning now will help you to learn more effectively as you go along; it will also mean that the final revision will not be the burden that it might be otherwise.

By going over your work constantly, reading through your notes, amending and improving them as your knowledge increases, and looking over textbooks and other material you have recently used, you will find that the pieces of the jigsaw will begin to make sense and will transfer from your short-term into the long-term memory, ready to be recalled during the examination.

Revision should be an ongoing process which begins in the first week of any long course of study leading to an examination. Even with continuous assessment, constant review will consolidate your learning and lead to a deeper understanding of the subject. It is also less stressful. Of course you will still need to go over, in some depth, the topics you are to be examined on but if you have managed to revise throughout your course this final revision will be more effective.

You may choose an informal approach, looking over your work at irregular intervals but ensuring that you cover all the material that you have been working on. A more structured approach to the entire course takes a short time to organise but once working will pay dividends as you go through the syllabus. It is just as useful for those taking a final examination as for those on continuous assessment. Because the earlier information is being kept at the forefront of the mind it is, in fact, easier to learn the *new* material. You then have a firm basis of knowledge and understanding for the integration of new information.

It is all too easy to learn material thoroughly, only to have to relearn it when a later assignment, project or examination requires it to be retrieved and used. The revision diary will help you to memorise and learn the material properly and will make current work more relevant. Reviewing initial learning stops the decay of memory, and an organised system of review at specific intervals will help the review process. Without constant review, learned information can easily be lost — and lost very quickly!

If possible, go over your work within ten minutes of the end of a lecture, broadcast or study session. Research has shown that memory reception is high at this time, and a short review immediately after learning can aid later recall quite considerably. To extend this way of reviewing you will need to write down the material to be reviewed and the dates of the reviews. You will find that regularity and involvement are essential if this learning method is to work for you. Use the revision diary outlined in Chapter Eleven.

By now you will have realised that to do any sort of revision it is important to be well organised. Think ahead, and build in constant reviews either in an informal or formal way; but never leave all the major revision until a couple of weeks before an examination. If you do, you will not be revising so much as relearning material that you had forgotten learning in the first place. Not everyone will find it easy to be totally organised and to keep faithfully to study and revision timetables. Perhaps your own approach will be more informal. But remember that although planned organisation appears to be restricting, it can save you a lot of anxiety when examination time looms close. By thinking through and carrying out a pattern of review and study you will find it becomes a familiar habit. Setting short-term and long-term revision goals leads to a self-discipline, and this is needed, not only when studying, but also in everyday life and work.

There are four main stages in learning and retention for recall in an examination:

> the original learning;
> immediate review (within ten minutes, one day, and one week after learning);

mid course review (within one month, three months, and six months after learning);
final revision before the examination.

Unless you decide to cram for your examination the day or so before it takes place, you will want to make a workable plan of action. Some people, and there are not many of them, can get away with cramming in the day or so before the examination; but for most students, cramming only makes for confusion and stress. It is very tiring to cram your revision into a short space of time, and to try to relearn material from the beginning of the course is extremely disheartening.

We will take it for granted that you have thoroughly learned the material in the first place; also that either formally with a revision diary, or informally with another method, you have reviewed the work while working through the course. The final examination revision plan now needs to be thought out.

### Final revision

There are two ways of planning your revision. You can either use *time* or *subject matter* as your starting point. The method you choose will depend on your own inclinations, the amount of time you have at your disposal and the material you need to revise.

### Time

You will probably need to begin your revision about four to six weeks before the examination. If you are already working to a study timetable it will be necessary to amend it so that you can fit in the revision sessions you need. If you have not got a written timetable it is certainly worth making one for the revision and examination period.

To begin with, you will need to draw out a chart similar to the course planner suggested in Chapter Eleven. Block out all the times when you cannot revise (these might include final study sessions). Only you can decide whether you will need to abandon some social or domestic arrangements for those few weeks to get the time you require. When the chart is drawn up, you are then ready to fit in all the revision sessions. Before you do that look at your timetable again; there may be times that you had not considered. For instance, driving to work can be a good time to listen to a tape if you have a cassette player in the car. Of course the traffic hazards on your route may make this undesirable!

When you know how much time you have at your disposal, then you should write down what you intend to cover in each revision block. To do this, you will have to think about the topics that need revising and put them in some sort of order. As revision is not just a matter of reading through your notes and hoping for the best, it is important to think about revision strategies. Later in the chapter there will be suggestions for different ways of revising. Use these and any others that you think of to make revision a positive and active process.

You must ask yourself:

(a) What material needs to be revised?
(b) Where is it to be found?

*What material needs to be revised?* Begin by taking each subject area and dividing it into key topics. A look at the original course syllabus can be useful here. For example:

> *The refraction of light at plane surfaces*
> Refractive index
> Law of refraction
> Ray tracing (algebraical)
> Ray tracing (graphical)
> Critical angle and total internal reflection
> Image formed by plane refracting surface

Start by putting each list in rank order, putting the *most* difficult to learn or remember at the head of the list. This will ensure that you cover all the work. A tendency all students have is to revise the easiest and most enjoyable subjects very thoroughly over and over again. This leads to a greater feeling of confidence but is little help in the examination hall.

When you have gone through all the material and made extensive lists, take the timetable and work out how much time you need to get it all in. Work backwards from the examination dates. Make sure that all the subjects are fitted in and that you have time to cover each one adequately. It is not always necessary to have long stretches of time; many small units can be revised in the odd half hour before a meal, or during a walk to work. Try to keep the overall perspective of the whole course, even when you are dealing in small parts of it. This action of planning is in itself a revision strategy. While you are thinking around a subject and being involved with preparation you are reinforcing the material you have learned, and making it easier to retain and recall when it is needed.

It is important to be realistic about the time you need for revision. Do not be afraid to change the timetable if necessary.

*Where is the material to be found?* Some of the material can be found in *books, technical journals, reports,* etc. With this type of material you must be selective. You may not have enough time to reread all the books and articles used. Concentrate on the important passages or chapters. These should have been noted as you read them during the course.

If possible try to read what different authorities have to say about the subject. Establish your own standpoint if that is applicable to your studies.

A second source of material is *past assignments, essays, projects,* etc. You should read your past assignments and projects critically. Did you go wrong? Do you now understand an idea correctly? Have you changed or deepened your understanding of the material? Have you taken your tutor's comments to heart?

Sharing assignments within a study group is useful. Try to get an assignment-sharing rota going, or photocopy good essays for distribution in the group.

*Notes* are another source of material. A comprehensive set of meaningful notes is essential. Note making is never an optional extra.

You may be working alone on an open-learning or distance-learning project. There may, however, be times when you can meet others taking the same or related subjects. A source of information and help is to set up a revision syndicate or self-help group. Regular if occasional meetings to discuss particular past examination questions, or to analyse the work done by members of the group, can be very helpful. Talking over a subject often clarifies it in your own mind, and you get a different perspective which can enlarge your understanding. More detailed advice for setting up self-help groups is dealt with earlier in the book. If you have set up a group, build the meetings into your revision timetable.

## Subjects

As with a conventional timetable you will have to draw up a revision chart. On this you insert all the subjects, which you have divided into topic areas. You can also put in tutorials, lectures you know you will be attending, group sessions, reading still to be done, and any aspect of the course that you know you will be covering before the final examination.

Display the chart where it can be see easily, at least six to eight weeks before the examination. As you read a chapter, learn a set of key points, do a timed essay or go to a lecture, tick it off on the chart. There may be some aspects of revision that you want to go over more than once; in this case use a different colour of tick for this activity. When a topic has been revised to your satisfaction, cross the square out firmly. This method has the advantage that you do not have to alter it if the timing has to be changed; and psychologically it is a good feeling to see the colours mount on the chart as you complete each revision unit. Number each unit, or colour code in order of importance.

Whichever method of organising your revision you use, the most important element will be your own involvement in the process. Passively reading through notes or books will never be of any use. It is essential that you think about the material to be revised and become really involved in the activity.

## Revision strategies

If you are planning a programme of strategies, you will soon realise that different subjects require different strategies. You will need to choose or design an appropriate strategy for each topic you are revising. Some revision methods have already been mentioned; below you will find a list of suggested strategies. Try some of them, adapt them to your needs and to the material you are studying. You may discover other ways which are equally as efficient. The main thing is to think about what you are doing (a revision ploy in itself). The passive student will never be as successful as the student who is constantly and actively involved in her or his own learning and revising.

(a)  Write out, in your own words, any handouts you were given or any passages from textbooks that are important.

(b) Summarise your own past essays or assignments.

(c) Go through notes, books and lecture notes, and underline all the key words or phrases. Mark important passages in books for quick review.

(d) Make a set of key points on cards. Write the question on one side and the answer on the other. Have a pack of at least ten. Test yourself often. Using a pencil, tick each card as you get it right, and cross it if it is wrong. When you have six ticks in a row, the material will have been consolidated in your memory for examination purposes. Keep topping up the cards and use them frequently. It is a good idea to keep the discarded cards and occasionally retest yourself.

(e) Using a tape recorder, 'explain' the topic you are revising, onto the tape. Go through the recording with your notes and check for detail.

(f) Plan out examination questions in detail; do some with your notes and books in front of you and some without (checking the latter afterwards).

(g) Practise maths problems frequently. Use those you have already worked. Rewrite them without the conclusions and redo them a week or so later.

(h) Read *all* your tutor's previous remarks on earlier assignments. Have you consolidated your knowledge?

(i) Prepare a brief talk about a topic and try it out on a friend who is not taking your course. If she or he can understand it, and if you can answer any questions, you have probably grasped the meaning well.

(j) Look at a diagram or graph and test yourself by writing about it in detail.

(k) Draw a diagram without any labelling; leave for a while and then fill in the appropriate wording.

(l) Practise doing timed examination questions.

(m) If you use pattern notes, make a note in the following way. First with one colour of pen, put down all you know about the subject. Do not use notes or textbooks. Then, with a second colour, add all the details that were left out, obtaining them from your notes and books. By doing this, you find out what you do not know, and you can make sure that you learn the material that you omitted the first time.

(n) Go through the index of a textbook, taking each relevant entry and writing brief notes on it. Check that you are correct.

(o) Take headings from textbooks, journals, reports, etc. Change the statements into questions. Answer the questions briefly, then look in the passage to see if you are right.

These are only a few revision strategies. You will probably be able to add more of your own. By taking responsibility for your learning and revision you will be more likely to achieve the success that you seek.

One word of warning: these are all good tactics to use in the time leading up to the examination. It is not a good thing to revise hard the night before an examination, or worse still on the actual morning of the examination. You will only confuse yourself and find it difficult to approach the questions with a clear overall understanding of the subject. By all means go over the key points and concepts of the examination subject the night before to get yourself into the right mental set. Another revision strategy would be to draw up a list of concepts and key points for particular use on the day before the examination.

## Why some students fail

There are many reasons why some students fail their examinations. Some of these are rooted in the inability of the students to organise themselves well enough. Or perhaps they have lacked the motivation and self-discipline to complete assignments on time, or have habitually handed in ill-prepared work. Trying to catch up with neglected work just before an examination is of little use.

It is important to think carefully about the examination itself, to consider the conventions of your examining board and to familiarise yourself with the way in which questions are phrased and presented.

If you have worked hard throughout the course and have learned the material thoroughly, it would be foolish to let yourself down by not developing good examination techniques. In this section of the chapter we will look at some of the difficulties that can arise in the examination room. Many of these problems could be eliminated by understanding how to cope with them.

For example, it is essential that you read the instructions about entering on the cover your name, examination number and probably the questions that you have answered. Failure to do this could mean, in extreme cases, that your paper will be invalidated. It *will* cause administration difficulties which could harm your chances.

There will probably be other important information about the examination in this rubric, including the equipment, tables, maps, calculators, etc. that you may or may not use. There may be diagrams or tables for your use. It is essential that you know where they are to be found. The number of questions to be answered, which are compulsory, and from which section they are to be taken, will also be here. This is probably the most important information. It is imperative that you answer the correct number of questions and that you take them from the right sections of the paper.

Try to get copies of past examination papers to look at before the examination. They will be useful for doing timed questions and for other revision strategies, and you will familiarise yourself with the way in which the paper is set out. This familiarity helps to eliminate the panic that occurs when you are confronted with an unfamiliar set of instructions, often in small print, in a small booklet. Finding your way around an examination paper helps to settle you down to do your best work. Of course, every now and then, these details will be changed; but this does not happen often and you can generally rely on the paper to look like that of the year before. This does not mean that you can relax, however. Read the paper through with great care, and carry out any instructions which are given to you.

Once you have read through the questions and have selected those that you wish to answer, read them through again. A common mistake is to read a few words of a question, imagine that you know what is required, and then to write a superb answer which will gain no marks because it has not answered the question. Half the battle in any examination is to understand what is wanted. Think hard about exactly what the examiner is asking, and then make sure that you answer that and only that.

If formulae, tables, maps or diagrams have been given out, discard any which you will not need to use. Familiarise yourself with the items relevant to the questions you will answer *before* you start to answer. If you only refer to items as you get well into the answer, you could miss crucial information, and possibly lose vital time while you see how to use them.

The time spent in thinking and planning an answer is never wasted, provided you are aware how much time you should allot to each question. If you do not submit a coherent and organised piece of work the examiner will find it impossible to mark it properly. Think carefully about what you want to write, and then jot down your plan, in as much detail as you can. You can use key words, a patterned note or some other method, and then concentrate on writing the answer in a clear and well-presented manner.

When writing your answer, make sure that you do not substitute your own opinions and prejudices for informed and logical evidence. Whenever you make a statement, back it with hard evidence. Make it quite clear when you are expressing your own thoughts and opinions on the subject. Examiners are looking for evidence that you know your subject, and you should give examples or quotes wherever possible.

If you are unsure of a subject, try not to waffle and pad it out. It is more sensible to go on to another question and do the best with that. You can always come back to a question later if you plan your time correctly.

Timing is crucial in an examination. You must know exactly how many questions are to be answered, and make sure that you spend the appropriate amount of time on each. Many examination papers will tell you how many marks are awarded for each question. Take this into consideration when planning the time. If the exam has three questions to be answered in three hours it would be foolish to imagine that you have one hour for each answer. Time has to be given for reading the paper through, thinking about which questions to select and for checking your answers at the end. None of these is an optional extra. This time will be built into the question paper, and you will be expected to spend a certain amount of time in carrying out these functions. As a rule of thumb, it will probably be necessary to spend at least ten minutes in reading through the paper and selecting the questions.

Leave at least five minutes at the end for checking the work through. Do not neglect to do this. When you are writing quickly and your mind is in top gear you can make mistakes very easily. The examiner will not know that you really know it is 1887 when you have written 1878. Obviously the surrounding text should make your meaning clear. But what if it doesn't? These slips of the pen happen frequently when you are working under pressure, and it really is important that you go over the work to correct it. Where figures are concerned, it is wise to check them during the work itself, as a small mistake can sometimes mean that the entire calculation is wrong.

If you have looked back at past papers you will have found words and phrases which occur frequently. Study the words in the question very carefully. Make sure that you know the implications of the wording. In examiners' reports, the main criticism about students is that many of them 'do not answer the question'. In other words they write about what they think has been asked instead of what the wording actually requests. Look at the key words in the question, and spend time determining exactly what is to be written and how it should be approached.

Some common phrases used in examination papers are as follows:

> *comment on; explain; evaluate; consider; prove; enumerate; summarise; outline; list; justify; give a brief account of; write short notes on; compare and contrast; show that; critically assess; as opposed to; discuss; describe; define; illustrate; interpret; relate; trace; review; state.*

Many of these instructions are very similar in meaning, but call for a different approach. Make sure that you understand their precise meaning. Your tutor should be of help if you are undecided about any of them. This is an instance where it is helpful to go over past papers, either in a group or with a tutor.

Research has been done on the marks awarded for the same examination essay copied out in different handwriting. On average, marks are considerably lower for an essay written in a poor hand, compared with those given for the same essay written in a tidy, legible hand.

It is worth getting a colleague to read some of your writing. Is it easy to read? When written with your normal pen, is it easy to decipher the words?

It is possible to improve your handwriting. If yours is particularly bad, seek help and practise until your handwriting improves. It would be foolish to sacrifice marks because the examiner is unable to read what you have written.

You will make sure, of course, that you know where the examination is to be held and at what time! Every year there are some candidates who turn up late or do not even arrive at all. Do not add to their number! If you do arrive, but feel flustered and anxious, you will be unlikely to do as well as you could have done.

A sure way to induce anxiety and near-panic is to wait outside the examination hall and discuss with others how terrible it will be and how you are sure to fail. Think in a positive way and go into the examination full of confidence. If you have worked well throughout the course and have revised as well as you could there will be no need to panic. There are a few unfortunate people who do find examinations extremely stressful, and at the end of the chapter I have included some simple exercises in stress control. If you get a moment of blind panic as you open the paper, take several deep breaths. It is virtually impossible to worry and breathe deeply at the same time — try it now!

## Types of examination questions

### The essay question

Never assume, in this type of question, that the examiner knows what you mean; padding and waffle are undesirable, but elaboration to show full understanding is important. Use illustrations and quotations (where relevant) to back up your argument or to show the implications of a statement. In some instances a sketched diagram may demonstrate that you see relationships between the varying factors you are writing about. In discussion it is wrong to merely list points; a balanced argument is necessary. The key to success with an essay question lies in the planning before you start to write.

### Multiple-choice questions

Because the material is printed and full recall of all salient points is not immediately necessary, some students believe that the

ELEM—Q

multiple-choice question is an easy option. This is not necessarily the case.

It is important to complete *all* the questions (even if you have to make an educated guess with some). Every question will have equal weight in marks, so you should work straight through, not hesitating too long on difficult ones. Return to these when you have reached the end; later questions often bring to mind what is needed to answer earlier ones.

Practise reading multiple-choice questions, looking carefully at the wording. The key words used in the construction of this type of question are all-important. If you feel you have time, it is sometimes an advantage to read through the entire section before you start to answer.

Make certain that you have read and can then *follow* directions such as 'list *all* the correct answers' or 'mark the *one* correct answer'.

In answering 'completion' questions, always fill in something, even if you are not convinced that it is a good answer. You may be given credit for being on the right lines.

### Interpretation of data questions

All the necessary information is given, and the student has then to interpret the material. The question examines whether or not the student has learned to use information correctly and can present a balanced answer, appropriately weighing the data. Not only does the student need to know the subject thoroughly, she or he must also be able to 'read' the forms in which the material is presented — tables of statistics, graphs, maps, etc.

### Question planning for a three-question paper

Consider this method of working. It exploits your brain's ability to think about one thing while doing another. The overall associations of words and concepts are recalled more easily with this technique.

(a) Plan out question 1.
(b) Plan out question 2.
(c) Write question 1.
(d) Plan out question 3.

    (e)  Write question 2.
    (f)  Check question 1.
    (g)  Write question 3.
    (h)  Check question 2.
    (i)  Check question 3.

As you are writing an answer, ideas and details for the next question are forming at the back of your mind, ready to rise to the surface when you begin the new question.

Many management and business studies courses include assessment procedures as well as the formal examination. These can take a variety of forms, all of which may contribute to the final marks which will determine your eventual grade. Continuous assessment can be a great advantage for students, as they can then monitor their own progress. There are several methods which might be used, including:

    tutor-marked essays and projects;
    an extended essay or dissertation;
    computer-marked assignments;
    oral examinations;
    group activity assessment;
    project work or practical submissions;
    practical examinations.

It is as well to find out at the start of any course how the overall assessment and examination marks are to be distributed. Concentration on a final examination will still be important, but good grades for course work may make this less of an ordeal.

## Control of stress

Although a certain amount of anxiety can get the adrenalin flowing and sharpen the wits, too much stress can lead to a miserable performance in an examination. It is important to have confidence in yourself and your ability to cope with pressure. Those who experience a high degree of stress will be thinking about their own feelings and fears rather than the tasks they have to do. Feelings of disorganisation and helplessness are felt by some students, and it is sensible to think about your own attitudes during the course and before any examination. By facing the fact of your anxiety and by thinking it through, it may be possible to come to term with your own feelings and to use them to your benefit.

*Flight* or *fight* are the basic methods of dealing with stressful situations. If your instinct is for flight, you will need to reduce the stress so that you can start to 'fight back'.

Well-organised study sessions and well-planned revision are the two most important factors for aiding confidence. If you know that your course work has been satisfactory and you are in control of your own learning, you will not need to worry extensively. This is why it is essential to plan your study from the very beginning of the course.

### Pre-examination stress: relaxation techniques

Try to arrange a time during the day when you can practise relaxation methods. Fifteen or twenty minutes would be adequate. If your instinctive reaction is to tense up at the very thought of spending time in relaxation, then it is even more important for you to practise.

You will need privacy and a comfortable place. Experiment with a chair or the floor and sit in different positions until you find a place in which you feel at ease. Sit with your arms relaxed by your side or loosely on your lap. The hands should be open, not clenched. Relax your shoulder and neck muscles, and try to relax the muscles in your head and face.

Clear your mind of outside thoughts. Breathe slowly and deeply, taking the breath from the bottom of your lungs rather than shallow breaths from only the top of the lungs. Count slowly up to ten, timing the words with each long breath. As you breathe, think only of your breathing; let the thoughts that come just drift through the mind. Dismiss them as they appear, but do not worry about them — just do not pursue where they lead. As you pause between breaths, you could say to yourself a word associated with a stress-free state: *peace, calm, pause,* or any word you feel happy with.

Repeat the sequence of ten breaths; aim for a state where you are conscious of your body breathing but where your mind is at rest.

As you breathe, let go of the tension in your body as you exhale. Listen to the air being released. Continue for 15—20 minutes. Do not worry about doing the exercise 'correctly'; there is no right or wrong way. Practise each day and you will find that you get progressively less tense and become more relaxed.

After a while you will find that you can begin to breathe in this way when you feel you are likely to become stressed. Use this type of exercise immediately before and at the start of an examination. Of course, you will not want to spend ten minutes or so in doing relaxation exercises during an examination; but once you have learned to clear your mind, you will find that only a few deep breaths will enable you to cope with 'exam nerves'.

Other exercises which you will find useful are those where you deliberately tense and then release muscles to achieve a state of relaxation. Take your arms, shoulders or stomach, for example. Tighten up each muscle and then relax it slowly, visualising the muscular activity as you consciously relax.

Finally, below you will find two checklists to use in the days before the examination, and on the examination day itself. Good Luck!

### Examination checklist

**The day before**

1 Run through the main points of the subject — do not try to learn any new detail now.

2 Try to get an overall perspective of the subject.

3 Check the time of the examination.

4 Make certain you know where the examination is to be held. (How do you get there? How long will the journey take?)

5 Check equipment:
    (a) pencils (HB for multiple-choice questions);
    (b) pen (cartridges may need to be refilled);
    (c) coloured pencils (avoiding felt tips which 'bleed');
    (d) mathematical instruments;
    (e) eraser;
    (f) mathematical tables (where allowed);
    (g) calculator;
    (h) Polo mints, tissues, etc.

With a calculator you should:
(a) check that it works before entering the hall;
(b) have spare batteries;
(c) leave behind any instruction books, cases or wallets belonging to the calculator;
(d) use your *own* calculator (do not borrow one unless you are sure that you know how to use it).

In some subjects you are allowed to take in certain equipment; be sure that you know what you may or may not take with you.

6 Get a good night's sleep.

**The examination day**

1 Get up in time to have a good breakfast. If the examination is in the morning, you may miss your usual coffee break. Hunger can depress your blood-sugar level and this could affect your concentration.

2 Arrive fifteen minutes before the start of the examination.

3 Wear suitable clothes; remember that some rooms can become too hot or too cold.

4 Check equipment again.

5 A three hour examination can be a long time — visit the lavatory before it begins. If it is essential, you may be escorted to the lavatory during the examination, but this will cut valuable minutes from your answering time.

6 Think positively! If you have worked well throughout the course and have revised efficiently, there will be no need for panic.

7 If you do feel a wave of panic, take several deep breaths. It is virtually impossible to worry and breathe deeply at the same time; try it out!

**The examination**

We have already looked at examination techniques and

questions. It is also advisable to familiarise yourself with the examination arrangements. If you are wise you will have looked at past papers and will recognise the format. Even so it is *essential* that you read the rubric through carefully as it may not be exactly the same as on previous papers.

When you are told, you may begin. You should:

1  Fill in your name and any other information required as soon as possible.

2  Take several deep breaths.

3  Read the *entire* paper through carefully and thoroughly.

4  Ask yourself:
    (a)  Which questions are compulsory?
    (b)  How many questions do I have to answer?
    (c)  Where do the questions have to be selected from?
    (d)  How much time can I allow for each question?

5  Familiarise yourself with formulae, tables, etc. before you begin.

6  Choose *all* the questions you want to answer at the beginning.

7  Make rough plans of the answers before starting them, where applicable.

8  Answer the 'best' question first. This gives you confidence.

9  Write simply, legibly and directly.

10  *Be relevant.* Glance back at the question every now and then, to make sure you are on the right lines.

11  Stop work on a question if the time runs out. If you are genuinely short of time, finish in note form using key words. The examiner will then at least know what you wanted to include.

12  During the final 5—10 minutes *check your work* for: ambiguity, sweeping generalisations, points made with no evidence to back them, words missed out, wrong names, dates or places, misquotations, etc. It is very easy to make a silly error because you are writing quickly and thinking under pressure.

## Group exercises

A review of memory, writing, planning skills and also reading strategies is useful in the weeks before any formal examination is taken.

## Revision

Encourage the students to think through their revision timetable and revision strategies. Group revision is helpful.

It is important to emphasise the need to check that the work has been learned and retained. Working timed examination questions is a valuable exercise.

Have a selection of past papers for the group to look through. Knowing the physical presentation of the paper is a confidence-booster in itself. An overview of the type used, colour, arrangement of questions and rubric is calming for pre-examination nervousness.

Group discussion on how to approach particular questions is a good revision strategy. Anything which helps students to 'know what they don't know' is a help. Knowing where understanding or knowledge is weakest makes for more positive revision.

Even with adults, examination times can be very traumatic. It is often a help to have an informal talk about the way the group feels about study and examination performance.

The questions below may be used as a basis for exchanging ideas. Finding that others also feel nervous is usually a great relief. The danger may lie in the group becoming negative about the examination. A positive and confident approach is vital if they are to go into the examination believing in their ability to achieve the results of which they are capable.

*Group discussion points for a pre-examination session*
Do you believe that:

(a) sensible planning is a key note to examination success?
(b) people who do well are lucky?
(c) if you fail it is because you have not worked hard enough?
(d) a well-planned timetable of work, study and leisure leads to good results?

(e) when things go badly it has been the staff, tutor or course material which has been at fault?
(f) competition is bad for you?
(g) it is difficult to study effectively at your age/with your responsibilities/with all your outside interests, etc?
(h) progress and success depend on liking all aspects of the course?
(i) it is natural to feel anxious about examinations, but you can use the extra adrenalin to boost your performance?
(j) personal responsibility for revision and examination performance is yours alone?
(k) panic is natural before an examination?
(l) panic can be controlled before and during an examination?

Positive advice from members of staff who have taken similar examinations can be a mixed blessing, but it may be worth recruiting a colleague (preferably successful) to talk briefly about what to expect. Professional boards can also be helpful if you contact them on behalf of your staff.

It will be of help to the students if you can find time to make them a simple checklist of times, venue, equipment allowed, etc. Of course, it is the responsibility of students to present themselves at the right time and place and with the correct equipment, but a double check for busy people is usually much appreciated.

Little has been said about practical examinations and field-work, as these vary so widely. The training department could perhaps make a checklist and give advice on specific problems as they occur.

Some people derive considerable benefit from using simple meditation techniques or deep breathing exercises. It may be helpful to give students information on this aspect of stress control, or arrange an appropriate course for them.

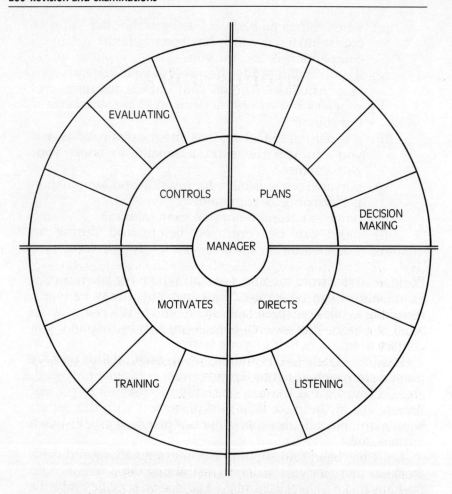

The effective manager recognises that learning never stops, and that there are always new skills to acquire and new experiences to draw from.

What learning skills will help YOU along the way?

# Bibliography

## Chapter 2

Atkinson, J. and Raynor, J., *Motivation and Achievement*, Wiley, 1974.
Honey, P. and Mumford, A., *The Manual of Learning Styles*, Honey & Mumford, 1982. (Available from Ardingley House, 10 Lindon Avenue, Maidenhead, Berks, SL6 6HB.)
Kolb, David A., *Experiential Learning*, Prentice Hall, 1984.
Kolb, Rubin and McIntyre, *Organizational Psychology*, Prentice Hall, 1979.
Lindsay, P. and Norman, D., *Human Information Processing*, Academic Press (International Edition), 1972.
Mace, C.A., *The Psychology of Study*, Pelican, 1982.
Morris, C.G., *Psychology*, Prentice Hall, 1985.
Peters, T.J. and Waterman, R.H., *In Search of Excellence*, Harper & Row, 1982.
Pyrah, Gill, 'Mind Games', *The Observer*, 29 Dec., 1985.
Robinson, F.P., *Effective Study*, Harper & Row, 1970.
Rowntree, D., *Learn How to Study*, Macdonald & James, 1978.
Russell, P., *The Brain Book*, Routledge & Kegan Paul, 1979.
Staw, B.M., 'Motivation in organisation: towards synthesis and redirection', in Staw, B.M. and Salanncik, G.R. (eds), *New Direction in Organisational Behaviour*, St Clair Press, 1977.
Vernon, M.D., *The Psychology of Perception*, Penguin, 1970.
Von Oech, R., *A Whack on the Side of the Head*, Angus & Robertson, 1986.

## Chapter 3

Gallway, W.T., *The Inner Game of Tennis*, Random House, 1974.
Maddox, H., *How to Study*, Pan, 1967.
New Zealand Council for Educational Research, *Study Habits Evaluation and Instruction Kit*, 1979.

'Partially sighted society', *Symposium* (Chartered Institution of Building Services Lighting Division/Partially Sighted Society), 1980.
Pedler, M. and Boydell, T., *Managing Yourself*, Fontana/Collins, 1985.

## Chapter 4

Barker, L.A., *Listening Behavior*, Prentice Hall, 1971.
Lundsteen, S., 'Listening, reading, and qualitative levels of thinking', in *Problem Solving: Vistas in Reading (Proceedings of the International Reading Association)* Part 1, 1967.
Hamblin, D.H., *Teaching Study Skills*, Basil Blackwell, 1981.
Lindsay, P. and Norman, D., *Human Information Processing*, Academic Press, 1972.
Spearritt, D., *Listening Comprehension: A Factorial Analysis*, G.W. Owen, 1962.

## Chapters 5 and 6

Brown, M., *Memory Matters*, David & Charles, 1978.
Cohen, G., Eysenck, M.W. and LeVoi, M., *Memory: A Cognitive Approach*, Open University Press, 1986.
Hunter, I.M.L., *Memory*, Penguin, 1978.
Lorayne, H. and Lucas, J., *The Memory Book*, Ballantine Books, 1975.
Luria, A.R., *The Mind of a Mnemonist*, Jonathan Cape, 1969.
Norman, D.A., *Memory and Attention*, Wiley, 1976.
Ornstein, R.E., *The Psychology of Consciousness*, Penguin, 1979.

## Chapter 7

Burnett, J., *Successful Study*, Hodder & Stoughton, 1979.
Buzan, T., *Use Your Head*, BBC Publications, 1975.
Carman, R.A. and Royce Adams, Jr, W., *A Student's Guide for Survival*, Wiley, 1976.
Gibbs, G., *Teaching Students to Learn*, Open University Press, 1981.
Howe, J.A. and Godfrey, J., *Student Note-taking as an Aid to Learning*, Exeter University Teaching Services, 1977.
Russell, P., *The Brain Book*, Routledge & Kegan Paul, 1979.

## Chapter 8

Barker, W.D., *Reading Skills*, Prentice Hall, 1974.
Gibbs, G., *Teaching Students to Learn*, Open University Press, 1981.
Maddox, H., *How to Study*, Pan, 1967.
Robinson, F.P., *Effective Study*, Harper & Row, 1970.

## Chapter 9

de Leeuw, E. and M., *Read Better, Read Faster*, Penguin, 1978.
Robinson, F.P., *Effective Study*, Harper & Row, 1970.
Vernon, M.D., 'The improvement of reading', *British Journal of Educational Psychology*, No. 26, pp. 85—93, 1956.
Vernon, M.D., *The Psychology of Perception*, Penguin, 1970.
Wenick, L.P., *Speed Reading*, Prentice Hall, 1983.

## Chapter 10

Bakewell, K.G.B., *Business Information and the Public Library*, Gower, 1987.
Bakewell, K.G.B., *How to Organise Information*, Gower, 1984.
Hoffmann, A., *Research*, Adam & Charles Black, 1979.
Parsons, C.J., *Thesis and Project Work*, Allen & Unwin, 1973.

## Chapter 11

Cooper, C.L., *The Stress Check*, Prentice Hall, 1981.
Garratt, S., *Managing Your Time*, Fontana/Collins, 1985.
Gibbs, G., *Teaching Students to Learn*, Open University Press, 1981.
Maddox, H., *How to Study*, Pan, 1967.
Reynolds, H. and Tramil, M.E., *Executive Time Management*, Prentice Hall, 1979.

## Chapters 12 and 13

Cooper, B.M., *Writing Technical Reports*, Penguin, 1983.
Gowers, Sir Ernest (Rev. by Sir Bruce Fraser), *The Complete Plain Words*, HMSO, 1977.
Mitchell, J., *How to Write Reports*, Fontana, 1984.
Rathbone, R.R. and Stone, J.B., *A Writer's Guide for Engineers and Scientists*, Prentice Hall, 1962.
Timm, P.R., *Managerial Communication*, Prentice Hall, 1986.

## Chapter 14

Maddox, H., *How to Study*, Pan, 1967.
Robinson, F.P., *Effective Study*, Harper & Row, 1970.
Rowntree, D., *Learn How to Study*, Macdonald & James, 1978.

# Index

abbreviations 96, 111
abstracting services 172
action learning 4
action learners 11
active listening 40, 44–47
affixes 134
age 5
  memory 60–61, 65
analytical learners 10
animal alphabet 79
Aslib 171–172
assignments 181, 200–223, 225, 229–230, 240
attention spans *see* concentration

bibliographies 161, 173, 228
biographies 173
body language 40–41
book lists 121–127, 160, 202
Books In Print 173
brain function 92

card indexes 214–216
catalogues, library 165–167
chaining 83
checklists 183, 251–252
classification, library 163–169
comprehension 146, 156
computer-based information 176
concentration 25, 43, 48, 60–61, 66, 156, 184–187
concept learners 11
concept trees 99–101
copyright libraries 162
course books 121–127, 202
courses 5

data bases 176
Dewey Decimal classification 163–167
diaries, revision 188–191
dictionaries 131–133
dissertations 161, 230–231
  (*see also* assignments)
distance learning 5

encyclopedias 174
environment 24–31
essays *see* assignments
examinations
  assessment 4, 232
  checklists 251–252
  failing 243–247
  planning 248–249
  questions 247–249
  revision 236–243
  stress 249–251
  techniques 244–247
  timing 245
exercise, value of 32
eye 142
  contact 40
  exercises 151–155
  fixations 144
  movements 142–143, 149, 150

field work 218
filing 15–17, 216 218
footnotes 210, 213, 229
furniture 26–27

glossaries 120, 228
graphics 120–121, 124, 231